Fundamentals of So

By

Kuntal Barua

Assistant Professor, Department of Computer Science and Engineering
SANGAM UNIVERSITY, Bhilwara.

Prof Dr Prasun Chakrabarti

Professor and Head-Department of Computer Science and Engineering
Sir Padampat Singhania University, Udaipur.

BPB PUBLICATIONS

FIRST EDITION 2017

Copyright © BPB Publications, INDIA

ISBN : 978-93-8655-156-6

Distributors:

BPB PUBLICATIONS
20, Ansari Road, Darya Ganj
New Delhi-110002
Ph: 23254990/23254991

BPB BOOK CENTRE
376 Old Lajpat Rai Market,
Delhi-110006
Ph: 23861747

COMPUTER BOOK CENTRE
12, Shrungar Shopping Centre,
M.G.Road, BENGALURU–560001
Ph: 25587923/25584641

DECCAN AGENCIES
4-3-329, Bank Street,
Hyderabad-500195
Ph: 24756967/24756400

MICRO MEDIA
Shop No. 5, Mahendra Chambers, 150
DN Rd. Next to Capital Cinema, V.T.
(C.S.T.) Station, MUMBAI-400 001 Ph:
22078296/22078297

Published by Manish Jain for BPB Publications, 20, Ansari Road, Darya Ganj, New Delhi-110002 and Printed him at Repro India Ltd, Mumbai

The fountain of inspiration "PARENTS"
(Mr. Kinchit Barua, Mrs. Bhadreswari Barua and Mr. Pradeep Kr. Das)
Mrs. Debashruti Barua, Mr. Abhijato Barua,
Mr. Saikat Mitra, Mrs. Sumana Mitra,
Ms. Aishi Mitra, Ms. Arohi Mitra

Preface

This book entitled "Fundamentals of Soft Computing" promises to be a very good starting point for beginners and an asset to advanced users too.

The authors are confident that the present work will come as a relief to the students wishing to go through a comprehensive work explaining difficult concepts in soft computing, offering a variety of numerical and conceptual problems along with their systematically worked out solutions and to top it, covering all the syllabi prescribed at various levels in universities.

This book is written as per the processes of soft computing, for the complete coverage of the syllabus for the courses of UG, PG and researchers. Concepts of Soft computing is given in an easy way, so that students can able to understand in an efficient manner.

Here the authors are open to any kind of constructive criticisms and suggestions for further improvement. All intelligent suggestions are welcome and the authors will try their best to incorporate such in valuable suggestions in the subsequent editions of this book.

KUNTAL BARUA
PROF. DR. PRASUN CHAKRABORTY

Acknowledgements

Life is a journey to excellence. Every milestone that one reaches, during this eternal journey, is marked by the guidance, help and support of the near and dear ones and this endeavor of mine is no exception. A teacher is a guide to life. The persons mentioned below have been a source of immense motivation to me all through this time. While some of them have given me keen insights into some topics covered herein, others have supported the cause by motivating me to achieve progressively higher standards. I take this opportunity to express my deep sense of gratitude to my teachers and guides as under:

1. Mr. Kinchit Barua
2. Mrs. Bhadreswari Barua
3. Mr. Pradeep Kr. Das
4. Prof. Prasun Chakroborty (Professor and HOD, Dept. of Computer Science, SPSU)
5. Prof. Kalyani mali (Reader, Dept. of Computer Science, University of Kalyani)
6. Prof. P.C. Deka (Vice Chancellor, SPSU)
7. Prof. Anirnban Mukhopadhaya (Associate Professor, Dept. of Computer Science, University of Kalyani)
8. Prof. Satadal Mal (Principal, Future engineering college)
9. Dr. Pradeep Das (HOD, Dept. of EE, KGEC)
10. Dr. Pritam Gayen (Associate Prof. Dept. of EE, KGEC)
11. Dr. Partha Sarati Bera (Associate Professor, Dept. of EE., KGEC)
12. Dr. Subabrata Roy Choudhary (Registrar, Techno Group)
13. Dr. Deepak Bera (Prof. Dept. CSE, KGEC)
14. Prof. Dr. Saikat Moitra (VC, MAKAUT)
15. Dr. Krishnendu Chakroborty (Principal, Ceramic Engg. College of Technology)
16. Dr. Debdas Ganguly (Dean of Management , HIT)
17. Dr. Suddhasatta Chakroborty (Associate Professor, Dept. of EE, Jadavpur University)
18. Dr. Atal Chodhary (HOD, Dept. of CSE, Jadavpur University)
19. Prof. B.B. Pal (Professor, Dept. of EE, Ramkrishna Mission Shilpo Mandir, Belur)
20. Prof. Dr. Debojyoti Mitra (Professor, Dept. of ME, KGEC)
21. Prof. Astam Sau (Professor, Dept. of EE, KGEC)
22. Dr. Sanjay Silakari, professor dept of computer science, RGPV, Bhopal, MP
23. Dr. Vivek Sharma, professor dept of computer science, RGPV, Bhopal,MP
24. Dr. Varsha Sharma, professor dept of computer science, RGPV, Bhopal, MP
25. Dr. A. K. Sinha, Dean academic, LNCT indore

26. Prof. Sumer Singh (Vice Chancellor, Sangam University)

27. Prof. Achinta Choudhary (Dean of school of Engineering, SPSU)

28. Prof. Premashish Roy (Deputy Dean, School of Management, Sangam University)

29. Prof. Manoj Kumar Rawat (Principal, LNCT, Indore)

30. Prof. B. P. Sarkar (Advisor, IMPS college of Engineering)

31. Mr. Shubhankar Saha Choudhury

32. Mr. Sandip Bhatore

I thank my colleagues at Sangam University, LNCT indore and AIMMT, barrackpore, Kolkata for the related discussion and my student Ms. Farha Khan from Ujjain, M.P. for helping to convert my manuscript into textbook. I am highly thankful to the publisher, BPB publication, New Delhi for transforming this dream into a reality.

KUNTAL BARUA

Contents

CHAPTER 1

Introduction to Neuro-Computing

I think the brain is essentially a computer, and consciousness is like a computer program. It will cease to run when computer is turned off. Theoretically, it could be recreated on a Neural Network, but that would require all one's memories.

-Stephen Hawking
Theoretical, physicist, cosmologist and author

Our today's computers are enormous at doing many tasks, like arithmetic operations on two digit numbers, factorization of very large numbers, speed, accuracy; in other words tasks which seeks accuracy and precision, and follow conventional rules to get accomplished. But on the other hand, tasks which require natural intelligence, common sense, self improvement by analyzing past experiences, like, image recognition (recognizing the image of a person, place or thing out of several similar instances), machine learning (learning through experiences and adapt itself according to circumstances, this feature is also useful in applications like forecasting and decision making), natural language (a machine which can follow our commands in our own language) etc, are a few tasks that are poorly dealt with our today's computers. But conversely these tasks are best handled by human brains. This draws the attention of researchers to study the worlds most brilliant and complex machines called, "Human Brains". Here, one question might arise in the minds of students, that, why our conventional computers are excellent at certain type of tasks, while human brains are good at other sort of tasks? This can be easily understood by understanding the problem handling techniques of both. Actually, our brains works in a parallel fashion, while conventional computers are good at handling tasks sequentially; tasks which require natural intelligence, common sense, consideration of past experiences etc, are best handled through parallel processing, however tasks like finding the sum of two number or other mathematical functions which needs to be answered precisely, are required to be handled serially; our conventional computers works serially, therefore they are best in calculation tasks but cannot perform tasks which require probabilistic reasoning.

In the chase of building such machines, which can act like human, think like human, handle problems like human; scientists are working hard to mimic human brains or *Biological Neural Networks*, and this procreated the idea of *neural networks*. Later on a new field of computing in the world of artificial intelligence emerged, specified as *"Soft Computing"*, which was apparently different from the conventional computing techniques.

The ideology of soft computing was first brought in light by Sir Lotfi A. Zadeh at the University of California, Berkley, U.S.A. He is proved to be a legend in the development of fuzzy mathematics, which is known to be the roots of Artificial Intelligence. Soft computing can tackle a collection of imprecise data and process on it to extract the useful information out of it, without exploiting and following the so called rules used to perform the particular task, thus it is thought to be useful in applications like image recognition, forecasting, optimization, natural language, making decision out of common sense etc. It is a combination of techniques and methods which help to deal with real practical problems in the same way human brains do.

Comparison of Hard Computing and Soft Computing

	Hard Computing	Soft Computing
1.	Hard computing requires precise inputs and produce precise outputs.	The main feature of soft computing is in dealing with the imprecise and approximate incoming data, and hence forth resulting to approximate answers.
2.	It is based on binary logic (two-valued logic), crisp system and numerical analysis.	It is based on Fuzzy Logic (many-valued logic), Neural Networks and Probabilistic Reasoning.
3.	Imprecision and uncertainty are strictly undesirable as these may lead to incorrect answers.	Build to handle imprecise and uncertain data, although this feature is exploited to achieve tractability, lower cost, High Machine Intelligence etc.
4.	Solve problems on the basis of fixed rules and written programs.	Can evolve their own programs according to the circumstances.
5.	These are deterministic in nature.	These are stochastic in nature.
6.	Perform tasks in a sequential fashion.	Handle problems by parallel computations.

The primary aspects of soft computing are, Neural Computing, Fuzzy Logic, Evolutionary Computation, Machine Learning and Probabilistic Reasoning. In this book, I am giving main priority to the first three principles; the latter two are somehow closely related to the former three. In this chapter we will discuss each of them in short, one after another.

1.1. Neural Computing

Neural Computing can be referred as the next major achievement in the industry of Artificial Intelligence. In simple words, neural computers can be defined as systems, comprised of artificial neural networks that are closely related to Biological Neural Networks in there technique of solving problems. The purpose behind building such systems is to mimic the natural processing of human brains.

Dr. Robert Hecht-Nielsen, the inventor of the first neuro-computers, defines a neural network as: "A computing system made up of a number of simple, highly interconnected processing elements, which process information by their dynamic state response to external inputs".

Thus one thing which is worth noticed here is that the most prominent component of neural computers is neural networks; both artificial and biological neural networks are prominently required to be discussed for building the basic concept of neural computing as well as soft computing. In this chapter, we will try to understand every aspect of neural- computing.

After many years of research on human brains, researchers discovered the fact that brains stores information in the form of patterns. Some of these patterns are highly complicated and give us the capability of recognizing faces from various angles. This technique of storing information in the form of patterns, exploiting those patterns in solving problems, evidenced to be the foundation of Neural Computing. This field does not utilize traditional programming mechanisms, rather involves the creation of massively parallel network and the training of those network to solve specific problems especially in situations where it is not possible to follow the so called protocols or rules that lead to the solution of a particular problem. Thus it is a promising field of computing, which can proved to be a boon especially in the applications of pattern recognition.

Every day research on biological neurons promise a basic understanding of the natural thinking mechanism. Neural Networks adopt various *learning mechanisms* of which supervised learning and unsupervised learning methods are very much popular and widely used in practical applications. In supervised learning, a learning signal (teacher) is assumed to be present during the learning procedure, i.e., the network tries to minimize the error between the target (desired) output presented by the 'teacher' and the actual output, to improve the performance. Whereas, in unsupervised learning, there is no teacher available to present the desired output; as a result, the network tries to learn by itself, by organizing and reorganizing the input instances of the problem.

Though NN architectures have been broadly classified as single layer feedforward networks, multilayer feedforward networks, and recurrent networks, with the need of more accurate and advanced systems, other NN architectures have also been evolved. Some of them include *backpropagation network, perceptron, ADALINE (Adaptive Linear Element), associative memory, Boltzmann machine, self-organizing feature map, adaptive resonance theory,* and *Hopfield network.*

Briefly, a neural network can be considered as a mystery device that is capable of predicting an output pattern after recognizing a presented input pattern. Once effectively trained (programmed), it is also capable of recognizing similarities when a new input pattern is presented, again resulting a predicted output pattern. Thus could be successfully applied to the field of pattern recognition, image processing, data compression, forecasting, optimization and many others.

Before moving further on the grounds of neural networks, let us first have a look at the other two important aspects of soft computing in short.

1.2.   Fuzzy Logic

The major difference between conventional computing (hard computing) and human brains is that, human brains have the capability to interpret the imprecise and unambiguous set of information provided as input by different organs like eyes, ears, tongue or other sensory organs. The aim of soft computing is to inhibit this property of human brain, and fuzzy logic plays a vital role in this task, by providing logical algorithms to handle such semantic information.

The origin of Fuzzy Logic is emerged from the theory of Fuzzy sets introduced by Sir Lotfi A. Zadeh in the mid '60s, it is also termed as 'many-valued logic' and deals with approximate rather than exact reasoning. Unlike traditional binary logic (used by traditional computers) which exhibits exact value as either 0(false) or 1(true), fuzzy logic variables acquires a truth value that ranges in probabilistic degree between 0 and 1. For example, in case of temperature sensing, a system exhibiting Fuzzy logic will answer slightly warm or fairly cold, rather than just warm and cold. Thus, it provides a foundation for the development of new tools for dealing with natural languages and natural decision making capabilities. The Fuzzy Logic is comprised of four fundamental aspects-

➢   Logical
➢   Set- theoretic
➢   Relational
➢   Epistemic

The first aspect, i.e., Logical, termed as *Fuzzy Logic* deals with logical systems in which solutions or results are not based on exact truth, rather to a certain extent or matter of degree of truth. The set-theoretic aspect encapsulated in the *Fuzzy set theory* provides a systematic algorithm to handle set of imprecise information linguistically and to perform mathematical operations on this information by imposing the membership functions. The relational aspect, comprised in the *fuzzy relations*, is focused on fuzzy dependencies, correlations and fuzzy rule sets. Most of the practical implementation of fuzzy logic to real world applications is related to Fuzzy reasoning. For instance, fuzzy if-then rules are served as a basis of many automated systems like temperature sensor, automatic toll booth gate controller, fire alarms, earthquake predictors etc. The epistemic aspect is mainly concerned with knowledge representation, natural languages, linguistics and *expert systems*. Probabilistic reasoning is also a part of it. Further, the right usage of fuzzy if then rules are very important for a fuzzy inference system (FIS) that can effectively model human like common sense in machinery. Fuzzy inference system can easily interpret the incoming imprecise information by sing fuzzy if-then rules, but the limitation of fuzzy inference system is its adequacy in dealing with the changing external conditions. Therefore a neuro-fuzzy expert system was developed by utilizing the learning algorithms of neural network. In soft computing, the term, Fuzzy logic has been used in two different notions:

(i)   Broadly, it is considered as a system comprised of concepts, principles, and methods for dealing with imprecise information that is supposed to be approximate rather than exact.

(ii)   Secondly, it is viewed as an abstraction of the various many-valued logics, which have been studied in the area of semantic logic since the beginning of the twentieth century.

We will discuss all these aspects of fuzzy, later in more detail in chapter-4.

1.3.   Evolutionary Computation

Some people would claim that things like joy, love and beauty belong to a different category from science and can-not be described in scientific terms, but I think they can now be explained by the theory of evolution.

- Stephen Hawking

Theoretical, physicist, cosmologist and author

If we look at the history of human evolution, we will find that our today's intelligence is not achieved over night. It is the outcome of countless years of biological evolution. A deep study of the biological evolutionary process, as to how the natural intelligence developed, from the brains of early-man to today's intelligent brains, could clear the point of developing intelligence in machines. Thus the field of Evolutionary Computation (EC) developed, that is also comprised of Genetic Algorithm (GA) which helps in understanding the principles of imitating the evolution of individual structures through processes of selection, mutation and reproduction.

Evolutionary Computation is also found to be practically advantageous in solving optimization problems. The evolutionary approach of computation can be applied to problems whose satisfactory heuristic solutions are not available. Involving the Heuristically informed search techniques, which enables to reduce the extremely large search space by utilizing GA as a candidate technique for the same purpose; it helps in inhibiting the capacity for population-based systematic random searches. Simulated annealing is also one algorithm for solving such heuristic search problems as well as optimization problems.

Evolutionary Computation is one of the most important aspects of soft computing and is globally applied to solve many problems including optimization, automatic programming, machine learning, operations research, bioinformatics, and social systems. In this book I am covering each and every aspect of EC including evolutionary strategies, evolutionary programming along with genetic algorithms (GA) and genetic programming. All these share fundamentally common principles. First of all a population of candidate solutions (for the optimization task) is initialized. Next, by applying reproduction operators (mutation and / or crossover), new solutions are created. The fitness of the resulting solutions are evaluated (which solution is best), and then suitable strategy like Schema theorem is applied to determine which solutions will be maintained into the next generation.

1.4. Biological Neural Networks

1.4.1. Computation in the brain

The neural system is not just the neural network; the overall neural system of the human body comprised of three primary constituents: Receptors, A neural network, and Effectors. The function of receptors is to receive the stimuli either internally (in the form of signals from internal organs like heart, liver etc.) or externally (through sensory organs, like eyes, ears, tongue etc.), this information is then passed onto the neurons in the form of electrical impulses. The neural network then in response to the incoming information took a decision of the outputs. At last, the effectors convert incoming electrical impulses out of the neural network into responses to the external signals received by the atmosphere. Lets understand this phenomena with a simple practical example, suppose, a ball of fire is coming with enormous speed towards you; then the receptors, will send this information to the neural network, the neural network will take a decision in response to the incoming danger, by generating a signal like run, or lean down, or move to right or left, according to the circumstances. In response to the generated signal, the effectors will make the body parts to respond, like legs will start running or anything like that. Figure 1.1 shows the bidirectional communication between stages for feedback.

The human brain consists of millions of **neural cells** that process information. Each cell performs like a simple processor. The collection and interconnection of all these cells makes a **neural network**. The primary component of the neural network is called a **neuron**. As shown in figure 1.2, a neuron is mainly comprised of three modules: **dendrites**, **soma**, and **axon**. A neuron functions by receiving signals from neighboring neurons through connecting points, called **synapses**. These signals are combined together, and if a fixed threshold or activation level is crossed, the neuron firing takes place; that is sending a signal further to other neurons associated or attached to it. *The presence or absence of firings in the synaptic connections between neurons is what is referred to as THINKING.* This phenomena might sound very simplistic until we recognize that there are approximately one hundred billion (100,000,000,000) neurons each connected to as many as one thousand (1,000) others in the human brain. The massive collection of neurons and the complexity of their interconnections results in a "thinking machine", your brain.

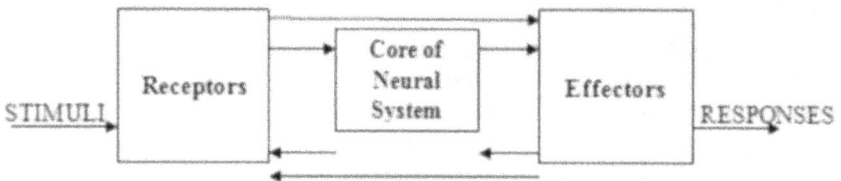

Fig. 1.1: Three stages of Biological neural network

Each neuron consists of a body, called the **soma**. The soma is similar to the body of any other cell. Inside the cell nucleus, various bio-chemical factories are present and other components that support ongoing processes. **Dendrites** are the tree-like structure that receives the signal from neighboring neurons, where each line is attached to one neuron. **Axon** is a like a fiber carrying information from the soma to the synaptic points of other neurons (dendrites and somas), muscles, or glands. Axon hillock is the point of summation for incoming information. At any instant, the collective impact of all neurons that transmits impulses to a given neuron will decide whether to initiate an action potential at the axon hillock or not. **Synapse** is the connecting point of two neurons or a neuron or a gland. The extreme point of the axon splits into numerous ends, called the **boutons.** The boutons are further connected to the dendrites of other neurons and the resulting interconnections are the synapses. (Actually, the boutons do not touch the dendrites; there is a small gap between them.) If a neuron has been fired, the generated electrical impulse triggers the boutons and this develops the electrochemical activity; this electrochemical activity results in the transmission of the signal across the synapses to the receiving dendrites.

The impulse signal coming from each synapse to the neuron is categorized into two types: excitatory and inhibitory. In order to cause firing, the excitatory signal should exceed the inhibitory signal by a fixed amount (threshold level) for a short period of time (latent summation). Each incoming impulse signal is assigned a weight; the excitatory signal possesses positive weight and the inhibitory signal hold negative weight. Thus we can conclude that, "A neuron fires only if the total weight of the synapses exceeds the threshold in the period of latent summation."

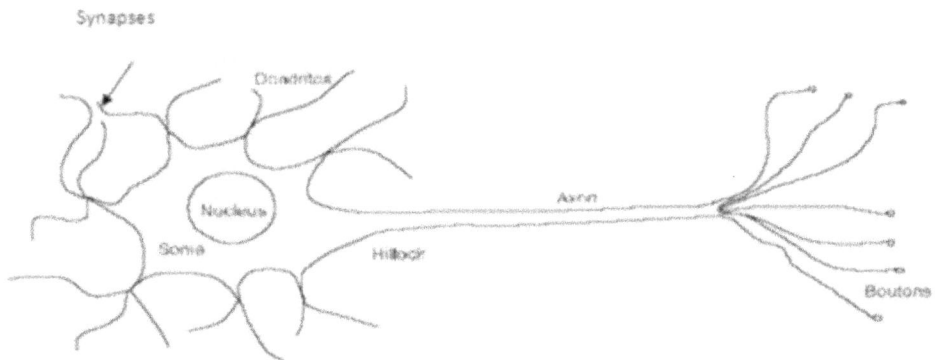

Fig. 1.2: A Biological Neuron

Summary

In neuroscience, a **biological neural network** is a pattern of interconnected neurons whose activation impulse defines an identifiable linear pathway. The network through which neurons interact with each other usually consists of several axon terminals connected through synapses to dendrites of other neurons. If the summation of the incoming input signals into one neuron exceeds a certain threshold level, the neuron generates an action potential (AP) and transmits it to the axon hillock and further this electrical signal is carried over to the axon. In contrast, a **neural network** can be seen as a functional unit of interconnected neurons that is capable of adjusting its own activity with the help of a feedback loop (similar to a control loop in cybernetics). Biological neural networks serve as an inspiration for the design of artificial neural networks.

The whole computation process in neural networks is summarized below-

➢ Dendrites receive activation from other neurons.

➢ Soma manages the incoming activations, performs various operations on them and results into output activations.

➢ Axons play the role of transmission lines to carry activations to other neurons.

➢ Synapses allow signal transmission between the axons and dendrites.

➢ The process of transmission is by diffusion of chemicals called neuro-transmitters.

1.4.2. Analogy between Biological Neural Network and Artificial Neural Network

	Biological Neural Network	Artificial Neural Network
1.	Soma	Node or unit
2.	Dendrite	Input
3.	Axon	Output
4.	Synapse	Weight

The main part of an artificial neural network is the artificial neurons. As in BNNs the body of neurons was called Soma, here in ANNs the main body of artificial neurons is often referred to as node or unit. They are physically connected to each other by wires that mimic the connection between biological neurons. The arrangement and connections of the neurons made up the network and mainly consist of three layers. The first layer is called the input layer, it transmits external signals to the neurons in the next layer, which is called a hidden layer. The hidden layer extracts relevant features or patterns from the received signals, which are then directed to the output layer.

1.4.3. The Brain Vs Conventional computers

At the state of rest, the neuron maintains an electrical potential of about 40-60 millivolts (inhibitory signal). When a neuron fires, an electrical impulse is created, this is the result of a change in potential to about 90-100 millivolts (excitatory signal). This impulse travels between 0.5 to 100 meters per second and lasts for about 1 millisecond (latent summation). Once a neuron fires, it is required to rest for several milliseconds before it can fire again. In some circumstances, the repetition rate may be as fast as 100 times per second, equivalent to 10 milliseconds per firing. If we compare this statistical values to a very fast electronic computer whose signals travel at about 200,000,000 meters per second (speed of light in a wire is 2/3 of that in free air), whose impulses last for 10 nanoseconds and may repeat such an impulse immediately in each succeeding 10 nanoseconds continuously, electronic computers have at least a 2,000,000 times advantage in signal transmission speed and 1,000,000 times advantage in signal repetition rate.

It is clear that if signal speed or rate were the sole criteria for processing performance, electronic computers would win hands down. What the human brain lacks in these, it makes up in numbers of elements and interconnection complexity between those elements. This difference in structure manifests itself in at least one important way; the human brain is not as quick as an electronic computer at arithmetic, but it is many times faster and hugely more capable at recognition of patterns and perception of relationships.

1. Brains are analogue; computers are digital

It's easy to assume that neurons are essentially binary in nature, by considering the factors that they fire an action potential if a certain threshold is exceeded and otherwise not. The signals travelling inside the brain or neural network are not in the form of 1s and 0s rather they are in the form of electrical impulses or electrochemical impulses which are analogue by nature. This superficial similarity to digital binary logic (1s and 0s) contradicts the continuous and non-linear processes that take place in neural networks.

For instance, one of the fundamental mechanisms of information transmission is the **rate** at which neurons fires. Similarly, networks of neurons can fire in synchronization to each other; this organization affects the strength of the signals received by the surrounding neurons. The inside mechanism of each and every neuron is similar to an integrator circuit, composed of a various ion channels.

2. The brain uses content-addressable memory.

In computers, if we want to retrieve any information stored in the memory, the computer will do this by polling its precise memory address. This phenomenon of polling and accessing is referred to as byte-addressable memory. In contrast, the brain uses content-addressable memory; any stored information can be retrieved from the memory through "spreading activation" phenomenon. This means terms which are closely related to each other. For example, thinking of the word "fox" may automatically spread activation to memories related to other clever animals, fox-hunting horseback riders, or any instances which happens in past related to fox.

We could conclude that our brain has a kind of "built-in Google," in which just a few key words are sufficient to cause a full memory to be retrieved. However, similar things can be done in computers, mostly by building lengthy and strenuous indices of stored data, which then also need to be stored and searched through for the relevant information.

3. The brain is a massively parallel machine; computers are modular and serial

Parallel processing assumes that some or all processes or computations involved in a cognitive task occur at the same time. For example, different parts of an image may be processed simultaneously. Human vision systems are naturally built to handle tasks in parallel fashion, whereas computer systems are sequential.

Serial processing fundamentally mean that one process should be completed before taking the next task into account, in other words, operations are performed sequentially in time whether or not they depend on each another. Sequential algorithms must be stingy with their resources or set protocols. We had already discussed this point at the beginning of this chapter.

4.   Processing speed is not fixed in the brain; there is no system clock

The processing speed of neural network processing is a matter of concern of a variety of constraints, including the time for electrochemical signals to travel through axons and dendrites, the effective time taken for neuronal firing and the time taken to generate an output signal out of this whole process. There is no central clock inbuilt in the brain, thus we could view the processing speed as a heterogeneous combination of all the speed constraints.

5.   Synapses are far more complex than electrical logic gate

It seems like brains might operate on the basis of electrical signals (action potentials) traveling along individual logical gates. But unfortunately, this is not the full truth. The signals which are propagated along axons are actually *electrochemical* in nature. They travel much more slowly than electrical signals in a computer, and that they can be modulated in multitude ways. For example, signal transmission is dependent not only on the putative "logical gates" of synaptic architecture but also by the presence of a variety of chemicals in the synaptic cleft, the relative distance between synapse and dendrites, and many other factors. This adds to the complexity of the processing taking place at each synapse – and it is therefore profoundly wrong to think that neurons function merely as transistors.

6.   Unlike computers, processing and memory are performed by the same components in the brain

Computers process information from memory using CPUs, and then write the results of that processing back to memory. These results are stored in the temporary memory, so if we want to retrieve this data in future, it is required to be saved manually in the permanent memory. *No such distinction exists in the brain*. As neurons process information they are also modifying (adapting) their synapses consequently. As a result, retrieval of information or past events after an infinite period of time is possible, with slight alternations (usually making them stronger, but sometimes making them less accurate).

7.   The brain is a self-organizing system

This point follows naturally from the previous point – experience profoundly and directly shapes the nature of neural information processing in a way that simply does not happen in traditional microprocessors. For instance, one of the most interesting characteristic of the brain is that it is a self-repairing circuit, i.e., *"injury-induced plasticity"* takes place after brain injury. It means that, if certain portion of brain got damaged due to some severe injury, brain cells around the damaged area underwent change in their behavior (function and shape) in order to mimic the functions of the damaged cells. Besides this, scientists also observed ***neuroplasticity*** in brain, under this phenomenon long lasting functional changes takes place in brain when a person learn new things or grasp new information. Although above mentioned characteristics are advantageous for brain development, or say overall development of a human being, but there are certain disorders whose base is plasticity, and which are severely harmful for human beings. For instance ***cognitive dysfunction***, which takes place after certain diseases like multiple sclerosis, depression, fibromyalgia and many other severe diseases. Under this, the patient lost intellectual functions like thinking capabilities, retrieving past memories and reasoning capabilities. The patient also has troubles in verbal recall, basic arithmetic and concentration.

Because of lack of studies in neuroplasticity, it is still beyond our scope to know how these neural adaptations takes place in brains by itself. And thus we fail in developing such algorithms in artificial intelligence.

The Journey of Neural Networks

Key Developments
McCulloch and Pitts (1943)
➢ Model of neurons
➢ Logic operations
➢ lack of learning
Hebb (1949)
➢ Synaptic modifications
➢ Hebb's learning law
Minsky (1954)
➢ Learning machines
Rosenblatt (1958)
➢ Perceptron learning and convergence
➢ Pattern classification
➢ Linear Separability constraints
Windrow and Hoff (1960)
➢ ADALINE- LMS learning
➢ Adaptive signal processing
Minsky and Papert (1969)
➢ Perceptron- Multilayer Perceptron (MLP)
➢ Hard problems
➢ No learning for MLP
Werbos (1974)
➢ Error backpropagation

Hopfield (1982)
➢ Energy analysis
➢ Boltzmann machine
➢ Generalized delta rule

In this book one by one we will discuss all these advancements along with the learning rules in a very much elaborative manner.

1.5. Artificial Neural Networks

An Artificial Neural Network (ANN) is a highly simplified model comprised of artificial neurons, inspired by the Biological Neural Networks. An ANN is comprised of a network of interconnected processing units. The processing unit basically consists of two parts, a summation unit and an output unit. The summation unit receives N number of input values, assigns a weight to each input value, and calculates the weighted sum. This weighted sum is called the activation value. The function of the output part is to receive this activation value and produce an output signal out of it. If the weight upholds a negative sign with it, it is called inhibitory signal, and if it possess positive sign, it is called excitatory signal. The inputs to a processing unit may come from other processing units or from external sources; similarly the output from each unit can be given to further processing units or to itself.

1.5.1. The First Artificial Neuron Model

Computational neurobiologists have constructed very elaborate computer models of neurons in order to run detailed simulations of particular circuits in the brain. As Computer Scientists, we mainly concentrate in the general properties of neural networks, independent of how they are actually "implemented" in the brain. This means that we can use much basic units called "neurons", which (hopefully) capture some of the essential properties of biological neurons, instead of trying to find out each and every stringent detail about them. McCulloch and Pitts (1943) are known as the inventors of the first neural network in the history artificial neural networks. They coupled many simple processing units (neurons) together that leads to an overall increase in computational power. They enlighten many ideas such as: a neuron has its threshold level and once that level is reached the neuron fires. It is still the most basic way in which ANNs operate. The McCulloch and Pitt's network had a constant set of weights.

1.5.1.1. McCulloch Pitt's Neuron Model

The first idea of McCulloch Pitt's Neuron Model came in light in 1943, in a paper published by two scientists- Warren S. McCulloch and Walter Pitts, a neuroscientist and a logician, "A logical calculus of the ideas immanent in nervous activity" in the *Bulletin of Mathematical Biophysics*. Through this paper the two scientists, tried to explain how the brain could produce highly complex patterns by using many basic cells coupled together. Neurons are nothing but these basic brain cells. McCulloch and Pitts presented a highly simplified model of a neuron in their paper. The **MCP neuron-** McCulloch and Pitts model of a neuron, already proved its potential in the field of computer science. In fact, we can find MCP neuron at most electronic stores, but with the name "threshold logic units." ANN- **Artificial neural network** is nothing but a group of MCP neurons that are connected together. If we compare it with human brain, the brain is a very large neural network, it consists of billions of neurons, and each neuron is connected further to thousands of other neurons. McCulloch and Pitts successfully illustrated how it is possible to encode any logical proposition by an appropriate network of MCP neurons. Thus theoretically anything that can be done with a computer can also be done with a network of MCP neurons. McCulloch and Pitts also showed in their paper that every network of MCP neurons encodes some logical proposition. Then if we consider brain as a neural network, then it must be able encode some complicated computer program. But, here comes the contrast; *the MCP neuron is not a real neuron*; it's only a highly simplified model. We must be very careful while drawing conclusions about real neurons based on properties of MCP neurons.

The research of the McCullough Pitts neuron is very must useful and informative for several reasons. The foremost reason is the evolution of a new type of computer model that gradually moves away from the classical conception of a **digital computer** to the emergence of what we call a **non-classical** computer. These non-classical computers are making a significant contribution in the research of artificial intelligence by understanding the workings of the human brain. However, we cannot ignore the vitally important contributions that **mathematicians** have made to the scientific study of the mind. This is a practical example of mathematics in science.

Figure 1.3 shows a simplified model of real neurons, also known as a Threshold Logic Unit.

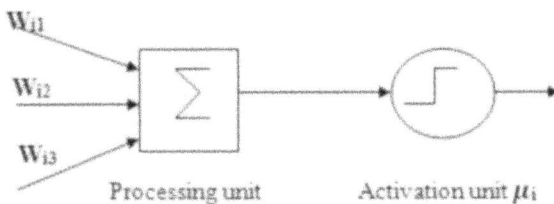

W_{i1}

W_{i2}

W_{i3}

Σ

Processing unit   Activation unit μ_i

Fig. 1.3: A simplified model of real neurons

➢ In the first step a group of inputs bringing in activations from other neurons are applied to a processing unit.

➢ Next, the processing unit sums the inputs, and then applies the sum to a non-linear activation function (μ_i in this case) over it.

➢ In the third step, the result is transmitted to other neurons through an output line.

In other words,

➢ The group of inputs arrives in the form of signals.

➤ The signals build up in the cell.
➤ Finally the cell discharges (cell fires) through the output.
➤ The cell starts building up signals again.

Below fig. 1.4 shows a more elaborative form of McCulloch Pitts neuron model.

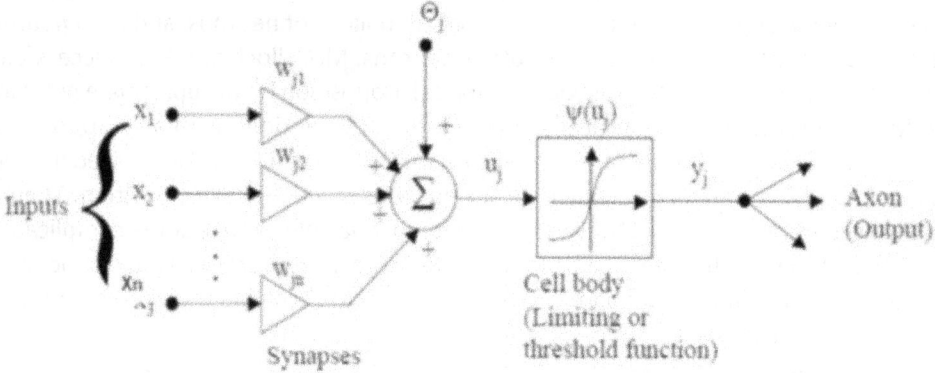

Fig. 1.4: McCulloch Pitt's Neuron Model.

The three fundamental constituents of a neuron are - weights, thresholds, and a single activation function.

$$Y_j = \psi\left(\sum_{i=0}^{n} W_{ji} x_i + \theta_j\right) \tag{1.1}$$

Where,

ψ : The node internal threshold. It is the magnitude offset also called as **activation function (A.F)**, which affects the activation of the node output Y.

Θ_j external threshold, offset or bias

W_{ji} : synaptic weights, the values W_{j1}, W_{j2},........ W_{jn} are weights to determine the strength of input vector x; x= [x_1, x_2........, x_n].

x_i : input

Y_j : output

The McCulloch-Pitts model of a neuron is so simple that it only produces a binary output, out of fixed weight and threshold values, yet it has substantial computing prospective. It also has an explicit mathematical definition. The neural computing algorithm is useful for a wide variety of applications. Thus, we need to obtain the neural model with more flexible computational features.

➤ Based on the McCulloch-Pitts model, the general form of an artificial neuron can be described in two stages shown in figure 1.4. In the first stage, the *linear combination* of inputs is calculated. Each input array corresponding to its weight value normally has values between 0 and 1. The summation function often takes an extra input value θ with weight value of 1 to represent threshold or *bias* of a neuron.

➢ The sum-of-product value is then passed onto the second stage to perform the activation function which generates the output from the neuron. The activation function "mortifies" the amplitude the output in the range of [0, 1] or [-1, 1] alternately. The behavior of the activation function will describe the characteristics of an artificial neuron model.

➢ The signals generated by actual biological neurons are the action-potential spikes. The biological neurons send the signal in the form of continuous *patterns* of spikes rather than single spike pulse. For instance, the signal could be a continuous string of pulses with various frequencies but with bounded range. The linear threshold function must be "softened".

1.5.1.2. Activation Function

An **activation function (AF)** is a function, used to perform mathematical operations on the output signal. Firing and the strength of the output signal are dealt with it. The activation function behaves like a mortifying function, such that the output of a neuron is between certain values (usually 0 and 1, or -1 and 1). More precisely the activation function can be said to as, "A function used to modify (transform) the activation level of an incoming unit (neuron) into an output signal." It also defines the unit type together with the PSP function (which is applied first). *Neural Networks* supports a large number of activation functions. However only a few of them are used by default; the others are available just for the customization purpose. The widely used activation functions are:

➢ Identity,
➢ Logistic,
➢ Hyperbolic,
➢ Exponential,
➢ Softmax,
➢ Unit sum,
➢ Square root,
➢ Sine,
➢ Ramp,
➢ Step.

     Identity: The activation level is passed on precisely as the output. It is used in a variety of networks such as linear networks, and the radial basis function's output layer.

     Logistic: This is an S-shaped (sigmoid) curve, with output in the range (0,1).

     Hyperbolic: The hyperbolic tangent function (tanh) is similar to sigmoid curve, like that of the logistic function, except that its output lies in the range (-1, +1). It is evidenced better in performance as compared to the logistic function because of its symmetry. Hyperbolic function is ideal for customization of multilayer perceptrons, especially the hidden layers.

     Exponential: The negative exponential function is ideal for use with radial units. The radial synaptic function along with negative exponential activation function results in units that model a Gaussian (bell-shaped) function with its center at the weight vector. The Gaussian function's standard deviation is given by the formula in equation 1.2, where *d* is the "deviation" of the stored unit in the threshold:

$$\sigma = \sqrt{1/d} \tag{2.2}$$

Softmax: It is an exponential function, with normalized results so that the activations sum across the layer is 1.0. It can be used in the output layer of multilayer perceptrons for pattern classification problems, so that the outputs can be defined as probabilities of class membership.

Unit sum: It normalizes the outputs to 1.0. It can be used in PNNs to allow the outputs to be defined as probabilities.

Square root: This function is used to transform the squared distance activations to the actual distance in a SOM network or Cluster network.

Sine: It is not used by default, but is useful in recognizing radially-distributed data.

Ramp: It can be viewed as a piece-wise linear form of the sigmoid function. However it is delimited because of relatively poor training performance, but is often used because of the potential of fast execution.

Step: This function gives outputs 1.0 or 0.0, depending on the positive or negative synaptic values. It can be used to model simple networks such as perceptrons.

The activation functions are decided according to the type of problem handled by the network. The mathematical representations of various activation functions are illustrated in the table below:

Activation Functions

Function	Definition	Range
Identity	x	$(-\inf, +\inf)$
Logistic	$\dfrac{1}{1-e^{-1}}$	$(0, +1)$
Hyperbolic	$\dfrac{e^{x}-e^{-x}}{e^{x}+e^{-x}}$	$(-1, +1)$
-Exponential	e^{-x}	$(0, +\inf)$
Softmax	$\dfrac{e^{x}}{\sum\limits_{i} e^{x_i}}$	$(0, +1)$
Unit sum	$\dfrac{x}{\sum\limits_{i} x_1}$	$(0, +1)$

Square root	$\sqrt{x}$	(0, + inf)
Sine	$\sin(x)$	[0, + 1]
Ramp	$\begin{cases} -x & \le -1 \\ x-1 & < x < +1 \\ +1 & x \ge +1 \end{cases}$	[-1, + 1]
Step	$\begin{cases} 0 & x < 0 \\ +1 & x \ge 0 \end{cases}$	[0, + 1]

Review Questions

1. Explain Biological Neuron and Artificial Neuron on the basis of structure and function of a single neuron.
2. Discuss the various techniques/ aspects of soft computing in short.
3. Discuss the taxonomy of neural network architecture.
4. Write short note on Activation Function.
5. Describe briefly Artificial Neural Network (ANN), and the first Artificial Neuron model.
6. Explain Biological Neural Networks along with the steps involved in neuronal-processing.
7. Differentiate between hard computing and soft computing.

CHAPTER 2

Training the Neural Networks

In this chapter we will discuss the most important aspect of Neuro-computing, i.e. training algorithms. At first we will discuss about various types of learning in neural network, than we will cover the algorithms portion, as it was seen in chapter 1 under the heading "the journey of neural networks" various advancements in the models of neural networks, here in this chapter we will cover those networks which supports supervised learning principle, namely, Perceptron, ADALINE, MADALINE, Backpropagation networks, Radial Basis Function Networks (RBFN); their corresponding learning rules, like, Gradient descent learning, Hebbian learning rule, LMS learning rule and winner takes all etc.

2.1. Learning

One of the most important parts of creating a Neural Network is the learning phase. The process of learning of a Neural Network can be interpreted in simple language as renovating a sheet of metal; this metal sheet represents the output (range) of the function to be mapped. The energy involved in bending the sheet of metal in a predefined shape or through pre-assigned points, is denoted by the training set (domain). However, the metal, by its characteristics, will resist such reshaping. So the network will try to fix to a zone of comfort (i.e. a flat/non-wrinkled shape) that satisfies the constraints (training data).

By learning rules we mean a systematic procedure for modifying the weights and biases of a network, or in other words, adapting the network's characteristics while training it to perform certain tasks. Training is nothing but this whole learning procedure. The learning in neural networks is broadly classified into three categories-

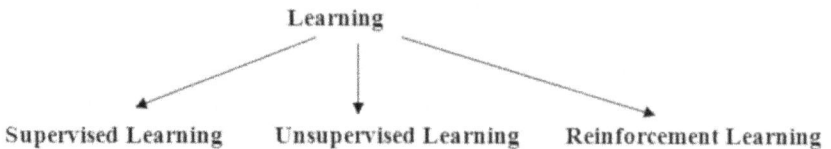

Learning

Supervised Learning   Unsupervised Learning   Reinforcement Learning

2.1.1. Supervised Learning

Supervised learning is a training mechanism employed to train the neural networks. The fundamental principle that differentiates supervised learning from other learning principles, is, "learning with a teacher". The training data contains some *training examples*. In supervised learning, each example consists of an input object (typically a vector) and a desired response (also called the *supervisory signal*). A supervised learning algorithm evaluates the training data and produces an implicit function, which can be further utilized for mapping new examples. Under optimal circumstances the algorithm will correctly determine the class labels for unseen examples. This requires the learning algorithm to guesstimate from the training data to unseen patterns (examples) in a logical methodology. The parallel task handling mechanism in human neuro-system is often specified as concept learning. A set of examples (the training set) is provided to the learning rule: $\{x_1, d_1\}$, $\{x_2, d_2\}$, ..., $\{x_n, d_n\}$

Where, x_n is the input to the network, d_n is the desired response. With the inputs applied to the network, the network outputs are analogized with the desired outputs. The learning rule is then used to adapt the network or in other words adjust the weights and the biases of the network in order to move the network outputs closer to the desired response.

In supervised learning we keep in mind that at each instant of time when the input is applied, the teacher presents the desired response of the system. This is shown in figure 2.3, the distance between the actual and the desired response serves as an error measure and is used to correct network parameter externally. For example, in learning the taxonomy of input patterns with known desired responses, the error is utilized for modifying the weights, so that the difference between the desired output and actual output can be minimized. This mode of learning is widely employed in a variety of applications, in which natural language learning, image recognition etc are required.

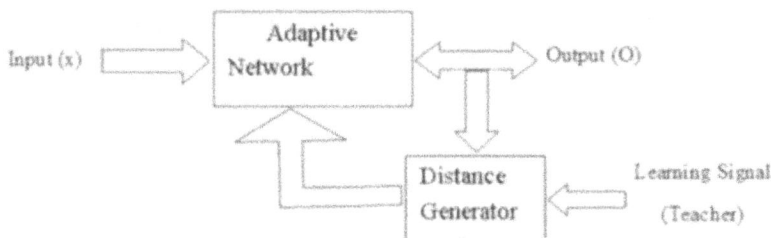

Fig.2.1: Block diagram for explanation of supervised learning.

2.1.2.   Unsupervised Learning

In unsupervised learning, the weights and biases are modified in response to network input only. There are no target outputs available. It is like there is no teacher to present the desired patterns and hence, the system learns by itself by discovering and adapting to structural features in the input patterns. This might seem impractical, how can you train a network if you don't know the desired response? This can be done by using clustering operation; the majority of these algorithms perform some kind of clustering operation. Under this methodology the input patterns are classified into a finite number of classes, which is particularly useful in applications such as vector quantization.

In learning without supervision the desired response is unknown; thus, to improve network behavior direct (straightforward) error information cannot be used. As no information is available regarding the correctness or incorrectness of responses, learning is accomplished somehow by the observation of responses to inputs that we have marginal or no knowledge about. Unsupervised learning algorithms use patterns that are redundant raw data, having no label regarding their class membership, or associations. In this mode of learning, the network discover itself about any possibly existing patterns, consistencies/ regularities, irregularities, etc., while discovering these characteristics network adapts its parameters. Unsupervised learning is sometimes referred to as learning without a teacher. However this terminology can-not be the most appropriate because mere learning without a teacher is not at all possible. Although, we agree with the point that the teacher does not have to be involved in every training step, but he is required to set objective even in an unsupervised learning mode.

Learning with feedback, from the teacher or from the environment, however, is more typical for neural network. Such learning is performed in steps and called incremental. The concept of feedback plays a vital role in learning. The concept is highly elusive and somewhat contradictory. In a broad sense it can be understood as an introduction of a pattern of relationships into the cause-and-effect path.

More on Supervised and Unsupervised Learning

Let us understand supervised and unsupervised learning with a simple real life example: Suppose you have a basket filled with fruits like, apple, guava, cherry, grapes. What you have to do is to rearrange the fruits, by making separate groups of same species fruits each. All these fruits are strange to you as you have seen them for the first time in your life. One after another we will see both supervised and unsupervised mechanisms for establishing the task.

Supervised mechanism:

So you are provided with the input patterns (basket of fruits), in supervised learning, a teacher will help you for accomplishing the task by telling you about the characteristics of each fruit (desired output), like-

➢   Big sized, red in color, with depression at the top means **Apple**.

➢   Small sized, red in color, with globular shape means **Cherry**.

➢   Big sized, green in color, having depression at the top means **Guava**.

➢   Small sized, green in color, with oval shaped means **Grapes**.

Thus, these are the desired responses provided to you by the teacher. By analyzing and keeping in mind all the illustrated points, you can easily accomplish the task by categorizing and rearranging the fruits in separate groups.

Unsupervised Mechanism:

Under this learning, the same bucket with the same fruits is provided, but this time, no teacher is available for helping you by providing the desired responses. What to do in this case?

Firstly, you will pick any one characteristic of the fruits, say color. You will start rearranging them on the basis of color. Your approach might be similar to this-

➤ Red color: **Apples** and **Cherries**.

➤ Green color: **Guavas** and **Grapes**.

You find the results unsatisfactory, so next, you will consider another characteristic, suppose, size. This time your approach will be like this-

➤ Red color + Big size: **Apple**

➤ Red color + Small size: **Cherry**

➤ Green color + Big size: **Guava**

➤ Green color + Small size: **Grape**

Task successfully accomplished. This is the procedure under unsupervised learning.

2.1.3. Reinforcement Learning

This method of learning although include a teacher, but the role of teacher here is not to present the desired patterns or examples, which help the system to learn, instead the teacher here only indicates if the computed output is correct or incorrect. We can analogize the information provided by the teacher, as rewards or punishments. A reward is provided for correct answer, and a punishment for the inaccurate answer. The system learns by figuring out, what it has done that made it get the reward or punishment. This method of learning is less popular as compared to supervised and unsupervised learning.

Supervised and unsupervised learning can be further classified based on learning rules as shown in below figure 2.2.

2.2. Learning Rules

In this section we will discuss various learning rules, which are shown in figure 2.2.

2.2.1. Gradient Descent Learning

At theoretical level, gradient descent is an algorithm based on the minimization of error E defined in terms of weights and activation function of the network. In this more advanced learning, weights are changed so that the network error is decreased as soon as possible. In other words, the learning rule moves the network down the steepest slope in error expanse. This is the basic meaning of gradient descent learning. It is the most common approach to training modern connectionist networks that use integration devices or value units as processors. The trick is to figure out HOW to adjust the weights. Intuitively, we know that if a change in a weight will increase (decrease) the error, then we needs to increase or decrease that weight. Mathematically, this means that we look at the derivative of the error with respect to the weight: $\partial E/\partial W_{ij}$, which represents change in the error given a unit change in the weight. Our main objective is to choose such value of weight (W_{ij}), so that the error (E) is at its minimum. There are three cases to consider:

➤ If $\partial E/\partial W_{ij} > 0$; then E increases with the increase in W_{ij}, So we have to decrease W_{ij}.

➤ If $\partial E/\partial W_{ij} < 0$; then E decreases with the increase in W_{ij}, So we have to increase W_{ij}.

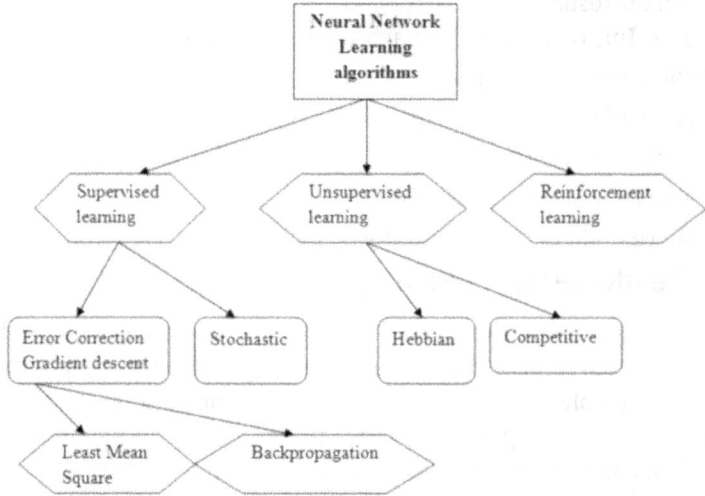

Fig.2.2: Classification of Learning based on learning rules

➤ If $\partial E/\partial W_{ij} = 0$; then E is at its maximum or minimum value, So we need not change W_{ij}.

In generalized form, we could say that, we can decrease E by changing W_{ij} by the amount:

$$\Delta W_{ij} = W_{ij}^{new} - W_{ij}^{old} = -\eta\ [\partial E/\partial W_{ij}] \qquad (2.1)$$

Where, η is a small positive constant also called the learning parameter, which specifies by how much amount we have to change W_{ij}; and $\partial E/\partial W_{ij}$ is the error gradient with respect to the weight W_{ij}.

Assuming η to be very small, and repeatedly using the eq (2.1), E will keep descending towards its minimum. Therefore, this procedure is termed as gradient descent minimization.

The Windrow and Hoffs/ Delta/ Least mean square (LMS) rule and Backpropagation learning rules are all examples of this type of learning mechanism.

2.2.2. Stochastic Learning

Under this algorithm, weights are adjusted in a probabilistic manner. One of the examples of stochastic learning is in simulated annealing- the learning mechanism employed by Boltzmann and Cauchy machines, which are a kind of NN systems.

2.2.3. Hebbian Learning

The Hebbian rule is the oldest and was the first learning rule that was developed by Donald Hebb in 1949 as learning algorithm of unsupervised neural network. Donald Hebb states that, "when an axon of cell A is near enough to excite a cell B and repeatedly or persistently participates in firing it, some development or metabolic changes occurs in one or both cells such that one cells efficiency of firing the other, is increased". This learning can also be referred to as correlational learning.

This statement may be summarized into a two-part rule:

(i)   If two neurons present on either side of a synapse are activated simultaneously, then the strength of that synapse is particularly enhanced.

(ii)   If two neurons present on either side of a synapse are activated asynchronously, then the strength of that synapse is particularly exhausted or eliminated.

This means that Hebb introduced the concept of increasing weights, but not decreasing weights. From pattern recognition perspective, this provides the means to strengthen weights when inputs are similar, and to weaken them when they're dissimilar. This type of synapse is called a Hebbian synapse. The four key mechanisms that characterize a Hebbian synapse are time dependent mechanism, local mechanism, interactive mechanism and correlational mechanism.

In the simplest form of Hebbian learning, the input- output pattern pairs (X_i, Y_i) are associated by the Weight matrix W. And is described by,

$$W_{ij} = \sum_{i=1}^{n} X_j Y_i T \qquad (2.2)$$

Where, X_j is the input, Y_i is the output, and W_{ij} is the weight that connects the input and output, Y_i^T is the transpose of the associated vector Y_i.

The Hebbian learning rule represents a purely feed forward, unsupervised learning. It states that if the cross product of output and input is positive, this result in increase of weight, otherwise the weight decreases. The NN that uses the Hebb's rule is a very simple network that utilizes some number of input cells, and identical set of output cells as shown in fig. 2.3.

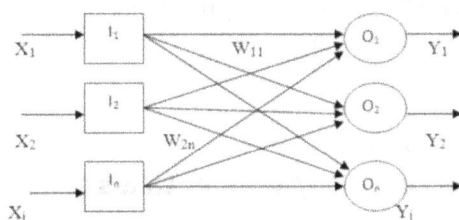

Fig.2.3: A simple feedforward network utilizing Hebb's learning rule

The network is fully interconnected, with weights connecting between each output cell and each input cell so that every input has some influence over the output. In order to train the network and build the association between input and output cells, the network must be provided with the input pattern and duplicate the value of the input at the output. Once the weights have been trained using Hebb's learning rule, the network can recall output patterns from those presented to the input. However, one major disadvantage with Hebb's rule is that it can only create map over orthogonal patterns of inputs. This is due to the lack of hidden layer within the network.

In some cases, the Hebbian rule needs to be modified to counteract unconstrained growth of synaptic weights, which takes place when excitations and response consistently agree in sign (because Hebbian rule states that weights can only increase). To resolve this problem, we might impose a limit on the growth of synaptic weights. It can be done by introducing a non-linear *forgetting factor* into Hebb's rule:

$$\Delta W_{ij} = \alpha\, Y_i X_j - \phi Y_i\, W_{ij} \tag{2.3}$$

Where, is the forgetting factor, its value usually falls in the interval between 0 and 1, typically between 0.01 and 0.1 to allow only a little "forgetting" while limiting the weight growth.

Step-wise illustration:

Step1: Initialization:

Set initial synaptic weights and thresholds to small random value, say in an interval [0,1].

Step2: Activation:

Compute the neuron output

$$Y_i = \sum_{i=1}^{n} X_j W_{ij} - \Theta_j \tag{2.4}$$

where n is the number of neuron inputs, and q_j is the threshold value of neuron j.

Step3: Learning:

Update the weights in the network

$$W_{ij}(P + 1) = W_{ij}(P) + \Delta W_{ij}(P) \tag{2.5}$$

Where, $\Delta W_{ij}(P)$ is the weight correction at iteration P.

The weight correction is determined by the generalized activity product rule:

$$\Delta W_{ij}(P) = \varphi Y_i(P)\, [\lambda X_j(P) - W_{ij}(P)] \tag{2.6}$$

Step4: Iteration:

Increase iteration P by one, go back to step 2.

2.2.4. Competitive Learning/ Winner takes all learning

The competitive learning rule was introduced in the early 1970s. Later after a decade, in 1980s, Teuvo Kohonen introduced a special class of artificial neural networks called **self-organizing feature maps**. These maps are based on competitive learning. We will discuss these maps in details in chapter 3, in this section we are going to learn about competitive learning rule.

In competitive learning, neurons present in the output unit compete with each other to be activated. While in Hebbian learning, several output neurons can be activated simultaneously, in competitive learning, only a single output neuron is active at any time. The output units are said to be in competition for input patterns. During training, the output unit that provides the highest activation to a given input pattern is declared the winner and is shifted closer to the input pattern, however the rest of the neurons are left unchanged. The output neuron that wins the "competition" is called the **winner-takes-all** neuron.

A neuron learns by shifting its weights from inactive connections to active ones. Only the winning neuron and its neighborhood are allowed to learn. If a neuron does not respond to a given input pattern, then learning cannot occur in that particular neuron. The **competitive learning rule** defines the change Δw_{ij} applied to synaptic weight w_{ij} as,

$\Delta w_{ij} = \alpha\,(x_i - w_{ij})$, if neuron j wins the competition

$\Delta w_{ij} = 0$, if neuron j loses the competition

where x_i is representing the input signal and *á* denotes the *learning rate* parameter. The principle objective of the competitive learning rule resides in bringing the synaptic weight vector W_j of the winning neuron j closer to the input pattern X. This matching methodology is simliar to the minimum **Euclidean distance** between vectors. The Euclidean distance between a pair of $n{:}1$ vectors X and W_j is mathematically represented by,

$$d = \| x - w_{ij} \| = \left[\sum\nolimits_{j=1}^{n} (x_i - w_{ij})^2 \right]^{1/2} \tag{2.7}$$

where, x_i and w_{ij} are the i_{th} elements of the vectors X and W_j, respectively.

To identify the winning neuron, j_x, that is closer to the input vector X, the following condition can be applied:

$j_x = \min \| X - W_j \|, j = 1,2,.....,m$ \hfill (2.8)

where m is the number of neurons in the Kohonen layer.

Step- wise illustration:

Step 1: Initialization:

Assign small random values to initial synaptic weights initially, let, in an interval $[0, 1]$, and allocate a small positive value to the learning rate parameter α.

Step 2: Activation and Similarity Matching:

Now activate the Kohonen SOM network by applying the input vector X, and determine the winner-takes-all (best matching) neuron j_x at iteration p, using the minimum-distance Euclidean criterion

$$j_x(p) = \min \| X - W_j \| = \left[\sum\nolimits_{j=1}^{n} (x_i - w_{ij})^2 \right]^{1/2}, \; j = 1,2,.......m \tag{2.9}$$

where n is representing the number of neurons present in the input layer, and m

is the total number of neurons present in the Kohonen map.

Step 3: Learning:

Update the synaptic weights,

$$W_{ij}(p + 1) = W_{ij}(p) + \Delta W_{ij}(p) \tag{2.10}$$

where $\Delta W_{ij}(p)$ denotes the weight correction at the pth iteration. The weight correction is determined by the competitive learning rule:

$$\Delta w_{ij} = \alpha (x_i - w_{ij}), j \in \Lambda_j (p)$$

$$\Delta w_{ij} = 0, j \in \Lambda_j (p)$$

where α is the *learning rate* parameter, and $\Lambda_j(p)$ = neighborhood function centered around the winner-takes-all neuron j_x at iteration p.

Step 4: Iteration:

Make advancement in the iteration p by one, repeat the process from Step 2 and continue until the minimum- Euclidian distance criterion is satisfied, and the feature map becomes stable with no noticeable changes.

2.2.5. Least Mean Square (LMS) / Windrow- Hoff Learning Rule

Bernard Windrow began his research on Neural Networks in the late 1950s. At nearly the same year, Frank Rosenblatt introduced the Perceptron Learning rule. In 1960, Windrow and Hoff brought in light ADALINE (ADAptive LInear NEuron) network. Its learning rule is called LMS (Least Mean Square) algorithm and is a supervised learning law.

The LMS algorithm minimizes mean square error, and therefore tries to move the decision boundaries as far from the training patterns as possible. This algorithm found many practical uses (like most long distance phone lines uses ADALINE network for echo cancellation).

Here, the change in the weight vector is,

$$\Delta W_i = \eta [t_p - O_p] x_i \tag{2.11}$$

Where, O_p = actual output and t_p = target output, the actual output of the ADALINE and given by,

$$O_p = W_i^T x_i \tag{2.12}$$

Hence,

$$\Delta W_{ij} = \eta [t_p - O_{pj}] x_{ij}, \qquad \text{for } j = 1,2,......,M \tag{2.13}$$

The change in the weight is made proportional to the negative gradient of the error between the desired output and the continuous activation value, which is also a continuous output signal due to linearity of the output function. Mathematically, this can be written as,

$$\partial E_p / \partial W_i = -2 (t_p - O_p) x_i \tag{2.14}$$

To decrease E_p by gradient descent the update formula of W_i given in equation 2.11 is used. It states that-

When $t_p > O_p$, we should increase O_p, by increasing $W_i x_i$; i.e., we should increase W_i if x_i is positive, and decrease W_i if x_i is negative.

Similarly, when $t_p < O_p$, we should decrease O_p by increasing $W_i x_i$.

Since in the whole algorithm our main objective is to minimize the square error, therefore, it is named as Least Mean Square algorithm.

Note: Backpropagation learning rule will be discussed later, with the explanation of backpropagation networks .

2.3. The Perceptron learning

In the late 1950s, Frank Rosenblatt and a group of researchers developed a class of Neural Networks called perceptrons. The neurons in these networks were much similar to those present in MCP model. Rosenblatt's crucially contributed in the history of artificial neural networks by discovering a learning rule for training perceptron networks to solve pattern recognition problems. Learning was very much simpler and automatic. Instances of proper behavior were portrayed to the network, which learned from experiences and past mistakes.

Inspite of the great contribution to artificial intelligence, perceptrons suffered with some severe limitations. These limitations were brought in light by two scientists Marvin Minsky and Seymour Paperts by their book Perceptrons. One of the major limitations of perceptron demonstrated by them was that, they could not learn those functions which are linearly inseparable. Rosenblatt had investigated more complex networks, which were thought to be beneficial in solving such problems, but he was always unable to extend the perceptron rule to such networks. During 1980s these limitations were overcome with improved *multilayer perceptron network*. Later in 1986 Rumelhart, Hinton and Wilham demonstrated a precise description of *backpropagation algorithm*; which was proved to be a systematic training algorithm for multilayer perceptron network.

Before proceeding on our further discussion on perceptron learning, it will be better to have a clear-cut idea about the various architectures of neural networks.

2.3.1. Architecture of Neural Networks

Neural Networks are known to be universal function approximators. Various architectures are available to approximate any nonlinear function. Different architectures allow for generation of functions of different complexity and power.

➢ Single layer Feedforward networks

➢ Multilayer Feedforward networks

➢ Recurrent or Feedback networks.

Table 2.1 shows classification of various neural networks according to their architectural types and learning methods.

Learning Method					
		Gradient descent	*Hebbian*	*Competitive*	*Stochastic*
Type of Architecture	*Single-layer feedforward*	ADALINE Hopfield Perceptron	AM Hopfield	LVQ SOFM	-
	Multilayer feedforward	Cascade Correlation MLFF RBF	Neocognitron	-	-
	Recurrent neural network	RNN	BAM BSB Hopfield	ART	Boltzmann machine Cauchy machine

Table 2.1: Classification of some NNs with respect to learning methods and architecture types

2.3.1.1. Feedforward Networks

A feed-forward neural network is a biologically inspired classification algorithm. It consists of a (possibly large) number of simple neuron-like processing units, organized in layers. Each unit in a layer is connected with all the units present in the previous layer. All these connections are not equal; each connection may exhibit different strengths or weights, especially when interconnections among the units do not form a directed cycle. The weight on these connections contains information about the network. The units in a neural network are also referred to as nodes. Data enters at the inputs and travels through the network, layer by layer, and finally arrives at the outputs. At the time of normal operation, when it behaves as a classifier, there is exactly no feedback present between the layers. This is the reason behind calling them feed-forward neural networks.

Fig. 2.4 shows an example of a 2-layered network with: 3 input units, a *hidden* layer with 4 units and an output layer with 5 units, respectively. The network has 3 input units.

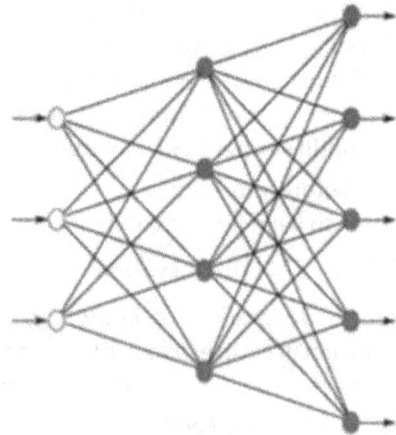

Fig. 2.4: Feed forward Network

The operation of this network can be divided into two phases:

1.   The learning phase
2.   The classification phase

These artificial neurons have nowadays little in common with their biological counterpart in the ANN standard; rather they are primarily used as computational devices, performing the task of problem solving: optimization, pattern classification, function approximation, real time prediction and many others.

2.3.1.1.1. Single Layer feedforward network

The simplest kind of neural network is a *single-layer* network (called Perceptron), which consists of a single layer of output nodes to which the inputs are fed directly through a series of weights. The model shown in Fig.2.5 can be considered the simplest kind of feed-forward network. The Perceptron is said to be a single-layer artificial network with just a single neuron. The sum of the products of the weights and the inputs is calculated at each node, and if the result is above the threshold value (typically 0) the neuron fires and takes the activated value (typically 1); otherwise it takes the deactivated value (typically -1). The neuron unit calculates the linear combination of its real-valued or Boolean inputs and passes it through a threshold activation function, according to Eq. 2.15.

$$O = Threshold\ (\Sigma_i x_i) \tag{2.15}$$

where x_i are the components of the input $x_e = (\ x_{e1},\ x_{e2},...,\ x_{ed}\ )$ from the set $\{(x_e, y_e)\}_{e=1}^{N}$ Threshold is the activation function defined as follows: Threshold $(\ s\ ) = 1$ if $s > 0$ and -1 otherwise.

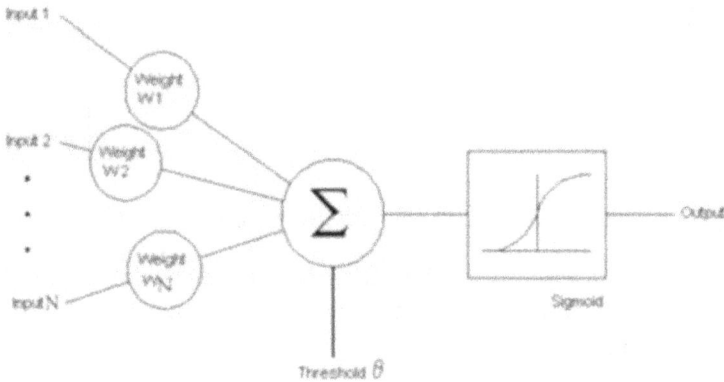

Fig.2.5: Perceptron

Neurons with this kind of activation function are also called artificial neurons or linear threshold units. The term Perceptron often refers to networks consisting of just a single unit of these units. A much alike neuron was discovered by Warren McCulloch and Walter Pitts in the early 1940s. The Perceptron is also known by the name threshold logic unit (TLU) since it distinguish the data on the basis of, whether the threshold value is lesser than the sum, i.e. $\Sigma_{i=1} w_i x_i > - w_0$ or the sum is less than the threshold value, i.e. $\Sigma_{i=1} w_i x_i < - w_0$. In the above formulation we imagine that the threshold value w_0 is the weight of an additional connection held constantly to $x_0 = 1$.

2.3.1.1.2. Multilayer feedforward network

Multi-Layer Feed-Forward neural networks that are trained by back-propagation learning algorithm are the most widely used neural networks. A wide scope of applications is present for various chemistry related problems. A Multi-Layer Feed-Forward neural network consists of neurons that are ordered into layers shown in Fig.2.6. The first layer represents the input layer, the last layer represents the output layer, and the layers between these two are the hidden layers.

For the formal description of the neurons we can use the so-called mapping function Γ, that assigns for each neuron i a subset $\Gamma_i \in V$ which consists of all ancestors of the given neuron. A subset $\Gamma_i^{-1} \in V$ than consists of all predecessors of the neuron i. A neuron present in any particular layer is connected with all neurons in the next layer. The weight coefficient w_{ij} represents the connection between the j_{th} neuron and the i_{th} neuron by the threshold coefficient ϑ_i.

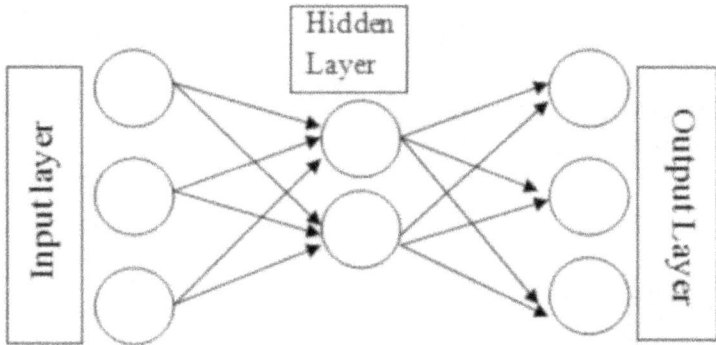

Fig.2.6: Typical feed forward neural network composed of three layers

The weight coefficient reflects the degree of importance of the given connection in the neural network. The output value (activity) of the i_{th} neuron x_i is determined by Equation 2.16. It holds that:

$$x_i = f(\xi_i) \tag{2.16}$$
$$\xi_i = \vartheta_i + \sum_{j \in \Gamma} W_{ij} x_j \tag{2.17}$$

Where ξ_i is the potential of the ith neuron and function $f(\xi_i)$ is the so-called transfer function (the summation in Equation 2.17 is performed over all neurons j transferring the signal to the i_{th} neuron). The threshold coefficient can be viewed as a weight coefficient of the connection with formally added neuron j, where $x_j = 1$ (so-called bias).

The adaptation process in supervised learning algorithm varies the threshold coefficients f_{ii} and weight coefficients w_{ij} to minimize the sum of the squared differences between the computed and required output values.

2.3.1.2. Recurrent Neural Network or Feedback Network

The fundamental feature of a *Recurrent Neural Network (RNN)* is that the network contains at least one *feed-back connection,* so that the activations can proceed round in a loop. This enables the networks to perform sequence recognition/reproduction or temporal association/prediction.

Recurrent neural network architectures can have many different forms. One common type consists of a standard Multi-Layer Perceptron (MLP) plus added loops. These can utilize the striking non-linear mapping potentials of the MLP, and also have some form of *memory.* Other types of RNN consist of more uniform structures, with each neuron connected to each others, and may also have stochastic activation functions.

For simple architectures and deterministic activation functions, learning can be achieved using similar gradient descent procedures to those leading to the back-propagation algorithm for feed-forward networks. For stochastic activations, simulated annealing approaches might be more suitable.

The most basic form of *fully recurrent neural network* is an MLP with the previous set of hidden unit activations feeding back into the network along with the inputs:

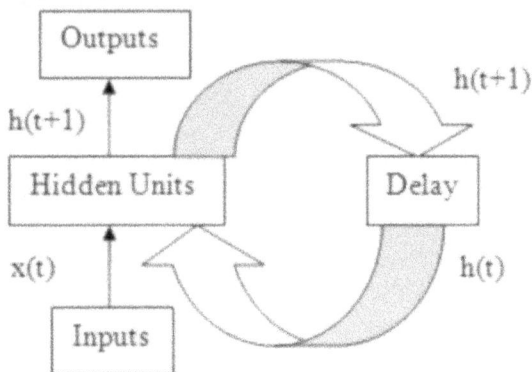

Fig.2.7: A fully recurrent neural network

Note that the time *t* has to be *discretized,* with the activations updating at each time step. The time scale might correspond to the operation of real neurons, or for artificial systems any time step size appropriate for the given problem can be used. A *delay unit* needs to be introduced to hold activations until they are processed at the next time step.

2.3.2. Perceptron Learning Rule

The operation of Rosenblatt's perceptron is based on the McCulloch and Pitts neuron model. The model comprise of a linear combiner followed by a hard limiter. The weighted sum of the inputs is applied to the hard limiter, which produces an output equal to +1 if its input is positive and -1 if it is negative. Fig.2.8 shows a general perceptron network.

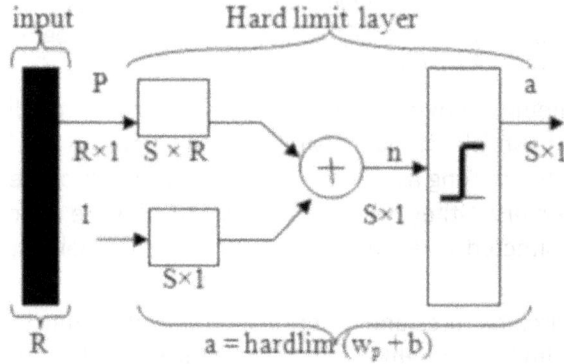

Fig. 2.8: Perceptron Network

The perceptron categorize inputs, $x_1, x_2, \ldots, x_n$, into one of two classes, say **A**$_1$ and **A**$_2$. In the case of a rudimentary perceptron, the n- dimensional space is divided by a *hyperplane* into two decision boundaries. The hyperplane is described by the ***linearly separable*** function as:

$$\sum_{i=1}^{n} x_i w_i - \theta = 0 \qquad\qquad (2.18)$$

Linear separability in perceptrons has been demonstrated in below figure 2.9.

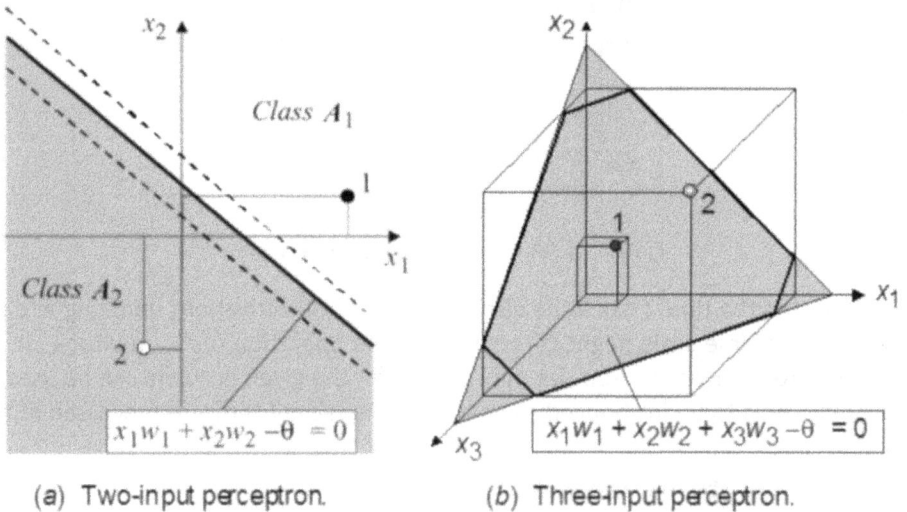

(a) Two-input perceptron.   (b) Three-input perceptron.

Fig.2.9: Linear Separability in the Perceptrons

Perceptron learns its classification task by making small adjustments in the weights to reduce the difference between the actual and desired outputs of the perceptron. Initially the weights are randomly assigned, usually in the range [-0.5, 0.5], and then updated to obtain the output consistent with the training examples. If at iteration *p*, the actual output is $Y(p)$ and the desired output is $Y_d(p)$, then the error is given by:

$$e(p) = Y_d(p) - Y(p) \tag{2.19}$$

where $p = 1, 2, 3, \ldots$

Iteration p here refers to the pth training example presented to the perceptron. The perceptron output $Y(p)$ is increased or decreased according to the error, $e(p)$. If the error, $e(p)$, is positive, we have to increase perceptron output $Y(p)$, however, if it is negative, we need to decrease $Y(p)$.

The perceptron learning rule follows:

$$w_i(p + 1) = w_i(p) + \alpha X_i(p).e(p) \tag{2.20}$$

where $p = 1, 2, 3, \ldots$

α = *learning rate-* a positive constant less than unity.

The perceptron learning rule was first brought in light by Rosenblatt in 1960. Utilizing this rule we can derive the perceptron training algorithm for pattern-classification applications.

Perceptron's Training Algorithm

Step 1: Initialization

Set initial weights $w_1, w_2, \ldots, w_n$ and threshold to random numbers in the range [-0.5, 0.5]. If the error, $e(p)$ is positive, the perceptron output $Y(p)$ is increased, but if it is negative, $Y(p)$ is decreased.

Step 2: Activation

Activate the perceptron by applying inputs $x_1(p)$, $x_2(p), \ldots, x_n(p)$ and desired output Y_d (p). Calculate the actual output at iteration $p = 1$

$$Y(p) = \text{Step} \left[\sum_{i=1}^{n} x_i(p) w_i(p) - \theta \right] \tag{2.21}$$

Where, n = number of the perceptron inputs, and *step* denotes the step activation function.

Step 3: Weight training

Update the weights of the perceptron-

$$w_i(p + 1) = w_i(p) + \Delta w_i(p) \tag{2.22}$$
$$\Delta w_i(p) = \alpha x_i(p) e(p) \tag{2.23}$$

Step 4: Iteration

Increase iteration p by one, go back to *Step 2* and repeat the process until convergence.

The perceptron is a linear classifier; therefore it will never get to the state with all the input vectors classified correctly if the training set is not linearly separable, i.e. if the positive examples cannot be separated from the negative examples by a hyperplane. But if the training set is linearly separable, then the perceptron will surely converge, however it is still undefined that how many times the perceptron will adjust its weights during the training.

The concept of perceptron initially was thought to be very much propitious, it was soon proved that perceptrons have many limitations in learning to recognize many classes of patterns. This led to the deterioration of the field of neural network research for many years, before it was recognized that a feedforward neural network with multiple layers (also called a multilayer perceptron) had far greater processing power than perceptrons with one layer (also called a single layer perceptron). Single layer perceptrons are only proficient in learning <u>linearly separable</u> patterns; in 1969 a famous book entitled *Perceptrons* by Marvin Minsky and Seymour Papert showed that it was impossible for these classes of network to learn an **XOR** function. Below figure 2.10 demonstrates the linear inseparability of XOR function.

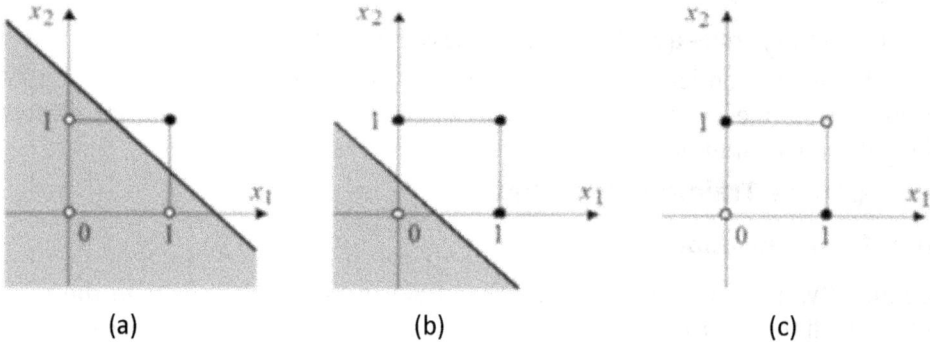

(a)   (b)   (c)

Fig.2.10: (a) AND $(x_1 \cap x_2)$, (b) OR $(x_1 \cup x_2)$, (c) Exclusive-OR $(x_1 \oplus x_2)$

Sets of points in two dimensional spaces are linearly separable if the sets can be separated by a straight line. It is evident from above figure 2.10 that it is possible to separate the even parity input patterns from the odd parity input patterns in the first two cases of AND and OR gates (fig. a and b), but it is inherently impossible to find a line separating even parity input patterns from the odd parity input patterns in the case of XOR gate (fig. c).

The XOR Problem

The truth table of XOR logical operation is given in table 2.2.

Inputs	Inputs	Output	
0	0	0	Even parity
1	1	0	
0	1	1	Odd parity
1	0	1	

Table 2.2: XOR truth table

The problem is to classify the inputs as odd parity or even parity. Here odd parity means odd number of 1 bits in the inputs, and even parity means even number of 1 bits in the inputs.

In this case of XOR function, it is impossible as is shown in fig. 2.11 (c), the perceptron is unable to find a line separating even parity input patterns from the odd parity input patterns. Now the question arises, why is the perceptron unable to find weights for non-linearly separable classification problems? This can be explained by means of a simple instance.

Consider a perceptron network with two inputs x_1 and x_2 and bias $x_0 = 1$ as shown in below figure 2.11. The weighted sum of the inputs.

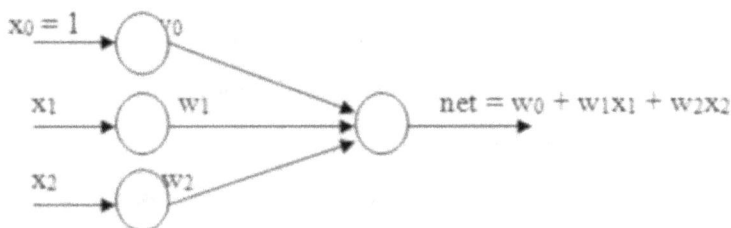

Fig. 2.11: A perceptron model with two inputs x_1, x_2.

$$net = w_0 + w_1x_1 + w_2x_2 \qquad (2.24)$$

eq 2.24 is similar to the equation of a straight line. The straight line acts as a decision boundary separating the points A_1 and A_2, above and below the line respectively (refer Fig. 2.10 (a)).

Minsky and Papert recognized that only multi-layer perceptrons have the potential of producing an XOR function. Later on Stephen Grossberg published a series of papers introducing networks capable of modelling differential, contrast-enhancing and XOR functions. Later in 1986 Rumelhart, Hinton and Wilham demonstrated a precise description of **backpropagation algorithm**; which was proved to be a systematic training algorithm for multilayer perceptron network. Before switching to the backpropagation algorithm, let's have a look at other networks say, ADALINE and MADALINE networks. Our next section is dedicated to these networks.

2.3.3. ADALINE Network

The Adaptive Linear Neural Element (ADALINE) Network is an early single layer neural network framed by Bernard Windrow and his graduate student Ted Hoff at Stanford University in the year 1960. It is based on the McCulloch Pitts neuron and makes use of supervised learning. Below figure 2.13 illustrates a simple ADALINE network.

Here, there is only one output neuron and the output values Y_k are bipolar (-1 or +1). However, the inputs x_k can be binary, bipolar or real valued. The bias weight is w_k with an input link of $x_k = + 1$. If the weighted sum of the inputs is greater than or equal to 0 then the output is 1 otherwise it is -1. There are 2^n possible input patterns. Thus there possible logic functions connecting n inputs to a single binary output.

The supervised learning algorithm adopted by ADALINE is similar to that of perceptron learning algorithm used in the standard (McCulloch–Pitts) perceptron. The only difference is that the adaline, after each iteration checks if the weight works for each of the input patterns; the perceptron just updates the weight after each new input pattern and does not go back and check.

In contrast, the ADALINE has two advantages:

➤   It is more accurate.

➤   It will tell the user if the adaline/perceptron is not suited for the given set of input patterns, because the adaline will keep on updating its weights and never stop if the adaline/perceptron can-not categorize the input patterns.

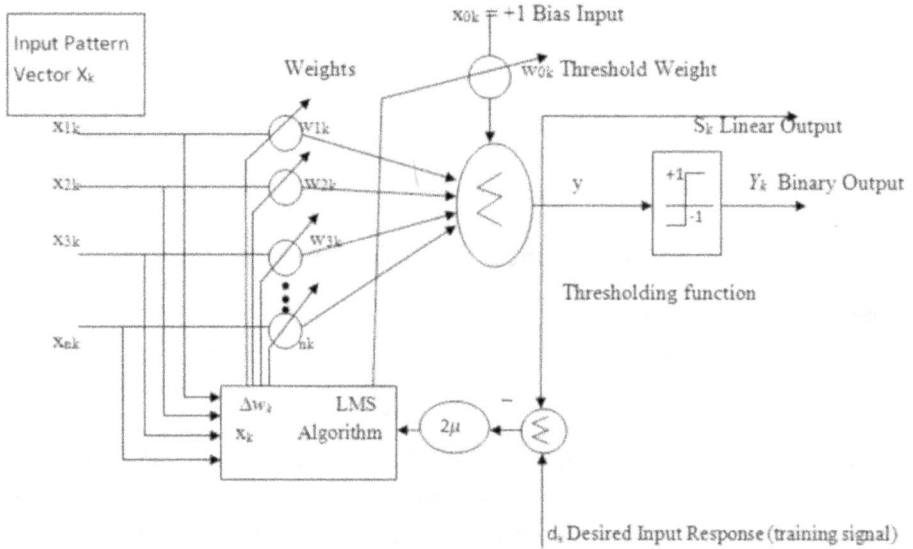

Fig.2.12: A simple ADALINE network

The learning algorithm used in ADALINE is also known as *Least Mean Square (LMS)* or *Delta rule*. This rule is very similar to perceptron learning rule. However their fundamentals basis are different; the perceptron learning rule is based on the Hebbian assumption, while the delta rule is based on gradient descent method. Also the perceptron learning rule converges after a finite number of learning steps, but the gradient descent approach continues forever, converging only asymptotically to the solution. The main object of the delta rule is to minimize the difference between net input to the output unit and the target value, by updating the weights. The rule is given by,

$$\Delta W_i = \eta \, [\, t_p - O_p \,] x_i \qquad\qquad (2.25)$$

Where, η is the learning coefficient, ΔW_i is the updating weight, t is the target output, O_p is net the computed output, given by, $O = \sum_{i=1}^{n} x_1 w_1$, and x_i is the input vector. This is the generalized formula for single output unit adaline network, in the case of several output units, the delta rule for adjusting the weights from i^{th} input unit to the jth output unit is given by,

$$\Delta W_{ij} = \eta[t_p - O_{pj}]x_{ij} \tag{2.26}$$

The adaline learning rule is justified by gradient descent rule:

$$\partial E_p/\partial W_i = (O_p - t_p)^2 / \partial W_i \tag{2.27}$$

$$= 2 (O_p - t_p) \partial O_p / \partial W_i \tag{2.28}$$

Since $O_p = \sum_{i=1}^{n} x_i W_i$, substituting this value in equation (2.28), we get,

$$\partial E_p/\partial W_i = 2 (O_p - t_p) x_i \tag{2.29}$$

Moving in the direction, $(O_p - t_p)$ increases the error, so the opposite direction will decrease the error, thus equation (2.29) can be rewritten as,

$$\partial E_p/\partial W_i = -2 (t_p - O_p) x_i \tag{2.30}$$

Thus we could say that, the change in the weight is made proportional to the negative gradient of the error between the desired output and the continuous activation value, which is also a continuous output signal due to linearity of the output function. Also,

When $t_p > O_p$, we should increase O_p, by increasing $W_i x_i$; i.e., we should increase W_i if x_i is positive, and decrease W_i if x_i is negative.

Similarly, when $t_p < O_p$, we should decrease O_p by increasing $W_i x_i$.

ADALINE network has been most widely employed in applications like high speed modems and telephone switching systems to cancel the echo in long distance communication circuits.

A single Adaline is capable of realizing only a small subset of these functions, known as the linearly separable logic functions or threshold logic function. These are the set of logic functions that can be obtained with all possible weight variations.

The linear classifier is limited in the number of distinct patterns it can learn correctly. The Adaline's pattern capacity is limited roughly to twice the number of adaptive weights in the classifier. To achieve higher pattern capacities, or to solve problems which are not linearly separable, nonlinear classifiers must be used.

There also exists an extension of ADALINE known as MADALINE.

2.3.4. MADALINE Network

A MADALINE (many ADALINE) network is a three-layer feedforward ANN architecture, created by combining a number of ADALINE units in its hidden and output layers. The use of multiple ADALINE networks helps solve the problem of non-linear separabilty. FOR instance, figure 2.14 shows a simple MADALINE network with two units, have the potential to counter the problem of non-linear separability and hence the XOR problem.

In this, each ADALINE unit receives the input bits x_1, x_2 and the bias input $x_0 = 1$ as its inputs. The weighted sum of the inputs is calculated and passed on to the bipolar threshold units. To obtain the final output, the logical AND of the two threshold outputs is calculated. Because of AND operation, if the two threshold outputs are (same) i.e. both +1 or -1 then the final output is +1, on the other hand, if the threshold outputs are different, i.e. (+1,-1) then the final output is -1. In other words, we could say that, the inputs with even parity produce positive outputs, and inputs with odd parity produce negative outputs. Below figure 2.14 shows the decision boundaries for the XOR problem while trying to classify the even parity inputs (positive outputs) from the odd parity inputs (negative outputs).

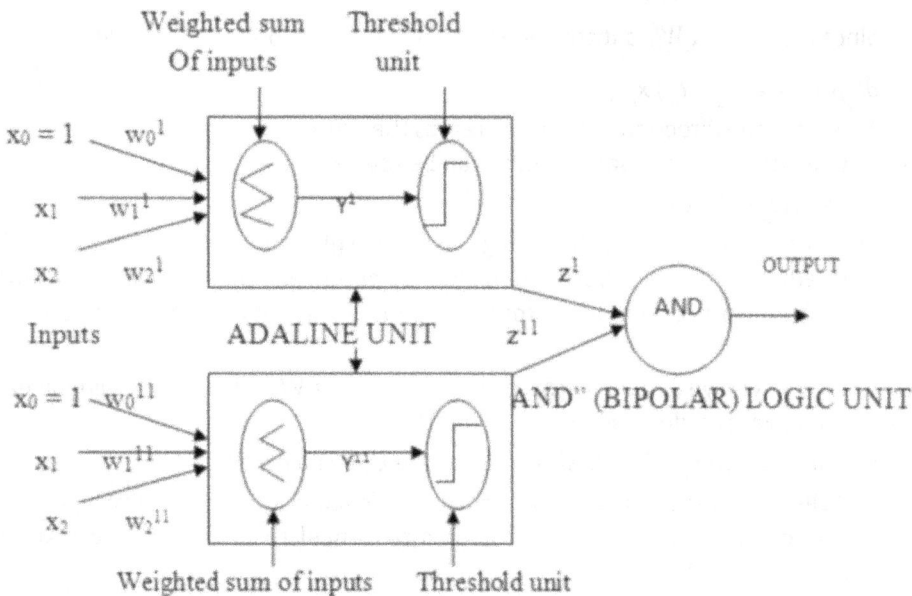

Fig.2.13: A two unit MADALINE network

The learning rule adopted by MADALINE network is termed as "MADALINE adaptation Rule" (MR) and is a form of supervised learning. The first MR rule was developed by Ridgway in the year 1962, and it was termed MR1, incorporating the principle of *minimal disturbance*. Ridgway's network was composed of a layer of ADALINEs whose outputs then fed into a single fixed logic element. The fixed logic element was typically an 'OR' element or a majority vote taker element. These logic elements could be realized using an ADALINE with appropriate weights. Thus Ridgway has a two layer feedforward network in 1962. The first layer had an arbitrary number of adaptive ADALINE processing elements, but the output layer was constrained to having a single non-adaptive output unit.

Later on an extension of MR1 was developed by Prof. Bernard Widrow and it was named MR2. MR2 removes these restrictions. The output layer may have as many adaptive units as desired. More than two adaptive layers are also possible. This greatly increases the power of the network to realize arbitrary input-output relationships presented to it.

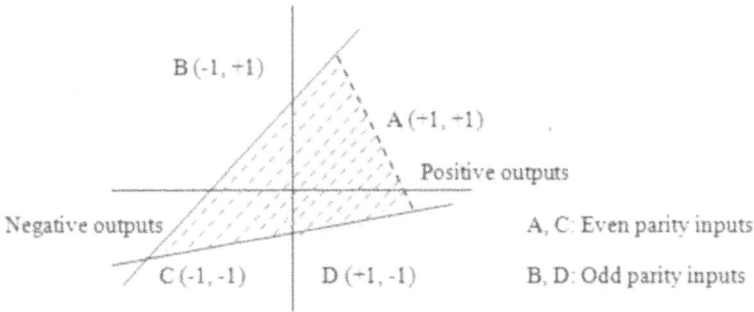

Fig. 2.14: Decision boundaries for the XOR problem

2.4. Backpropagation Networks

As it is discussed in section 2.3.2 that, single perceptron networks are limited to solving only linearly separable functions, to achieve greater computational capabilities larger networks with neurons arranged in layers or stages are required. These larger networks were termed as *Multilayer feedforward networks (MLFF)*. Arranging neurons in layers or stages is supposed to mimic the layered structure of certain portions of brain. Here the question arises, why it is necessary to mimic exactly the structure of brain.

This could be explained by taking a simple example. Consider an image recognition task of recognizing an object out of a couple of different objects, and a simple addition task of 2+2 = 4. A small child, who is not very much familiar with mathematics, might not answer the addition problem correctly, but he can easily recognize the image of object. This happens because image recognition requires parallel processing, and the addition task is required to be solved serially. Human brain is quite efficient in parallel processing but is not that efficient in processing serially as compared to machines. On the other hand machines are proved to be excellent in serial processing rather than handling task in a parallel fashion. We are trying to inbuilt the parallel processing capabilities in today's computers and artificial intelligence for applications such as image and pattern recognition, machine learning etc. This led us to mimic human brain and enter into a whole new world of neuroscience.

For many years, the whole research on neural networks was stagnated, as researchers failed in finding out a sound algorithm for training MLFF networks. The solution came with the invention of backpropagation algorithm. In 1986, Rumelhart, Hinton and Wilham developed this systematic method of training multilayer artificial neural network. Even though, it has its own limitations, but it has proved its potential in a wide range of practical applications.

Under this section, we will cover Multilayer Feedforward (MLFF) network with back propagation algorithm. This type of network is often referred as a multilayer perceptron because of it similarity to perceptron networks with multiple layers.

2.4.1. Single Layer Artificial Neural Network

A single neuron can efficiently perform certain simple pattern detection problems, for greater computational potentials, and in order to mimic the structure of brain, layered networks are required. Let's have a look at the single feedforward neural network as shown in below figure 2.16.

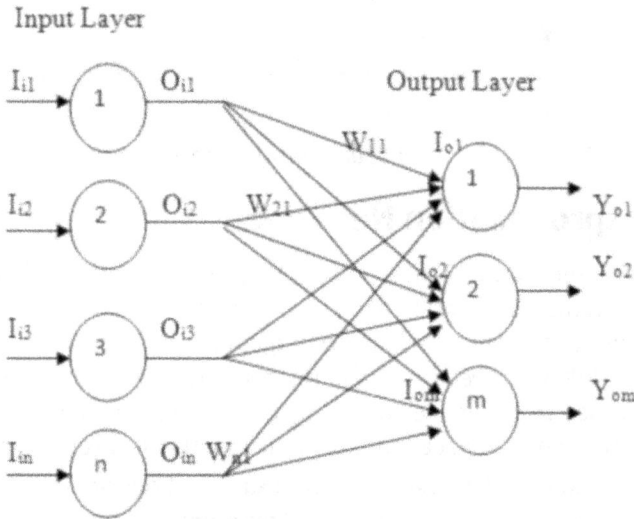

Fig.2.15: Single layer feedforward neural network

The most common way to connect neurons into a network is by layers. The simplest form of layered network is shown in figure 2.15. The nodes at the left represent the *input layer*. The input layer consists of n neurons and their task is to just pass and distribute the inputs and perform no computation. Thus, the only true layer of neurons is the one on the right representing the *output layer,* and consists of m neurons. Each of the inputs I_{i1}, I_{i2},...I_{in} is connected to every artificial neuron in the output layer through the connection weight. Since every value of outputs Y_{o1}, Y_{o2}...Y_{on} is calculated from the same set of input values, each output is varied based on the connection weights. However the network given in figure 2.16 is *fully connected*, the true biological neural network may not have all possible connections - the weight value of zero can be represented as "no connection".

The inputs of the input layer and the corresponding outputs of the output layer are given as:

$$I_i = \begin{Bmatrix} I_{i1} \\ I_{i2} \\ I_{in} \\ n \times 1 \end{Bmatrix} O_o = \begin{Bmatrix} O_{o1} \\ O_{o2} \\ O_{om} \\ m \times 1 \end{Bmatrix} \tag{2.31}$$

Assume, we use linear transfer function for the neurons in the input layer and the unipolar sigmoidal function for the neurons in the output layer.

$$\{O_j\} = \{I_j\} \text{ (linear transfer function)} \tag{2.32}$$

$$\text{n} \times 1 \quad \text{m} \times 1$$

$$I_{oj} = W_{ij} I_{l1} + W_{2j} I_{l2} + \dots\dots + W_{nj} I_{iN} \tag{2.33}$$

Hence, the input to the output layer can be given as,

$$\{I_o\} = [W]^T \{O'\} = [W]^T \{I_j\} \tag{2.34}$$

$$\text{m} \times 1 \quad \text{m} \times \text{n} \quad \text{n} \times 1$$

where, W = weight matrix or connection matrix.

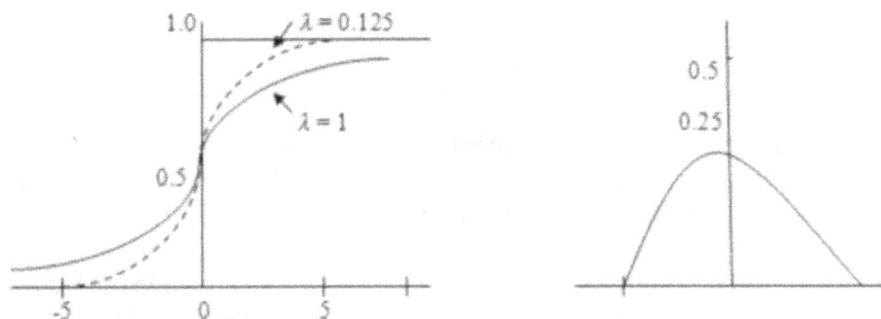

Fig. 2.16 (a): Squashed-S function for various values of Fig. 2.16 (b): Squashed-S slope

Using the unipolar sigmoidal or squashed –S function and the slope of this function for neuron in the output layer as shown in figure 2.16(a) and (b) respectively, the output is given by,

$$O_{ok} = \frac{1}{1 + e^{-\lambda y / O_K}} \tag{2.35}$$

Where, λ = sigmoidal gain.

2.4.2. Multilayer Artificial feedforward Network

To achieve higher level of computational capabilities, a more complex structure of neural network is required. Figure 2.17 shows the *multilayer neural network* which distinguishes itself from the single-layer network by having one or more *hidden layers*. In this multilayer structure, the input nodes pass the information to the units in the first hidden layer, then the outputs from the first hidden layer are passed to the next, and so on. Multilayer networks can also be regarded as cascading of groups of single-layer networks. The level of complexity in computing can be seen by the fact that many single-layer networks are combined into this multilayer network. The designer of an artificial neural network should consider how many hidden layers are required, depending on complexity in desired computation.

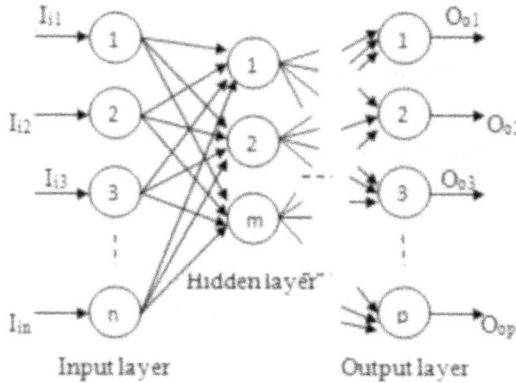

Fig.2.17: Multilayer Perceptron

The three- layer network shown in figure 2.17 show that the activity of neurons in the input layer represents the raw information that is fed into the network. The activity of neurons in the hidden layer is determined by the activities of the neurons in the input layer and the connecting weights between the input and hidden units. Similarly, the activity of the output units depends on the activity of neurons in the hidden layer and the weight between the hidden and output layer. The neurons in the hidden layers are free to construct their own representations of the input.

The input-output mapping of multilayer perceptron is represented by,

$$O = N_3 [N_2 [N_1 [I]]] \tag{2.36}$$

Where, N_1, N_2, and N_3 represent nonlinear mapping provided by input, hidden and output layers respectively. Multilayer perceptron provides no increase in computational power over a single layer neural network until and unless there is a nonlinear activation function between layers. Most of the potentials of neural networks, such as nonlinear functional approximation, learning, generalization etc. are in fact due to nonlinear activation function of each neuron.

2.4.3. Learning in Backpropagation Networks

Backpropagation networks, and multi layered perceptrons, in general, are *feedforward networks* with distinct input, output, and hidden layers. The units function basically like perceptrons, except that the transition (output) rule and the weight update (learning) mechanism are more complex. The figure 2.18 represents the architecture of backpropagation networks. There may be any number of hidden layers, and any number of hidden units in any given hidden layer. Input and output units can be binary {0, 1}, bi-polar {-1, +1}, or may have real values within a specific range such as [-1, 1]. Note that units within the same layer are not interconnected.

In general, every unit in a given layer is connected to every other unit in the preceding layer. However, there are no interconnections among units in the same layer.

Activation of the network proceeds from the input units, layer by layer of hidden layers, up to the output unit.

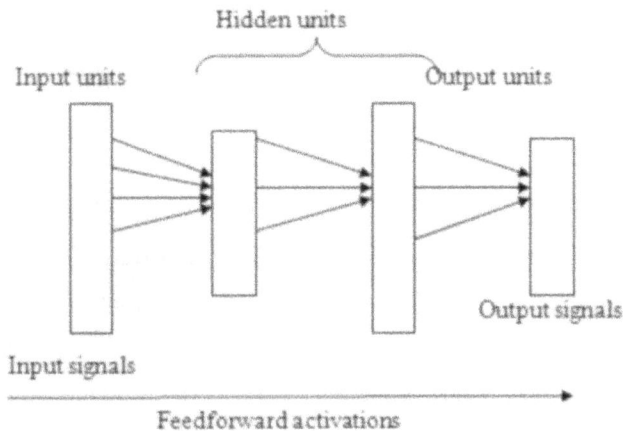

Fig.2.18: Architecture of Backpropagation Networks

In feedforward activation, units of hidden layer 1 compute their activation and output values and pass these on to the next layer, and so on until the output units will have produced the network's actual response to the current input. The activation value a_k of unit k is computed as follows.

$$a_k = \sum_{i=1}^{n} W_{ik} . I_i \tag{2.37}$$

where, I_i is the input signal, W_{ik} is the weight of the connection between unit k and unit i.

This is basically the same activation function of *linear threshold units* (McCulloch and Pitts model). Unlike in the linear threshold unit, the output of a unit in a backpropagation network is no longer based on a threshold. The output O_{ok} of unit k is computed as follows:

$$O_{ok} = f(a_k) \text{ and } f(x) = 1/(1+ e^{-x}) \tag{2.38}$$

The function $f(x)$ is referred to as the output function. It is a continuously increasing function of the *sigmoid* type, asymptotically approaching 0 as x decreases, and asymptotically approaches 1 as x increases. At $x = 0$, $f(x)$ is equal to 0.5. As shown in below figure 2.19. In some implementations of the backpropagation model, it is convenient to have input and output values that are bi-polar. In this case, the output function uses the hypertangent function, which has basically the same shape, but would be asymptotic to -1 as x decreases. This function has value 0 when x is 0. As shown in figure 2.20.

$$f(x) = 1/(1+e^{-x})$$

$$f(x) = (e^x - e^{-x})/(e^x + e^{-x})$$

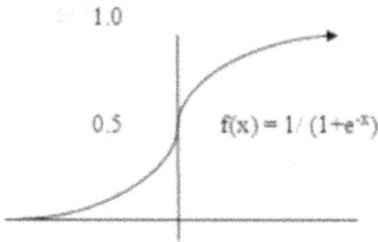

Fig.2.19: the output function   Fig.2.20: The hypertangent function

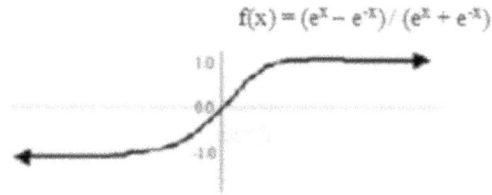

Once activation is fed forward all the way to the output units, the network's response is compared to the desired output O_i^d which accompanies the training pattern. There are two types of error. The first error is the *error at the output layer*. This can be directly computed as follows:

$$e_i = O_i^d - f(a_i) \tag{2.39}$$

The second type of error is the *error at the hidden layers*. This cannot be computed directly since there is no available information on the desired outputs of the hidden layers. This is where the retropropagation of error is called for.

Essentially, the error at the output layer is used to compute for the error at the hidden layer immediately preceding the output layer. Once this is computed, this is used in turn to compute for the error of the next hidden layer immediately preceding the last hidden layer. This is done sequentially until the error at the very first hidden layer is computed. The retropropagation of error is illustrated in the figure 2.21. Computation of errors e_i at a hidden layer is done as follows:

$$e_h = \sum_{i=1}^{n} W_{ih} . e_i \tag{2.40}$$

The errors at the other end of the outgoing connections of the hidden unit h have been earlier computed in equation 2.40. These could be error values at the output layer or at a hidden layer. These error signals are multiplied by their corresponding outgoing connection weights and the sum of these is taken.

After computing the error for each unit, whether it be at a hidden unit or at an output unit, the network then fine-tunes its connection weights W_{kj}^{t+1}. The weight update rule is uniform for all connection weights.

$$W_{kj}^{t+1} = W_{kj}^{t} + \alpha e_k f(a_k) f^1(a_k) \tag{2.41}$$

The learning rate α is typically a small value between 0 and 1. It controls the size of weight adjustments and has some bearing on the speed of the learning process as well as on the precision by which the network can possibly operate. $f'(x)$ also controls the size of weight adjustments, depending on the actual output $f(x)$. In the case of the sigmoid function above, its first derivative (slope) $f'(x)$ is easily computed as follows:

$$f^1(x) = f(x)(1 - f(x)) \tag{2.42}$$

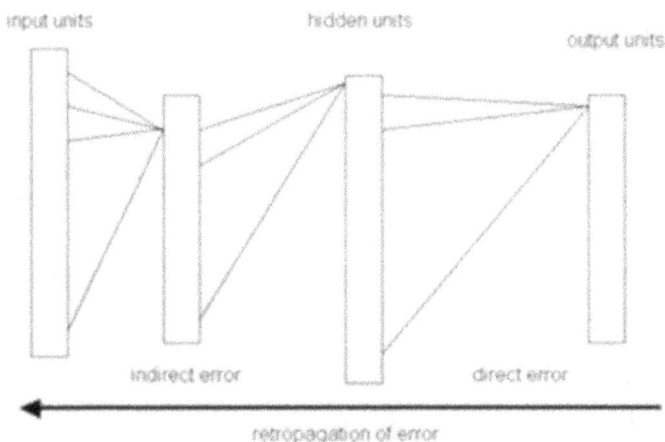

Fig.2.21: the retropropagation of error

We note that the change in weight is directly proportional to the error term computed for the unit at the output end of the incoming connection. However, this weight change is controlled by the output signal coming from the input end of the incoming connection. We can infer that very little weight change (learning) occurs when this input signal is almost zero. The weight change is further controlled by the term f^1 (a_k). Because this term measures the slope of the function, and knowing the shape of the function, we can infer that there will likewise be little weight change when the output of the unit at the other end of the connection is close to 0 or 1. Thus, learning will take place mainly at those connections with high pre-synaptic signals and non-committed (hovering around 0.5) post-synaptic signals.

Step by step illustration of Backpropagation learning algorithm

Step 1: Initialisation

Set all the weights and threshold levels of the network to random numbers uniformly distributed inside a small range say, $-2.4/n$, $+2.4/n$.

Where n is the total number of inputs of neuron *i* in the network. The weight initialisation is done on a neuron-by-neuron basis.

Step 2: Activation

Activate the back-propagation neural network by applying inputs $I_{i1}, I_{i2},..., I_{in}$ and desired outputs $O_d^1, O_d^2,..., O_d^n$.

(a)   Calculate the actual outputs of the neurons in the hidden layer:

$$O_o = \text{sigmoid}\left[\sum_{i=1}^{n} I_I \cdot W_{ih} - \theta_j\right] \qquad (2.43)$$

Where, *n* is the number of inputs of neuron *j* in the hidden layer, and *sigmoid* is the *sigmoid* activation function.

(b)   Calculate the actual outputs of the neurons in the output layer:

$$O_{ok} = \text{sigmoid} \left[\sum_{j=1}^{m} I_{ik} \cdot W_{ik} - \theta_k \right] \tag{2.44}$$

where *m* is the number of inputs of neuron *k* in the output layer.

Step 3: Weight training

Update the weights in the back-propagation network propagating backward the errors associated with output neurons.

(a)   Calculate the error gradient for the neurons in the output layer:

$$\delta_k = O_{ok} \cdot [1 - O_{ok}] \cdot e_i \tag{2.45}$$

$$e_i = O_d^i - O_{ok} \tag{2.46}$$

$O_{ok} = f(a_k)$ from equation 1.22.

Calculate the weight corrections:

$$W_{jk}^{t+1} = \alpha \cdot O_o \cdot \delta_k \tag{2.47}$$

Update the weights at the output neurons.

(b)   Calculate the error gradient for the neurons in the hidden layer:

$$\delta_h = O_o \cdot [1 - O_o] \cdot \sum_{k=1}^{l} \delta_k \cdot w_{jk} \tag{2.48}$$

Calculate the weight corrections:

$$W_{ih}^{t+1} = \alpha . I_i . \delta_i \tag{2.49}$$

Update the weights at the hidden neurons.

Step 4: Iteration

Increase iteration *t* by one, go back to *Step 2* and repeat the process until the selected error criterion is satisfied.

2.5.   Radial Basis Function Network

Radial basis function (RBF) networks are feed-forward networks trained using a supervised training algorithm. They are typically configured with a single hidden layer of units whose activation function is selected from a class of functions called basis functions. While similar to back propagation in many respects, radial basis function networks have several advantages. They usually train much faster than back propagation networks. They are less susceptible to problems with non-stationary inputs because of the behavior of the radial basis function hidden units.

Popularized by Moody and Darken (1989), RBF networks have proven to be a useful neural network architecture. The major difference between RBF networks and back propagation networks (that is, multi layer perceptron trained by Back Propagation algorithm) is the behavior of the single hidden layer. Rather than using the sigmoidal or S-shaped activation function as in back propagation, the hidden units in RBF networks use a Gaussian or some other basis kernel function. Each hidden unit acts as a locally tuned processor that computes a score for the match between the input vector and its connection weights or centers. In effect, the basis units are highly specialized pattern detectors. The weights connecting the basis units to the outputs are used to take linear combinations of the hidden units to product the final classification or output.

2.5.1. The Structure of the RBF Networks

Radial Basis Functions are first introduced in the solution of the real multivariable interpolation problems. Broomhead and Lowe (1988), and Moody and Darken (1989) were the first to exploit the use of radial basis functions in the design of neural networks. The structure of an RBF networks in its most basic form involves three entirely different layers (Figure 2.23).

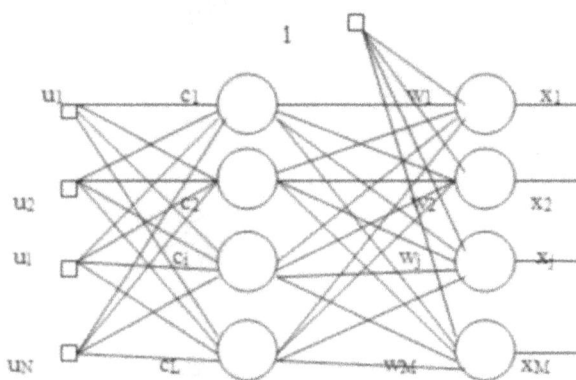

Fig. 2.22: Structure of the Standard RBF network

The input layer is made up of source nodes (sensory units) whose number is equal to the dimension p of the input vector u.

2.5.1.1. Hidden layer

The second layer is the hidden layer which is composed of nonlinear units that are connected directly to all of the nodes in the input layer. It is of high enough dimension, which serves a different purpose from that in a multilayer perceptron. Each hidden unit takes its input from all the nodes at the components at the input layer. As mentioned above the hidden units contains a basis function, which has the parameters center and width. The center of the basis function for a node i at the hidden layer is a vector c_i whose size is the as the input vector u and there is normally a different center for each unit in the network.

First, the radial distance d_i, between the input vector u and the center of the basis function c^i is computed for each unit i in the hidden layer as

$$d_i = \mid u - c_i \mid \tag{2.50}$$

using the Euclidean distance.

The output h_i of each hidden unit i is then computed by applying the basis function G to this distance,

$$h_i = G\,(d,\,\sigma_i) \tag{2.51}$$

As it is shown in Figure 2.23, the basis function is a curve (typically a Gaussian function, the width corresponding to the variance, σ_i) which has a peak at zero distance and it decreases as the distance from the center increases.

For an input space $u \in R^2$, that is $M = 2$, this corresponds to the two dimensional Gaussian centered at c_i on the input space, where also $c_i \in R^2$.

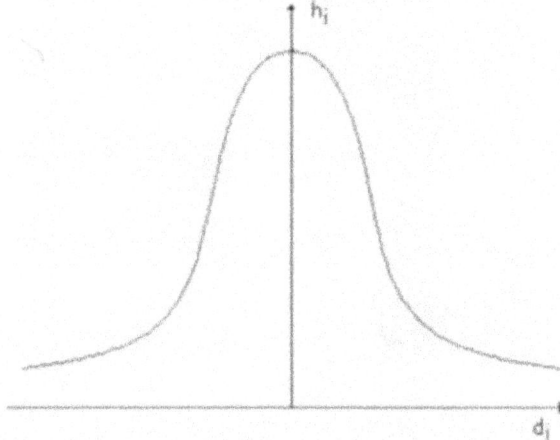

Fig.2.23: the response region of an RBF hidden node around its center as a function of the distance from this center.

2.5.1.2. Output layer

The transformation from the input space to the hidden unit space is nonlinear, whereas the transformation to the hidden unit space to the output space is linear. The jth output is computed as,

$$x_j = f_j(\mathbf{u}) = w_{oj} + \sum_{i=1}^{L} w_{ij} h_i \tag{2.52}$$

where, $j = 1,2,.., M$

Mathematical model

In summary, the mathematical model of the RBF network can be expressed as: $x = f(u)$, $f: R^N \rightarrow R^M$

$$x_j = f_j(u) = w_{oj} + \sum_{i=1}^{L} w_{ij} G(|u - c_i|) \tag{2.53}$$

Function Approximation

Let $y = g(u)$ be a given function of u, $y \in R$, $u \in R$, $g: R \rightarrow R$, and let G_i $i=1..L$, be a finite set of basis functions.

The function g can be written in terms of the given basis functions as,

$$y = g(u) = \sum_{i=1}^{L} w_i G_i(u) + r(u) \tag{2.54}$$

where $r(u)$ is the residual.

The aim is to minimize the error by setting the parameters of G_i appropriately. A possible choice for the error definition is the $L2$ norm of the residual function $r(u)$ which is defined as

$$|r(u)|_{L2} = \int r(u)^2 \tag{2.55}$$

Approximation by RBFNN

Now, consider the single input single output RBF network shown in Figure 1.27. Then x can be written as

$$x = f(u) = \sum_{i=1}^{L} w_i G_i(|u - c_i|) \tag{2.56}$$

By the use of such a network, y can be written as,

$$y = \sum_{i=1}^{L} w_i G(|u - c_i|) + r(u) = f(u) + r(u) \tag{2.57}$$

where, $f(u)$ is the output of the RBFNN given in Figure 2.24 and $r(u)$ is the residual. By setting the center c_i the variance σ_i and the weight w_i the error appropriately, the error can be minimized. Whatever we discussed here for $g:R{\rightarrow}R$, can be generalized to $g:R^N{\rightarrow}R^M$ easily by using an N input, M output RBFNN given in figure 2.24 previously.

Data Interpolation

Given input output training patterns (u^k, y^k), $k = 1,2, ..K$, the aim of data interpolation is to approximate the function **y** from which the data is generated. Since the function **y** is unknown, the problem can be stated as a minimization problem which takes only the sample points into consideration:

Choose $w_{i,j}$ and c_i, $i = 1, 2...L$, $j = 1,2...M$ so as to minimize

$$J(w, c) = \sum_{k=1}^{K} |y^k - f(u^k)|^2 \tag{2.58}$$

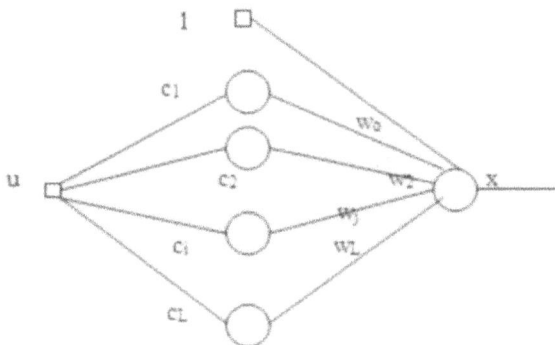

Fig.2.24: Single input, single output RBF network

2.5.2. Training RBF Networks

The training of a RBF network can be formulated as a nonlinear unconstrained optimization problem given below:

Given input output training patterns (u^k, y^k), $k = 1, 2, ..K$, choose $w_{i,j}$ and c_{j}, $i = 1$, $2...L$, $j = 1, 2...M$ so as to minimize,

$$J(w, c) = \sum_{k=1}^{k} [y^k - f(u^k)]^2 \tag{2.59}$$

Note that the training problem becomes quadratic once if **c**i's (radial basis function centers) are known.

2.5.2.1. Adjusting the widths

In its simplest form, all hidden units in the RBF network have the same width or degree of sensitivity to inputs. However, in portions of the input space where there are few patterns, it is sometime desirable to have hidden units with a wide area of reception. Likewise, in portions of the input space, which are crowded, it might be desirable to have very highly tuned processors with narrow reception fields. Computing these individual widths increases the performance of the RBF network at the expense of a more complicated training process.

2.5.2.2. Adjusting the centers

Remember that in a back propagation network, all weights in all of the layers are adjusted at the same time. In radial basis function networks, however, the weights into the hidden layer basis units are usually set before the second layer of weights is adjusted. As the input moves away from the connection weights, the activation value falls off. This behavior leads to the use of the term "center" for the first-layer weights. These center weights can be computed using Kohonen feature maps, statistical methods such as K-Means clustering, or some other means. In any case, they are then used to set the areas of sensitivity for the RBF network's hidden units, which then remain fixed.

2.5.2.3. Adjusting the weights

Once the hidden layer weights are set, a second phase of training is used to adjust the output weights. This process typically uses the standard steepest descent algorithm. Note that the training problem becomes quadratic once if **c**i's (radial basis function centers) are known.

2.6.   Some Applications of Neural Networks

Out of several applications of Neural Networks, image compression and data forecasting, are the two most promising and widely used domains. Here in this section, we are going to discuss these two domains.

2.6.1.   Image compression

The meaning of Image compression is to minimize the size in bytes of a graphics file without degrading the quality of the image to a suboptimal level. The diminution in file size allows more images to be stored in a given amount of memory space. This is a key feature in artificial intelligence, as more number of images stored in the artificial brains, led to the more promising approach in the image recognition and optimization tasks. As neural networks can accept a vast array of input immediately, and can perform various functions on it instantly, they are proved to be very much useful in image compression.

2.6.1.1. Bottleneck-type Neural Net Architecture for Image Compression

Here in figure 2.25 we are presenting Neural Network architecture suitable for image compression application. The structure shown is considered as a bottleneck type network. It consists of equal sized input layer and an output layer, with a comparatively small sized intermediate layer in-between. The ratio of the size of the input layer to the size of the intermediate layer is said to be the compression ratio. For using the network for image compression it is splitted into two as shown in the Figure 2.26 below. The transmitter encodes and then transmits the output of the hidden layer. At receiver the 16 hidden outputs are received and decoded and henceforth 64 outputs are generated.

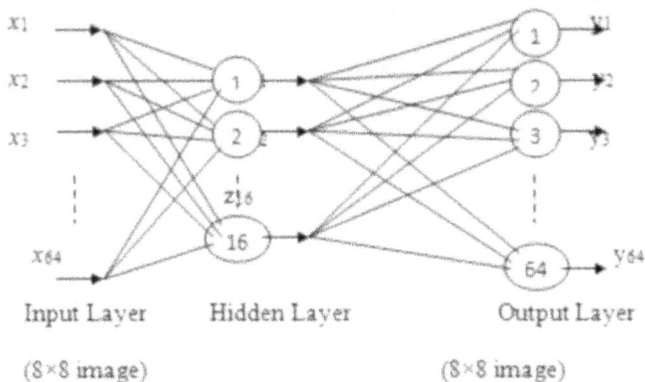

Fig. 2.25: Bottle-neck type Neural Network Architecture

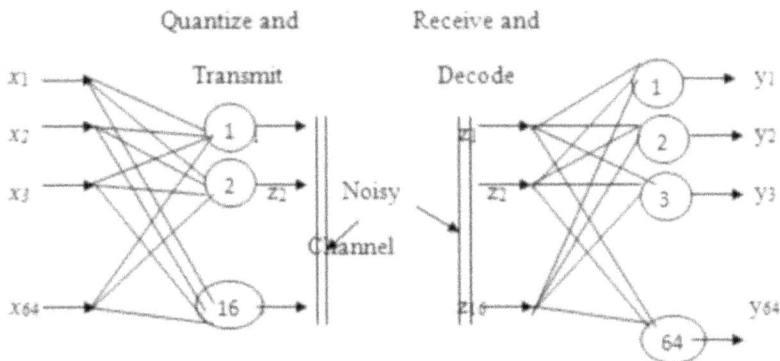

Fig 2.26: The Image Compression Scheme using the Trained Neural Net

The Quantization of Hidden Unit Outputs

Although the bottleneck network reduced the number of nodes from 64 to 16, but actual compression has not occurred because the outputs of the hidden layer are real valued integers (between -1 and +1), unlike the 64 original inputs which are 8-bit pixel values. Thus, requires possibly an infinite number of bits to transmit. The actual image compression takes place when the hidden layer outputs are **quantized** before transmission. A typical quantization scheme is presented in the figure 2.27. It uses 3 bits to encode each input. In this case, 8 possible binary codes may be formed, viz, 000, 001, 010, 011, 100, 101, 110, 111 respectively. Each code represents a range of values for a hidden unit output.

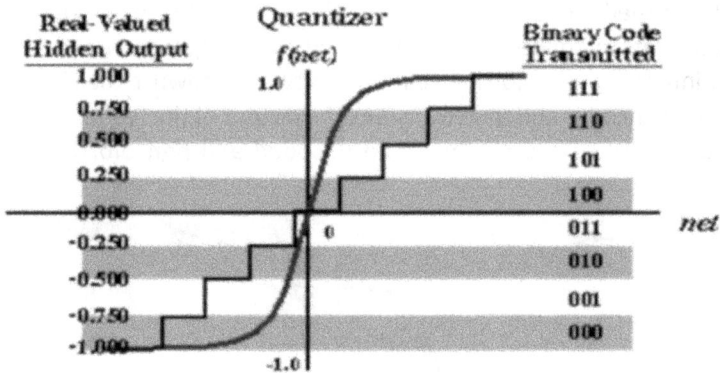

Fig.2.27: a typical quantization scheme

To compute the amount of image compression (measured in bits-per-pixel) for this level of quantization, we consider the ratio of the total number of bits transmitted to the total number of pixels in the original image (64 in this case) so, the compression rate is given as bits/pixel.

Training

A 256 x 256 training image is used to train the bottleneck type network to assimilate the required identity map. From the image the training input-output pairs are produced by extracting small 8x8 portions of the image. These portions are randomly chosen at different locations in the image. Now the question is how to decide which random portion to select and which to leave? The easiest way to chose and extract such random portion is to generate a pair of random integers, these integers serve as the upper left hand corner of the extracted portion. Here, we are choosing random integers i and j, that lies between 0 and 248, and (i, j) is the upper left hand corner coordinate of the extracted portion of the image. The pixel values of the extracted image portions are moved from left to right, from top most to bottom most part through the pixel-to-real mapping to construct the 64-dimensional neural net input.

Once training phase is accomplished, the next is the *recall phase*. Under this phase, the neural network with 8x8portions of the image is still presented, but now instead of randomly selecting the location of each portion, we select the portions sequentially from left to right and from top to bottom. For each such 8 x 8 portion, the output of the network can be evaluated and displayed on the screen to visually observe the performance of neural net image compression.

2.6.2. Forecasting

Forecasting planning tool helps management in its attempts to deal with the uncertainty of the future. It relies mainly on data from the past and present and analysis of latest trends in the world. Forecasting starts with certain presumptions, which are based on the management's past experiences, knowledge about present market trends, and decision making accuracy.

These estimates are outlined into the coming months or years using one or more techniques such as *Box-Jenkins models, exponential smoothing method, Delphi method, regression analysis method, moving averages method,* and *trend projection.* Since any misinterpretation in the presumptions will result in a similar or magnified destruction in forecasting, the sensitivity analysis technique is used which assigns a range of values to the uncertain factors (variables).

Neural networks are said to be "Universal Approximators", it is a crucial task to find a suitable model for the data forecasting problem in reality, and it might be done only by trial-and-error. We may take the data forecasting problem for a kind of data processing problem.

Steps in data forecasting modeling using neural network Data Collection and Analysis

Design of data forecasting model goes through following steps-

1. **Choosing variables & Data collection:** Determining the variable which is related directly or indirectly to the data that we require forecasting. If the variable does not have any effect to the value of data that we need to forecast, then we should wipe it out of consider. Beside it, if the variable is concerned directly or indirectly then we should take it on consider.

2. **Data preprocessing:** Analyze and transform values of input and output data to put focus on the main features, observe the trends and the dispensation of data. Normalize the input and output real values into the interval between max and min of transformation function (generally in [0, 1] or [-1, 1]

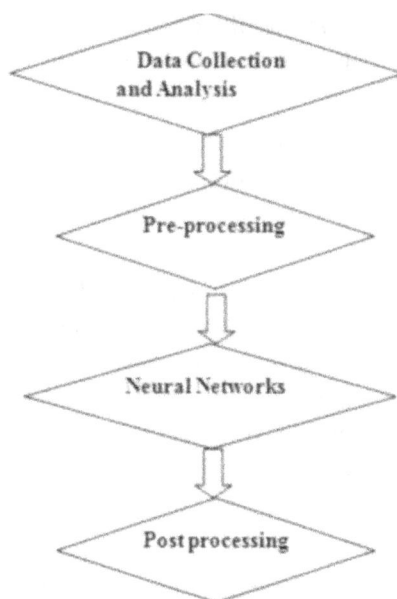

Fig.2.28: Flow chart of Data-Forecasting

intervals). The most common methods are following:

SV = ((0.9 - 0.1) / (MAX_VAL - MIN_VAL)) * (OV - MIN_VAL)

Or

SV = TFmin + ((TFmax - TFmin) / (MAX_VAL - MIN_VAL)) * (OV - MIN_VAL)

Where, SV: Scaled Value

      MAX_VAL: Max value of data

      MIN_VAL: Min value of data

      TFmax: Max of transformation function

      TFmin: Min of transformation function

      OV: Original Value

3. **Dividing the data set into smaller sets:** Divide the whole patterns set into the smaller sets:
   - ➢ Training set
   - ➢ Test set
   - ➢ Verification set.

   The training set is usually the biggest set employed in training the network. Often 10% to 30% of training set is included in the test set for testing the generalization. And the verification set is set at balance between the needs of enough patterns for the purpose of training, testing and verification.

4. **Determining network's topology:** This step verifies the links between neurons, number of hidden layers, and number of neurons in each layer. It works on the basis of following questions like:
   - ➢ How the neurons are linked to each other in the network.
   - ➢ How many hidden layers are present? They should not exceed two.
   - ➢ The number of neurons present in the hidden layers. However, there is no particular method to find the most optimum number of neurons used in hidden layers.

   ⇒ Issue 2 and 3 can only be done by trial and error since it is depended on the problem that we are dealing with.

5. **Determining the error function:** To estimate the network's performance before and after training process. Function used in evaluation is usually a mean squared errors. Other functions may be: percentage differences, least absolute deviation, asymmetric least squares etc.

   Performance index

   $F(x) = E[e^T e] = E[(t-a)^T(t-a)]$

   Approximate Performance index

   $F(x) = e^T(k)e(k)] = (t(k) - a(k))^T(t(k) - a(k))$

   The latest quality determination function is usually the Mean Absolute Percentage Error - MAPE.

6. **Training:** Training tunes a neural network by adjusting the weights and biases that is expected to give us the global minimum of performance index or error function.

7. **Implementation:** This is the last step after we determined the factors related to network's topology, variables choosing, etc. The environment will be Electronic circuits or PC. The interval to re-train the network might be depended on the times and also other factors related to our problem.

Review Questions

1. Explain supervised and unsupervised learning with the help of examples.
2. Explain the Gradient descent learning rule.
3. State and explain the Hebb's leaning rule.
4. Describe Delta rule for the training of Neural Networks.
5. Draw and discuss the configuration of recurrent network.
6. Explain Feedforward networks and feedback networks.
7. Explain the problem of linear separability. How XOR gate problem can be implemented using Artificial Neural Networks.
8. Explain linear separability. Why a single layer of perceptron can-not be used to solve linearly inseparable problem?
9. Illustrate using an example that Multilayer perceptron can successfully implement XOR logic, while simple perceptron can-not.
10. Distinguish between linearly separable and linearly inseparable problems, giving example for each.
11. Explain ADALINE and MADALINE networks, with their algorithms.
12. Explain back propagation networks along with the backpropagation algorithm.

CHAPTER 3

The Unsupervised Networks

"I can-not articulate enough to express my dislike to people who think that understanding spoils your experience...How would they know?"

- **Marvin Minsky**
American Cognitive Scientist

In the previous chapter we had discussed, various learning methods including supervised learning, unsupervised learning and reinforcement learning. We had also studied about various networks such as Perceptron, ADALINE, MADALINE, backpropagation networks, radial basis function networks etc, and their corresponding learning algorithms. Here, one point is worth noticeable, that all these networks were based on one fundamental learning rule- *supervised learning*.

Now, in this chapter we are going to study some more models of neural networks and their corresponding learning algorithms, but the fundamental learning rule is *unsupervised learning*.

3.1.   Self Organizing Maps

The self organizing map (SOM) network is the most prominent type of artificial neural network model that is trained using unsupervised learning algorithm and comes under the category of competitive learning networks. As it is based on unsupervised learning, it means that no human intervention is required during the training phase and a very little information about the characteristics of the input data is needed.

The Self Organizing Map or SOM was first introduced by Professor Teuvo Kohonen, at the academy of Finland in the 1980s, and therefore it is also called as *Kohonen SOM* or network.

These are quite different from other artificial neural networks in their basic principle that they use a neighborhood function to conserve the topological properties of the input space. In other words, it provides a topological preserving mapping from the high dimensional space to Lower dimensional space. The term topology preserving means that the relative distance between the points are preserved during the mapping. Points that are closest to each other in the input space are mapped to adjacent map portions in the SOM. The SOM can thereby serve as a cluster analyzing technique for high dimensional data. Also, the SOM is capable of generalizing. Generalization capability refers to the recognition or characterization capability of the input data.

Like most of the Artificial Neural Networks, SOMs also exhibits two operating modes: training and mapping. "Training" refers to the building of map using input examples (vector quantization), while "mapping" refers to the classification of a new input vector. A SOM consists of elements called nodes or neurons. Each node is assigned with a weight vector (of the same dimension as the input data vectors) and a map space is associated along with it. The nodes are usually arranged in a two-dimensional regular spacing, such as hexagonal or rectangular grid pattern as shown in figure 3.1.

In simple words, the SOMs can be considered as an arrangement of two-dimensional assembly of neurons:

$$M = \{M_1, \ldots \ldots M_{pq}\} \tag{3.1}$$

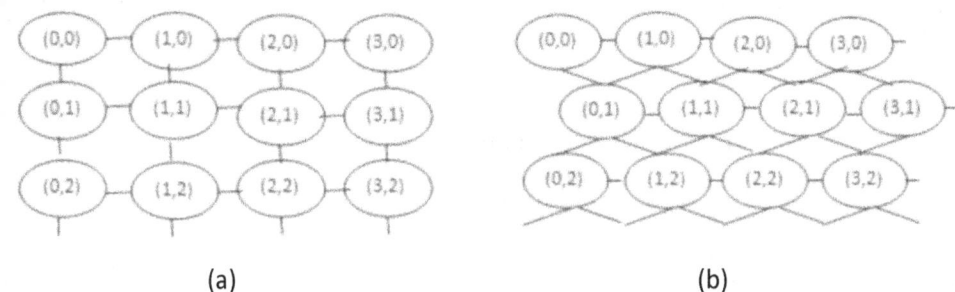

(a)   (b)

Fig. 3.1: (a) Rectangular grid pattern, (b) Hexagonal grid pattern

SOMs provide a methodology of representing multidimensional data (three dimensional), in lower dimensional spaces (one or two dimensional), and this transformation occurs in a topologically ordered fashion. This process of reducing the dimensionality of vectors is a data compression technique, also known as vector quantization. Furthermore, the Kohonen approach builds a network that is also capable of storing information with all the topological relationships maintained within the training set.

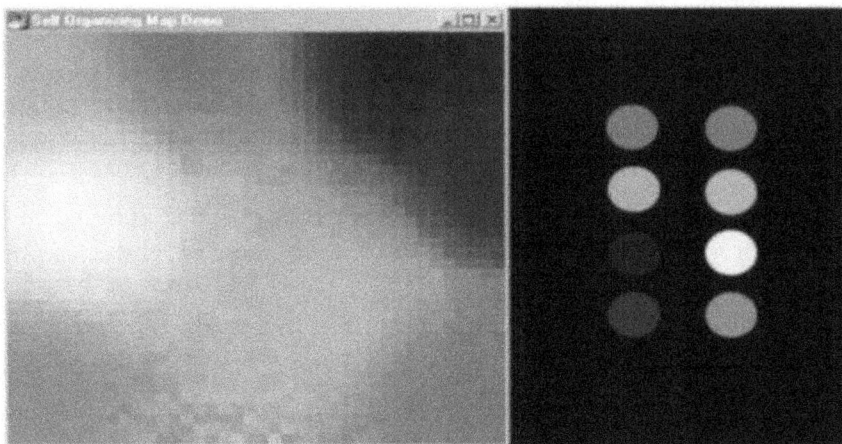

Fig.3.2: Image of the demo program (left) and the colors classified by it (right)

A simple example, to clarify the fundamentals behind SOMs, is the mapping of colors for their three dimensional constituents, say- red, green and blue, into a two dimensional space. Figure 3.2 shows an example in which a SOM is trained to identify and represent the eight different colors in a two dimensional space, out of the colors present in a three dimensional space. One point which is worth noticed her, is that along with clustering the colors into distinct regions, the network has also placed the regions of similar characteristics alongside each other. As already illustrated above, one of the key features of SOMs is that they learn to classify data without supervision.

Architecture of SOM

Figure 3.3 shows the architecture of a two dimensional SOM. The network is created from a two dimensional lattice of nodes; each node is fully connected to the source node in the input layer. However the lines showing the connection between the nodes in figure 3.3 are not laterally present, they just signify the adjacency between the nodes instead of the connections. Consequently, this network represents a fully feedforward structure with a single computational layer consisting of neurons arranged in a two dimensional or one dimensional rectangular or hexagonal space.

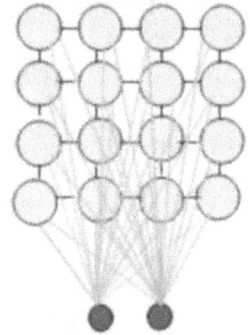

Fig.3.3: A simple Kohonen Network architecture

Figure 3.3 shows a simple Kohonen network of 4 X 4 nodes connected to the input layer (shown in purple) representing a two dimensional vector.

3.1.1.   Algorithm for training SOMs

A SOM does not require a target output to be specified unlike many other types of networks. Instead, the area where the node weight matches the input vector, is selectively optimized to more closely resemble the data for the class, whose member is the input vector. From the initial classification of random weights, and after going through several iterations, the SOM finally settles into a map of stable sectors. Each sector is efficaciously a feature classifier, so we can conclude the graphical output as a type of feature map of the input space. As you can see in figure 3.2, the blocks of similar color represents the individual sectors.

The algorithm utilized for the self organization of the network is based on three fundamental processes:

➢   Competition;

➢   Cooperation;

➢   Synaptic Adaptation;

A detailed description of all the three mentioned processes is presented next.

3.1.1.1. Competition

First of all, each node's weights are initialized; typically small standardized random values are set for these. A vector is selected randomly from the set of training data and introduced over the lattice. Each node's weight is investigated to determine whose weights are most alike the input vector. The winning node is referred to as the B.M.U.-Best Matching Unit. To determine the best matching unit, here we will utilize the technique of iterating across all the nodes and calculating the Euclidean distance between a pair of n:1 vectors, i.e., each node's weight vector w_j and the current input vector x. The node having the weight vector nearest to the input vector is categorized as the winning node or the BMU. This whole process is presented in a more detailed fashion below:

➤ Let the dimension of the input space is denoted by *m*. A pattern chosen randomly from input space is denoted by:

$$x = [x_1, x_2, ..., x_m]^T \tag{3.1}$$

➤ Each node's synaptic weight in the output layer has the same dimension as the input space. The weight of neuron j is denoted as:

$$w_j = [w_{j1}, w_{j2}, ..., w_{jm}]^T, \quad j = 1, 2, ..., n \tag{3.2}$$

Where, *n* = total number of neurons present in the output layer.

➤ In order to determine the best match of the input vector *x* with the synaptic weights w_j we use the Euclidean distance. The Euclidean distance between a pair of *n*:1 vectors *X* and W_j is mathematically represented by,

$$d = \| x - w_{ij} \| = \left[\sum_{j=1}^{n} (x_i - w_{ij})^2 \right]^{1/2} \tag{3.3}$$

where, x is the input vector (current) and w is the node's weight vector. For example, to calculate the distance between the input vector, the color red (1, 0, 0) with an arbitrary weight vector (0.1, 0.4, 0.5),

distance, d = [(1 − 0.1)² + (0 − 0.4)² + (0 − 0.5)²]^{1/2}

   = [(0.9)² + (−0.4)² + (−0.5)²]^{1/2}

   = [0.81 + 0.16 + 0.25]^{1/2}

   = (1.22)^{1/2} = 1.1061.106

➤ The neuron with the infinitesimal distance is called *i*(x) and is given by:

$$i(x) = \arg\min_j \| x - w_j \|, j = 1, 2, ..., l \tag{3.4}$$

➤ The neuron (i) that fulfills the above condition is called *best-matching* or *winning neuron* for the input vector *x*.

➤ The above equation leads to the following observation: *By deploying the process of competition between the neurons present in a vector, a continuous input space of activation patterns is mapped upon a discrete output space of neurons.*

➤ Depending on the application's interest the response of the network is either the index of the winner (i.e. coordinates in the lattice) or the synaptic weight vector that is nearest to the input vector.

3.1.1.2. Cooperation

Now, under this step, the radius of the BMU's neighbourhood is calculated. The value initially starts at large and typically set to the 'radius' of the lattice, but diminishes with each iteration. All the nodes that are present within this radius are considered to be inside the BMU's neighbourhood. After determining the BMU, next we have to observe the other nodes within the BMU's neighbourhood. All these nodes' weight vectors will be adjusted in the next step. This can be done by simply calculating the radius of the neighbourhood, and then applying the Pythagoras theorem to determine whether each node is present within the radial distance or not. Figure 3.4 shows an example of the size of a typical neighbourhood at nearly the commencement of the training.

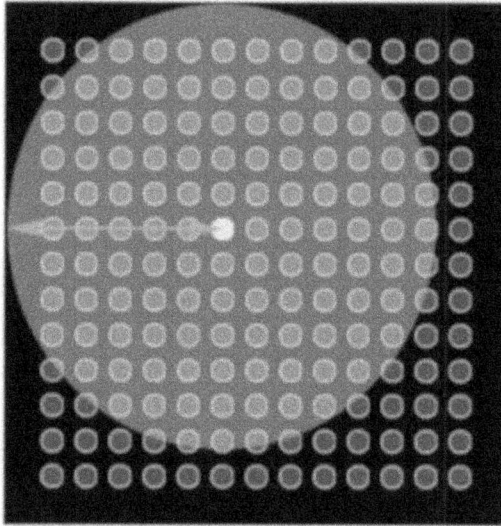

Fig. 3.4: The BMU's neighbourhood

You can see that the neighbourhood shown in figure 3.4 is centered about the BMU (colored yellow) and incorporates most of the other nodes. The green arrow shows the radius

➢ The winning neuron effectively locates the center of a *topological neighbourhood*.

➢ From neurobiology we know that a winning neuron excites more than average the neurons that exist in its immediate neighbourhood and inhibits more the neurons that they are in longer distances.

➢ Thus we observe that the neighbourhood must be a diminishing function of the *lateral distance* between the neurons.

➢ In the neighbourhood are included only excited neurons, while inhibited neurons exist outside of the neighbourhood.

➢ If d_{ij} is the lateral distance between neurons i and j (assuming that i is the winner and it is located in the centre of the neighbourhood) and we denote h_{ji} the *topological neighbourhood around neuron i*, then h_{ji} is a *unimodal function of distance* which satisfies the following two requirements:

- • The topological neighbourhood h_{ji} is symmetric about the maximum point defined by $d_{ji}=0$; in other words, it attains its maximum value at the winning neuron i for which the distance is zero.

- • The amplitude of the topological neighbourhood h_{ji} decreases monotonically with increasing lateral distance d_{ij} decaying to zero for $d_{ij} \to \infty$; this is a necessary condition for convergence.

➢ A typical choice of h_{ji} is the Gaussian function i.e. independent of the location of the winning neuron:

$$h_{ji(x)} = \exp(-d_{ij}^2 / 2\sigma^2) \tag{3.4}$$

where, σ is the "effective width" of the neighbourhood. It measures the degree up to which the excited neurons in the area of the winning neuron participate in the learning process.

➢ The distance among neurons is defined as the Euclidean metric. For example for a 2D lattice we have:

$$d_{ij}^2 = \| r_j - r_i \|^2 \tag{3.5}$$

➢ Where the discrete vector r_j describes the position of excited neuron j and r_i defines the position of the winning neuron in the lattice.

➢ Another characteristic feature of the SOM algorithm is that the size of the neighbourhood *shrinks* with time. This requirement is satisfied by making the width of the Gaussian function decreasing with time.

➢ A popular choice is the exponential decay function described by:

$$\sigma(n) = \sigma_0 \exp(-n / \tau_1); n = 0, 1, 2,..... \tag{3.6}$$

Where σ_0 is the value of σ at the initialization of the SOM algorithm and τ_1 is a *time constant*.

➢ Correspondingly the neighbourhood function assumes a time dependent form of its own:

$$h_{ji(x)} = \exp(-d_{ij}^2 / 2\sigma(n)^2) \tag{3.7}$$

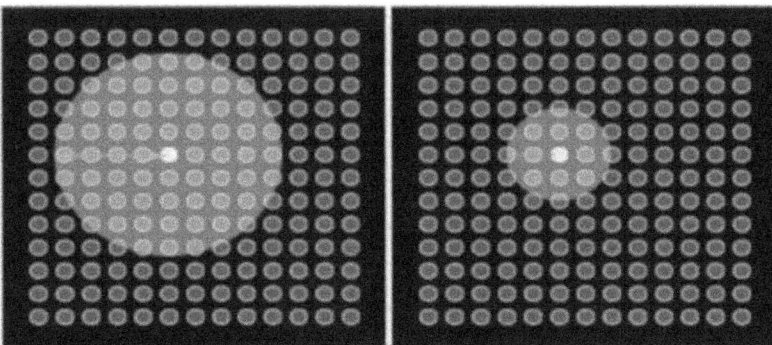

Fig.3.5: The shrinking radius

➢ Thus as the number of iterations increases, the width decreases in an exponential manner and the neighbourhood shrinks appropriately. Figure 3.5 shows how the neighbourhood in Figure 3.4 decreases over time (the figure is hypothetical, assuming the neighbourhood remains centered on the same node, but practically the BMU will move around depending on the presented input vector to the network) .

3.1.1.3. Adaptation

Now as we determined the radius, it is an easy task to iterate through all the nodes in the lattice to determine whether they lay within the radius or not. If a node is present in the neighbourhood then its weight vector is adjusted, in order to make them more alike to the input vector. The rate of alteration in the weights of the node, depends on its distance from the BMU, the node situated closer to the BMU, will go through more amount of alteration in the weight. A more elaborated discussion over this process is presented below.

➢ The adaptive process modifies the weights of the network so as to achieve the self-organization of the network.

➢ Just the weight of the winning neuron and that of neurons inside its neighbourhood are adapted. All the other neurons have no change in their weights.

➢ A method for deriving the weight update equations for the SOM model is based on a modified form of Hebbian learning. There is a forgetting term in the standard Hebbian weight equations.

➢ Let us assume that the *forgetting term* ϕ has the form $g(y_j)w_j$ where y_j is the response of neuron *j*.

➢ The only requirement for the function $g(y_j)$ is to make the constant term in its Taylor series expansion to be zero when the activity is zero, i.e.:

$$g(y_j) = 0 \text{ for } y_j = 0 \tag{3.8}$$

➢ The modified Hebbian rule for the weights of the output neurons is given by:

$$\Delta W_{ij} = \alpha Y_i X_j - \phi Y_i W_{ij} \tag{3.9}$$

Where α is the *learning rate parameter and* $\phi = g(y_j)w_j$.

➢ To satisfy the requirement for a zero constant term in the Taylor series we choose the following form for the function $g(y_j)$:

$$g(y_j) = \alpha y_j \tag{3.10}$$

We can simplify further by setting:

$$y_j = h_{ji(x)} \tag{3.11}$$

Combining the previous equations we get:

$$\Delta w_j = \alpha h_{ji(x)} (x - w_j) \tag{3.12}$$

Finally using a discrete representation for time we can write:

$$w_j(n+1) = w_j(n) + \eta(n) h_{ji(x)}(n) (x - w_j(n)) \tag{3.13}$$

    The above equation moves the weight vector of the winning neuron (and the rest of the neurons in the neighbourhood) near the input vector *x*.

➤ The algorithm leads to a *topological ordering* of the feature map in the input space in a way that neurons that are adjacent in the lattice tend to have similar synaptic weight vectors.

➤ The learning rate is also required to be time varying as it should be for stochastic approximation. Thus it is given by:

$$\eta(n) = \eta_0 \exp(-n/\tau_2);\ n = 0,1,2\ldots\ldots \tag{3.14}$$

Where η_0 is an initial value and τ_2 is another time constant.

➤ The adaptive process can be decomposed in two phases:

- A *self-organizing or ordering phase;*
- A *convergence phase.*

We explain next the main characteristics of each phase.

➤ Ordering Phase: During this phase of the adaptive process the topological ordering of the weight vectors occurs. The ordering phase may go through 1000 iterations of the SOM algorithm or more. One should choose carefully the learning rate and the neighbourhood function:

- The learning rate should begin with a value close to 0.1; thereafter it should decrease gradually, but remain above 0.01. These requirements are satisfied by making the following choices:

  $\eta_0 = 0.1,\ \tau_2 = 1000$

- The neighbourhood function should initially include almost all neurons in the network around the winning neuron i, and then shrink slowly with time. Specifically during the ordering phase it is allowed to reduce to a small value of couple of neighbours or to the winning neuron itself. Assuming a 2D lattice the value of σ_0 is chosen identical to the "radius" of the lattice. Correspondingly we may set the time constant t_1 as:

➤ **Convergence phase:** This second phase is needed to fine tune the feature map and therefore to provide an accurate statistical quantification of the input space. In general the number of iterations needed for this phase is 500 times the total number of neurons present in the lattice.

- For good statistical accuracy, the learning parameter must be maintained during this phase to a small value, on the order of 0.01. It should not allowed to go to zero, otherwise the network may stuck to a *metastable state* (i.e. a state with a defect);

- The neighbourhood should contain only the nearest neighbours of the winning neuron which may eventually reduce to one or zero neighbouring neurons.

Summary of the algorithm:

1.   Initialize each node's synaptic weight .

2. Select a vector randomly from the set of input vectors and present it to the network.

3. Examine each node to determine whose weights are most alike the input vector. The winning node is referred to as the (BMU) Best Matching Unit.

4. Next the radius of the neighbourhood of the BMU is being computed. Initially its value starts from large, set to the 'radius' of the network, but diminishes each time-step. Any node which is situated within this radius is considered to be within the BMU's neighbourhood.

5. Each neighbouring node's (the nodes found in step 4) weights are adjusted so as to make them more equivalent to the input vector.

6. Again return to step 2 for N iterations.

The whole algorithm has also been shown in the form of flow diagram, in figure 3.6.

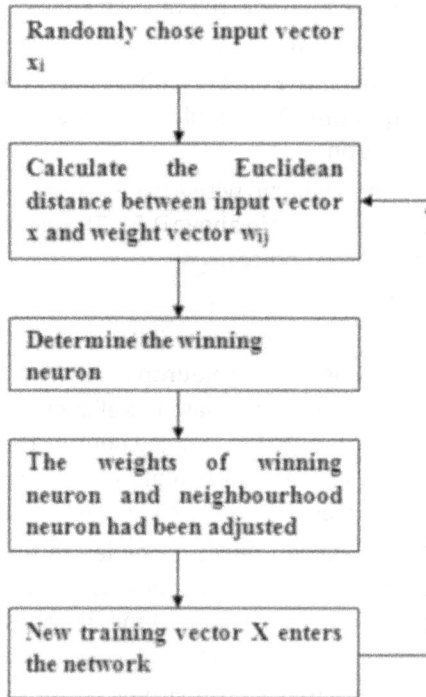

Fig. 3.6: Flow diagram of Kohonen SOM algorithm

3.1.2. Properties of SOM

➤ **Approximation of the Input Space**: The feature map Φ, represented by the set of synaptic weight vectors $\{w_j\}$ in the output space, delivers a fine estimation to the input space.

➤ **Topological Ordering**: The feature map Φ computed by the SOM algorithm is topologically ordered apparently because the spatial location of a neuron in the network corresponds to a specific domain or aspect of the input patterns.

➤ **Density Matching**: The feature map Φ reflects variations in the enumeration of the input distribution; regions within the input space from which sample vectors *x* are obtained with a high probability of occurrence are mapped onto larger domains of the output space, and with better resolution, whereas the regions in input space from which sample vectors *x* are drawn with a low probability of occurrence are mapped onto smaller domains of the output space.

➤ **Feature Selection**: Suppose a data is presented from an input space with a nonlinear distribution, the self-organizing map is capable of choosing a set of best features for the approximation of the elementary distribution.

3.2. Counter Propagation Networks

The Counter Propagation Networks (CPN) were introduced by Professor Robert Hecht-Nielson in the year 1987, as a network which combines the principles of unsupervised learning and supervised learning, thus it could be seen as a semi-supervised network. As the network is thought to as a combination of competitive network and Grossberg's outstar network, it is also sometimes called as a hybrid network. The architecture of CPN is shown in figure 3.7.

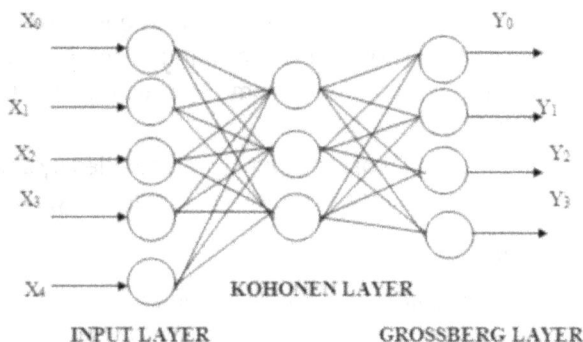

Fig. 3.7: Architecture of Counter Propagation Network

From the figure 3.7 it is clear that the CPN is composed of three layers:

➤ An **Input layer** that reads input patterns from the training set and forwards them to the succeeding network.

➤ A **Hidden layer** that works in a competitive fashion and links each input pattern with one of the hidden units, thus calculates a net input value and a competition takes place among the neurons to determine which unit has the largest net-input value. This is made up of number of processing elements known as *instar*.

➤ The **Output layer** which is trained via a delta learning algorithm whose main objective is to reduce the mean square error (MSE) between the actual output and the target output linked with the current input vector, this is basically a structure known as an *outstar*.

In the next section, we will elaborate the basic components of these three layers.

There are so many things that categorize CPN a unique network, unlike other networks till now we discussed. Instead of employing a single learning algorithm throughout the network, the CPN uses a different learning procedure on each layer. This allows the CPN to train quite rapidly with respect to other networks that we have studied so far. The drawback of CPN is that it might not always yield sufficient accuracy for some applications. Nevertheless, they remains a good choice for some class of applications like, data compression, function approximation and pattern association.

3.2.1. Building Blocks of CPN

The Counter Propagation Network is build up of four major constituents: an **input layer** that process on the incoming data, a processing element called an **instar**, a layer of instar known as a **competitive network**, and a structure known as an **outstar**.

3.2.1.1. The Input Layer

The most basic and commonly known purpose of this layer is to distribute the incoming external input pattern vector to the feedforward portion of the network. But this task is not that simple, as it seems to be. Although the input vectors may contain the same pattern information, these patterns may be of varying magnitude. Furthermore, for any processing by a unit, the input is required to be bounded to certain limits. Also, the input layer should not feed the background noise to the feedforward portion of the competitive network. This well known noise-saturation dilemma for input vectors can be handled by feeding the actual inputs from the environment to a layer of input processing units as shown in figure 3.8.

The noise saturation problem of the input layer is handled by a shunting activation model, with on-centre off-surround configuration, it is given by,

$$x_i = -Ax_i + (B - x_i)I_i - (C + x_i) \cdot \sum_{j \neq i} I_j \tag{3.15}$$

The ith unit's steady state activation value is given by,

$$x_i(\infty) = [(B + C)I_I - CI]/[A + I] = [(I_i / I) - (C/(B + C))] \cdot (B + C)/(1 + A/I) \tag{3.16}$$

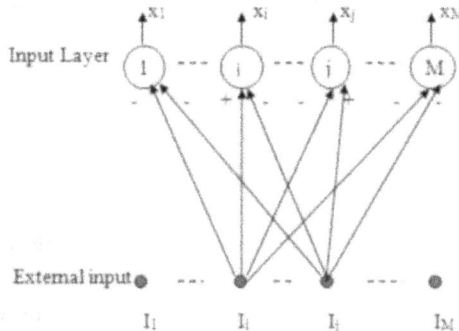

Fig. 3.8: Input layer with M processing units showing some of the connections with external inputs

where, $I = \sum_{i=0}^{M} I_I$, and all the inputs are positive. The above equation shows that in the steady state the activation value of the ith units lies under the range $[-C, B]$. The output function of these units is assumed to be linear for $x > 0$, i.e.,

$$f(x) = x; \quad \text{for } x \geq 0;$$
$$\quad\quad = 0; \quad \text{for } x < 0;$$

The output of the units will be zero as long as the inputs $I_i < CI / (B + C)$; i.e. the input is required to be greater than a certain value, before it could make the activation of the unit positive. Thus, the units in the input layer will not respond to noise input, if the value of noise input is below some threshold value. Therefore the input of the feedforward portion is always positive and is limited to a maximum value of B. thus it is clear that the input layer not only normalizes the data values, but also carefully handle the noise saturation problem with an on-line input data.

3.2.1.2. The Instar and The Outstar

The hidden layer of the CPN is comprised of an array of processing elements known as instar. In this section we will discuss instar individually and we will also examine the set of instars that operate together to form the CPN hidden layer.

Let us consider two layers K_1 and K_2 with M and N processing units respectively. By providing connection to the jth unit in the K_2 layer from all the units in the K_1 layer as shown in figure 3.9. Two network structures are shown in fig (a) and (b), instar and outstar, which have fan-in and fan-out geometries respectively. During the training, the normalized weight vector $w_j = (w_{j1}, w_{j2}, \ldots w_{jM})^T$ in instar approaches the normalized input vector, when an input vector $x = (x_1, x_2, \ldots x_M)^T$ is presented at the K_1 layer. Thus,

the activation $w_j^T a = \sum_{i=1}^{M} w_{ij} x_k$ of the jth unit in the diagram.

K_2 layer will reach its maximum value during learning. Each time the input is projected to K_1, the jth unit of the K_2 will be activated to the maximum extent. Thus the operation of an instar can be viewed as content addressable memory.

In the case of an outstar, during learning the weight vector for the connections from the jth unit in K_2 approaches the activity pattern in K_1, whenever an input vector x is presented at F_1. During recall, whenever the unit j is activated, the signal pattern $(y_j w_{1j}, y_j w_{2j} \ldots y_j w_{Mj})$ will be transmitted to K_1, where y_j represents the output of the jth unit. This signal pattern produces the original activity pattern corresponding to the input vector x, even though the input is absent. Thus the operation of an outstar can be viewed as memory addressing the contents.

When all the connections between the units of K_1 and K_2 layer is set as shown in fig. (c), we obtain a heteroassociation network. This network can be viewed as a group of instars, if the flow is from K_1 to K_2. On the other hand, if the flow is from K_2 to K_1 then the network can be viewed as a group of outstars.

(a) Instar

(b) Outstar

(c) Group of instars

(d) Group of outstars

(e) Bidirectional Associative Memory

(f) Auto-associative memory

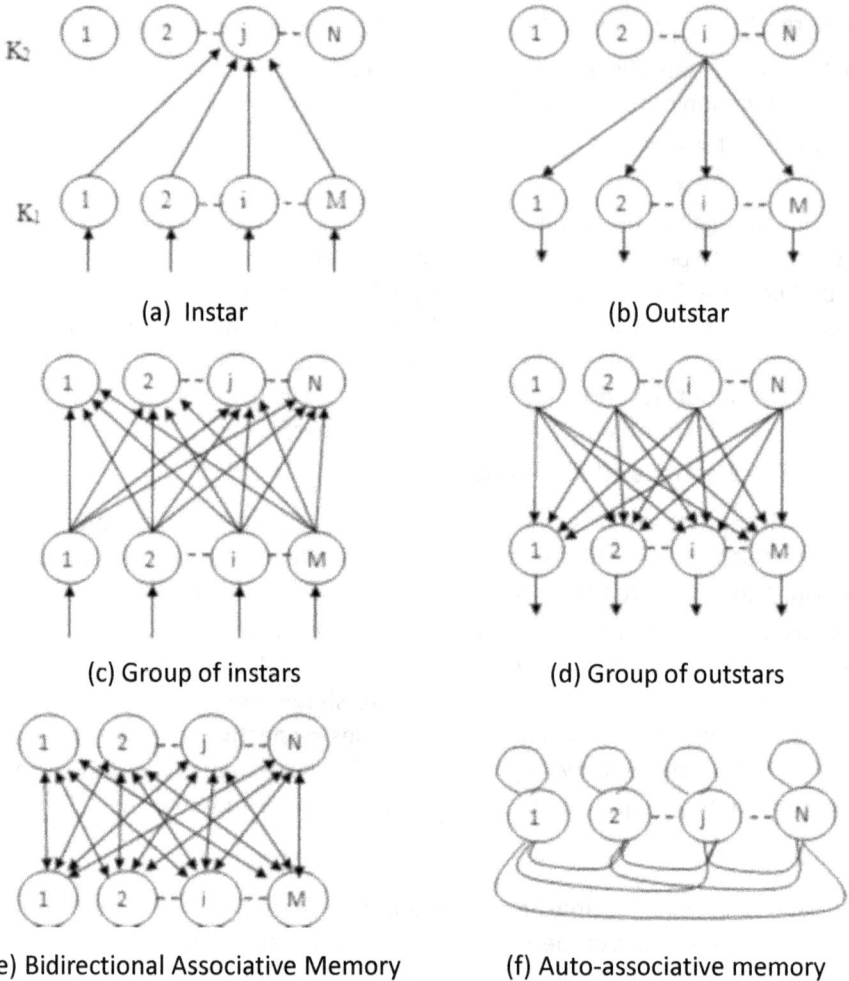

Fig. 3.9 some basic structures of artificial neural networks

When the flow is bidirectional, we get a bidirectional associative memory as shown in figure (e), where either of the layers can behave as input or output layer.

If the two layers K_1 and K_2 coincides and the weights are symmetric, i.e., $w_{ji} = w_{ij}$, $I \neq j$, then we obtain an autoassociative memory in which each unit is connected to each other unit and also to itself.

3.2.2. Training the CPN

The training process of the counter-propagation network is said to be a two stage procedure: during the first stage the process the synaptic weights adaptation takes place between the input and the Competitive layer; while in the second stage the synaptic weights between the Kohonen and the Grossberg layer are updated. Next we will see a more detailed description of the training algorithm of the counter – propagation network:

Stage I- Adjusting the weights between the input and the Kohonen layer (hidden layer):

This phase of training may be called as In-star modeled training.

Step 1: The synaptic weights of the network between the input and the Kohonen layer are set to small random values in the interval [0, 1].

Step 2: A vector pair (x, y) of the training set, is selected at random.

Step 3: The input vector x of the selected training pattern is normalized.

Step 4: The normalized input vector is sent to the network.

Step 5: In the hidden competitive layer the distance between the weight vector and the current input vector is calculated for each hidden neuron *j* utilizing the equation (3.3) as-

$$d = \left[\sum_{j=1}^{n} (x_i - w_{ij})^2 \right]^{1/2}$$

where *n* is the number of the hidden neurons and w_{ij} is the weight of the synapse that joins the ith neuron of the input layer with the jth neuron of the Kohonen layer.

Step 6: The winner neuron F of the Kohonen layer is identified as the neuron with the minimum distance value *d*.

Step 7: The synaptic weights between the winner neuron F and all M neurons of the input layer are adjusted according to the equation

$$F_{wi}(t+1) = F_{wi}(t) + \alpha(t)(x_i - F_{wi}(t)) \tag{3.17}$$

In the above equation (3.17) α is a coefficient known as the Kohonen learning rate. The training process starts with an initial learning rate value α_0 that is gradually decreased during training according to the equation

$$\alpha(t) = \alpha_0 (1 - t/T) \tag{3.18}$$

where *T* is the maximum iteration number of the stage A of the algorithm. A typical initial value for the Kohonen learning rate is a value of 0.7.

Step 8: The steps 1 to 6 are repeated until all training patterns have been processed once. For each training pattern *p* the distance Dp of the winning neuron is stored for further processing. The storage of this distance is performed before the weight update operation.

Step 9: At the end of each epoch the training set mean error is calculated according to the equation

$$E = 1/P \sum_{k=1}^{p} d_k \tag{3.19}$$

Where, *P* is the number of pairs in the training set, d_k is the distance of the winning neuron for the pattern *k* and *i* is the current training epoch.

The network converges when the error measure falls below a user supplied tolerance value. The network also stops training in the case where the specified number of iterations has been performed, but the error value has not converged to a specific value.

Stage II- Performs the training of the weights from the hidden to the output nodes:

This phase may be called the Out-star modeled training. The weight updation is done by the Grossberg learning rule, which is only for out-star learning. In out-star learning, no competition is assumed among the units, and the learning occurs for all units in a particular layer. The weight updation rule involves following steps,

Step 1: The synaptic weights of the network between the Kohonen and the Grossberg layer are set to small random values in the interval [0, 1].

Step 2: A vector pair (x, y) of the training set, is selected in random.

Step 3: The input vector x of the selected training pattern is normalized.

Step 4: The normalized input vector is sent to the network.

Step 5: In the hidden competitive layer the distance between the weight vector and the current input vector is calculated for each hidden neuron j according to the equation,

$$d = \left[\sum\nolimits_{j=1}^{n} (x_i - w_{ij})^2 \right]^{1/2}$$

where n is the number of the hidden neurons and w_{ij} is the weight of the synapse that joins the ith neuron of the input layer with the jth neuron of the Kohonen layer.

Step 6: The winner neuron W of the Kohonen layer is identified as the neuron with the minimum distance value Dj. The output of this node is set to unity while the outputs of the other hidden nodes are assigned to zero values.

Step 7: The connection weights between the winning neuron of the hidden layer and all N neurons of the output layer are adjusted according to the equation,

$$F_{wi}(t+1) = F_{wi}(t) + \beta(t)(x_i - F_{wi}(t)) \qquad (3.20)$$

In the above equation the β coefficient is known as the Grossberg learning rate.

Step 8: The above procedure is performed for each training pattern. In this case the error measure is computed as the mean Euclidean distance between the winner node's output weights and the desired output, that is,

$$E = 1/P \sum\nolimits_{j=1}^{P} d_j = 1/P \sum\nolimits_{k=1}^{N} [(y_k - w_k)^2]^{1/2} \qquad (3.21)$$

As in stage A, the network converges when the error measure falls below a user supplied tolerance value. The network also stops training after exhausting the prescribed number of iterations.

Although CPN is inferior as compared to other neural network's models such as back propagation networks, but it has so many advantages too; it's simple architecture and forms a good statistical model for its input vector environment. Can be trained rapidly and is also useful for rapid prototyping of systems.

In the following subsection types of CPN are discussed.

3.2.3.   Classification of CPN

Counter Propagation Network is broadly classified into two types:

➢   Full counter propagation network

➢   Forward only counter propagation network

3.2.3.1. Full counter propagation network

The Full CPN acquire the capability of generalization, i.e., it is seem to be tolerant to a certain imprecision, or in other words we could say that it could efficiently handle a partial incorrect or incomplete input vector and produce a correct output out of it. By constructing a look-up table, it could represent large number of vector pairs, *x:y*.

As we had already discussed that the training algorithm of CPN consists of two phases, so do the full CPN, in this section we will again discuss the training algorithms of both the types of CPN individually. In full CPN, during the first phase of training, the training vector pairs are ought to form clusters. This clustering is accomplished either by dot product or Euclidean distance formula. But we usually prefer Euclidean distance methodology for the task, to avoid the normalization. During the second phase of training, the weights are adjusted between the cluster units and the output units. First we will go through the architecture of full CPN. Figure 3.10 shows the architecture of full CPN.

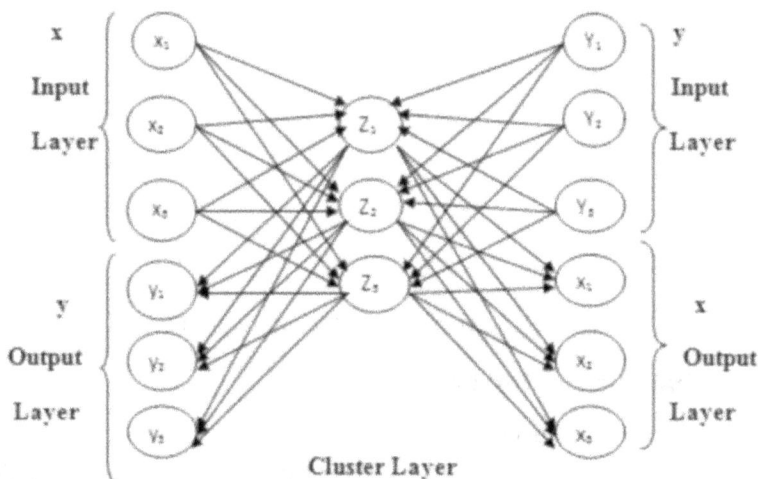

Fig.3.10: Architecture of full CPN

As we had already discussed in previous section that CPN learns in two phases, in spite of it, a CPN also operates in two modes; in the first mode, the input vectors are accepted and outputs are produced, while in second mode, the input vectors are applied and the weights are adjusted to obtain the desired output vectors.

Below figures 3.11 and 3.12 shows the two phases of full CPN learning algorithm.

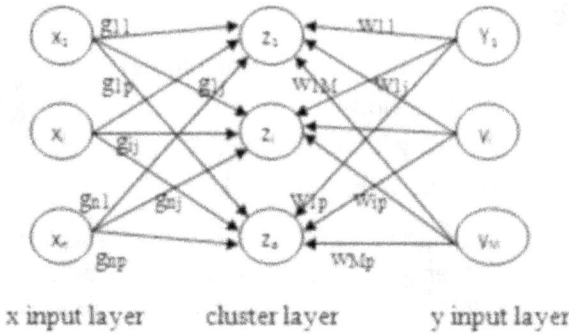

x input layer   cluster layer   y input layer

Fig.3.11: First phase of full CPN learning

The architecture of full CPN consists of Grossberg instar and outstar model. It has two input layers and two output layers with the hidden layer common to both input and the output layer. The portion which connects the input layer to hidden layer is the instar model and the portion which connects the hidden layer to output layer behaves as outstar model. The first phase of training is performed by instar and the second phase of training is performed by the outstar.

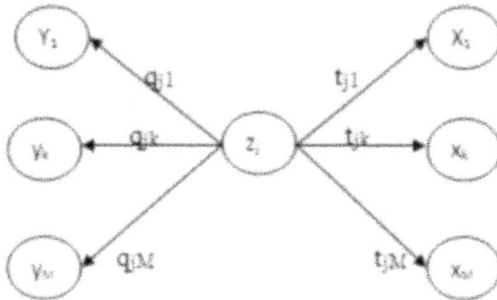

Fig.3.12: Second phase of feedforward CPN

3.2.3.1.1. Training the full CPN

The full CPN training is achieved in two phases.

First phase: This phase of training may be called as In-star modeled training. The active units here are the units in the x-input, z-cluster and y-input layers. Generally in CPN, the cluster unit does not assume any topology, but the winning unit is allowed to learn. The winning unit uses our standard Kohonen learning rule for its weight updation. The rule is given by,

$$g_{ij}^{(new)} = g_{ij}^{(old)} + \alpha(x_i - g_{ij}^{(old)})$$
$$= (1 - \alpha) \, g_{ij}^{(old)} + \alpha x_i ; \quad i = 1 \text{ to } n \tag{3.22}$$
$$W_{kj}^{(new)} = w_{kj}^{(old)} + \beta(y_k - w_{jk}^{(old)})$$
$$= (1 - \beta) \, w_{kj}^{(old)} + \beta y_k; \quad k = 1 \text{ to } m \tag{3.23}$$

Second phase: In this phase, we can find only the J unit remaining active in the cluster layer. The weights from the winning cluster unit J to the output units are adjusted, so that vector of activation of units in the y output layer, y, is the approximation of input vector y; and x is an approximation of input vector x. This phase may be called the Out-star modeled training. The weight updation is done by the Grossberg learning rule, which is only for out-star learning. In out-star learning, no competition is assumed among the units, and the learning occurs for all units in a particular layer. The weight updation rule is given as,

$$q_{jk}^{(new)} = q_{jk}^{(old)} + \alpha(y_k - q_{jk})^{(old)}$$
$$= (1 - \alpha)\alpha_{jk}^{(old)} + \alpha y_k; \quad k = 1 \text{ to } m \tag{3.24}$$

$$t_{ji}^{(new)} = t_{ij}^{(old)} + b(x_i - t_{ij}^{(old)})$$
$$= (1 - \beta)\,'t_{ij}^{(old)} + bx_i; \quad i = 1 \text{ to } n \tag{3.25}$$

Training Algorithm for Full CPN:

Step 1: Set the weights and the initial learning rate.

Step 2: Perform step 2 to 7 if stopping condition is false for phase I training.

Step 3: For each of the training input vector pair x:y presented, perform step 3 to.

Step 4: Make the X-input layer activations to vector X. Make the Y-input layer activation to vector Y.

Step 5: Find the winning cluster unit. If dot product method is used, find the cluster unit zj with target net input; for $j = 1$ to p,

$$z_i n_j = \sum x_i \cdot g_{ij} + \sum y_k \cdot w_{kj} \tag{3.26}$$

If Euclidean distance method is used, find the cluster unit zj whose squared distance from input vectors is the smallest:

$$d_j = \sum (x_i - g_{ij})^2 + \sum (y_k - g_{kj})^2 \tag{3.27}$$

If there occurs a tie in case of selection of winner unit, the unit with the smallest index is the winner. Take the winner unit index as J.

Step 6: Update the weights over the calculated winner unit zj.

For $i = 1$ to n, $g_{ij}^{(new)} = g_{ij}^{(old)} + \alpha[x_i - g_{ij}^{(old)}]$

For $k = 1$ to m, $w_{kJ}^{(new)} = w_{kJ}^{(old)} + \hat{a}[y_k - w_{kJ}^{(old)}]$

Step 7: Reduce the learning rates.

$$\alpha(t + 1) = 0.5\alpha(t); \quad \beta(t + 1) = 0.5\beta(t) \tag{3.28}$$

Step 8: Test stopping condition for phase I training.

Step 9: Perform step 9 to 15 when stopping condition is false for phase II training.

Step 10: Perform step 10 to 13 for each training input vector pair x:y. Here α and β are small constant values.

Step 11: Make the X-input layer activations to vector x. Make the Y-input layer activations to vector y.

Step 12: Find the winning cluster unit (Using the formula from step 4). Take the winner unit index as J.

Step 13: Update the weights entering into unit z_j.

For $i = 1$ to n, $g_{ij}^{(new)} = g_{ij}^{(old)} + \alpha[x_i - g_{ij}^{(old)}]$

For $k = 1$ to m, $w_{kj}^{(new)} = w_{kj}^{(old)} + \beta[y_k - w_{kj}^{(old)}]$ 　　　　　　(3.29)

Step 14: Update the weights from unit z_j to the output layers.

For $i = 1$ to n, $t_{ji}^{(new)} = t_{ji}^{(old)} + \beta[x_i - t_{ji}^{(old)}]$

For $k = 1$ to m, $q_{jk}^{(new)} = q_{jk}^{(old)} + \alpha[y_k - q_{jk}^{(old)}]$ 　　　　　　(3.30)

Step 15: Reduce the learning rates α and β.

$\alpha(t + 1) = 0.5\alpha(t); \ \beta(t + 1) = 0.5\beta(t)$ 　　　　　　(3.31)

Step 16: Test stopping condition for phase II training.

Numerical 3.1. Consider the following full CPN, having input pairs $x = (1,0)$, $y = (0, 1)$. By performing the first stage of training, find out the activation of the cluster layer units and update the weights using learning rates of 0.3.

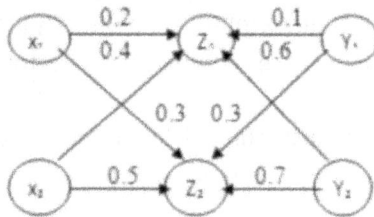

Solution: As only first stage of training is to be performed, so the corresponding steps are as follows:

Step 1: Initialize the weights

$$V = \begin{Bmatrix} 0.2 & 0.3 \\ 0.4 & 0.5 \end{Bmatrix}, \ W = \begin{Bmatrix} 0.1 & 0.3 \\ 0.6 & 0.7 \end{Bmatrix}$$

Initialize the learning rates, $\alpha = \beta = 0.3$;

Step 2: Begin the training.

Step 3: Present the input vector pair;

$X = (1,0)$, $Y = (0,1)$;

Step 4: Set the activations of input and output to x and y.

Step 5: Determine the winner unit, by using the Euclidean distance formula,

$d_j = \Sigma(x_i - g_{ij})^2 + \Sigma(y_k - g_{kj})^2$

$d_1 = (1 - 0.2)^2 + (0 - 0.4)^2 + (0 - 0.1)^2 + (1 - 0.6)^2 = 0.97$

$d_2 = (1 - 0.3)^2 + (0 - 0.5)^2 + (0 - 0.3)^2 + (1 - 0.7)^2 = 0.92$

since, $d_2 < d_1; j = 2$

Step 6: Updating the weights on the winner unit. The weight updation is given by,

$$g_{ij}^{(new)} = g_{ij}^{(old)} + \alpha[x_i - g_{ij}^{(old)}]$$

$$g_{12()} = g_{12(0)} + \alpha[x_1 - g_{12(0)}]$$

$$g_{12(0)} = 0.3 + 0.3[1 - 0.3] = 0.51$$

$$g_{22(0)} = 0.5 + 0.3[0 - 0.5] = 0.35$$

Also,

$$w_{kj}^{(new)} = w_{kj}^{(old)} + \beta[y_k - w_{kj}^{(old)}]$$

$$w_{12}(x) = 0.3 + 0.3\,(0 - 0.3) = 0.21$$

$$w_{22}(x) = 0.7 + 0.3\,(1 - 0.7) = 0.79$$

Thus, the first iteration is performed, the updated weights are

$$g = \begin{Bmatrix} 0.2 & 0.51 \\ 0.4 & 0.35 \end{Bmatrix}, \quad w = \begin{Bmatrix} 0.1 & 0.21 \\ 0.6 & 0.79 \end{Bmatrix}$$

3.2.3.2. Forward only CPN

Forward only CPN is a simplified form of full CPN. It is different from full CPN only in the sense that it uses only x-vectors to form the clusters on the Kohonen units during the first phase of training. It consists of three layers: input layer, cluster layer and output layer. Its architecture resembles the back-propagation network, but in CPN there exists interconnections between the units in the cluster layer.

The architecture of forward only CPN is shown in below figure 3.13.

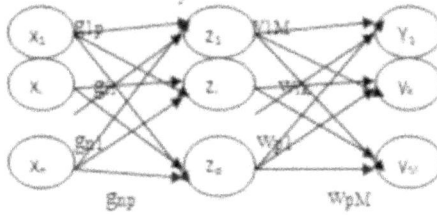

Fig.3.13: Forward only CPN

Training Algorithm for Forward-only CPN:

Step 1: Initialize the weights and learning rates.

Step 2: Perform step 2 to 7 when stopping condition for phase I training is false.

Step 3: Perform step 3 to 5 for each of training input X.

Step 4: Set the X-input layer activation to vector X.

Step 5: Compute the winning cluster unit J. If dot product method is used, find the cluster unit z_j with the largest net input:

$$z_j n_j = \sum x_i \cdot g_{ij} \tag{3.33}$$

If Euclidean distance is used, find the cluster unit z_j square of whose distance from the input pattern is smallest:

$$d_j = \sum (x_i - g_{ij})^2 \tag{3.34}$$

If there exists a tie in the selection of winner unit, the unit with the smallest index is chosen as the winner.

Step 5: Perform weight updation for unit z_j. For $i = 1$ to n,

$$g_{ij}^{(new)} = g_{ij}^{(old)} + \alpha[x_i - g_{ij}^{(old)}] \tag{3.35}$$

Step 6: Reduce learning rate α:

$$\alpha(t+1) = 0.5\alpha(t) \tag{3.36}$$

Step 7: Test the stopping condition for phase I training.

Step 8: Perform step 9 to 1 when stopping condition for phase II training is false.

Step 9: Perform step 10 to 13 for each training input pair $x{:}y$.

Step 10: Set X-input layer activations to vector X. Set Y-output layer activation to vector Y.

Step 11: Find the winning cluster unit J.

Step 12: Update the weights into unit z_j. For $i = 1$ to n,

$$g_{ij}^{(new)} = g_{ij}^{(old)} + \alpha[x_i - g_{ij}^{(old)}] \tag{3.37}$$

Step 13: Update the weights from unit z_j to the output units.

For $k = 1$ to m, $w_{jk}^{(new)} = w_{jk}^{(old)} + \beta[y_k - w_{jk}^{(old)}]$ (3.38)

Step 14: Reduce learning rate β,

$$\beta(t+1) = 0.5\beta(t) \tag{3.39}$$

Step 15: Test the stopping condition for phase II training.

Numerical 3.2. Consider the following forward only CPN, having input pairs $x = (1, 0)$, $y = (0, 1)$. By performing the first stage of training, find out the activation of the cluster layer units and update the weights using learning rates of $\alpha = 0.5$ and $a = 0.1$.

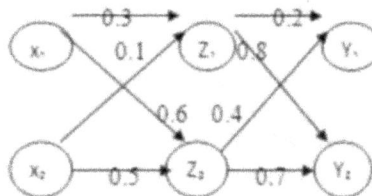

Solution: As only first stage of training is to be performed, so the corresponding steps are as follows:

Step 1: Initialize the weights

$$V = \begin{cases} 0.3 & 0.6 \\ 0.1 & 0.5 \end{cases}, \quad W = \begin{cases} 0.2 & 0.8 \\ 0.4 & 0.7 \end{cases}$$

Initialize the learning rates, $\alpha = 0.5$, $a = 0.1$;

Step 2: Begin the training.

Step 3: Present the input vector;

$x = (1, 0)$

Step 4: Set the activations of $x = (1, 0)$.

Step 5: Determine the winning cluster unit, by using the Euclidean distance formula,

$d_j = \Sigma(x_i - g_{ij})^2$

$d_1 = (1 - 0.3)^2 + (0 - 0.1)^2 = 0.5$

$d_2 = (1 - 0.6)^2 + (0 - 0.5)^2 = 0.41$

since, $d_2 < d_1; j = 2$

Step 6: Updating the weights on the winner unit. The weight updation is given by,

$g_{ij}^{(new)} = g_{ij}^{(old)} + \alpha[x_i - g_{ij}^{(old)}], i = 1$ to 2

$g_{12()} = g_{12(0)} + \alpha[x_1 - g_{12(0)}]$

$g_{12(0)} = 0.6 + 0.5[1 - 0.6] = 0.8$

$g_{22(0)} = 0.5 + 0.5[0 - 0.5] = 0.25$

the updated weights are,

$$g = \begin{matrix} 0.3 & 0.8 \\ 0.1 & 0.25 \end{matrix}$$

Step 7 and 8: keeping α- same constant value for using it in the second stage. If stopping condition is mentioned, check or move to next step.

Step 9: Begin the second stage of training.

Step 10: Present input vector pair x and y.

Step 11: set the activations to x (1,0) and y (0,1)

Step 12: Calculate the winning cluster unit.

$d_j = \Sigma(x_i - g_{ij})^2$

$d_1 = (1 - 0.3)^2 + (0 - 0.1)^2 = 0.5$

$d_2 = (1 - 0.8)^2 + (0 - 0.25)^2 = 0.1025$

since, $d_2 < d_1; j = 2$

Step 13: Update the weights into cluster unit:

$g_{ij}^{(new)} = g_{ij}^{(old)} + \alpha[x_i - g_{ij}^{(old)}], i = 1$ to 2

$g_{12()} = g_{12(0)} + \alpha[x_1 - g_{12(0)}]$

$g_{12(0)} = 0.8 + 0.5[1 - 0.8] = 0.9$

$g_{22(0)} = 0.25 + 0.5[0 - 0.25] = 0.125$

Step 14: Update the weights from the cluster unit to the output unit:

$w_{kj}^{(new)} = w_{kj}^{(old)} + \beta[y_k - w_{kj}^{(old)}]; k = 1$ to 2;

$w_{12}(x) = 0.4 + 0.1 (0 - 0.4) = 0.36$

$w_{22}(x) = 0.7 + 0.1 (1 - 0.7) = 0.73$

Thus, the first iteration is performed, the updated weights are

$$g = \begin{Bmatrix} 0.3 & 0.9 \\ 0.1 & 0.125 \end{Bmatrix}, \quad w = \begin{Bmatrix} 0.2 & 0.5 \\ 0.36 & 0.73 \end{Bmatrix}$$

The next step can be carried out depending on the stopping condition or by further reduction of learning rates.

3.3.   Adaptive Resonance Theory

The Backpropagation Network which we discussed in chapter-2 was very efficient in simulating any continuous function with the help of a certain number of hidden layer and certain form of activation functions. But training a BPN is a hectic and time consuming task, as it took thousands of epochs for the network to reach equilibrium and it is not guaranteed that it can always result in the global minimum. Once a BPN is trained and the number of hidden neurons and the weights are fixed, the network cannot learn from new patterns unless the network is retrained from the very beginning. Thus we land to the conclusion that the BPN don't have plasticity.

Assuming that the number of hidden neurons can be kept constant, the plasticity problem can be solved by retraining the network on the new patterns using on-line learning rule. However, it will cause the network to forget about old knowledge completely, therefore, such algorithm can be said stable. Such contradiction between plasticity and stability is called plasticity/stability dilemma. This dilemma is about:

Any system is required to learn with continuous changes in the environment, this property is called plasticity; but the constant variations in the environment could make the system unstable, because, a system can only learn new information, when it forgets about everything it has learned so far. This is what we meant by plasticity-stability phenomena.

Adaptive Resonance Theory (ART) is a new type of Neural Network, introduced by Grossberg in 1976 to solve this plasticity/stability dilemma and on aspects of how the brain processes information. ART has a self regulating control structure that allows autonomous recognition and learning. It requires no supervisory control structure that allows autonomous recognition and learning and describes a number of neural network models which use supervised and unsupervised learning methods, and capable of handling problems like pattern recognition and prediction. The basic perception behind the designing of ART model is that generally the object identification and recognition is an outcome of the linkage between the 'top-down' observer predictions with the 'bottom-up' sensory information. The model postulates that 'top-down' predictions take the form of a memory template or patterning which is then compared with the genuine characteristics of an object as perceived by the sensory organs. This correlation between prediction and genuine characteristics arise a measure of category relationship. As long as this difference between sensation and prediction does not exceed a predefined threshold level defined by the *'vigilance parameter'*, the sensed object will be believed to be a member of the predicted class. Thus to a certain extent, we could say that the 'plasticity/stability' problem is solved, i.e. the ability of grasping new knowledge without forgetting about the existing or past knowledge.

The first version of ART, i.e., ART-1 was proposed by Gail Carpenter and Stephen Grossberg in 1987, is used to cluster binary data. Since then, several versions of ART have been developed.

The most prominent ones are: ART-2, ART-3 extensions of ART-1, based on unsupervised algorithm and used to cluster analog data and introduce the concept of *resonance*; ARTMAP, a supervised learning mechanism for binary data, here the algorithms cluster both the inputs and targets and associate two sets of clusters; and fuzzy ARTMAP, a supervised learning algorithm of analog data. A detailed description about the classification of all these networks is given in below figure 3.14.

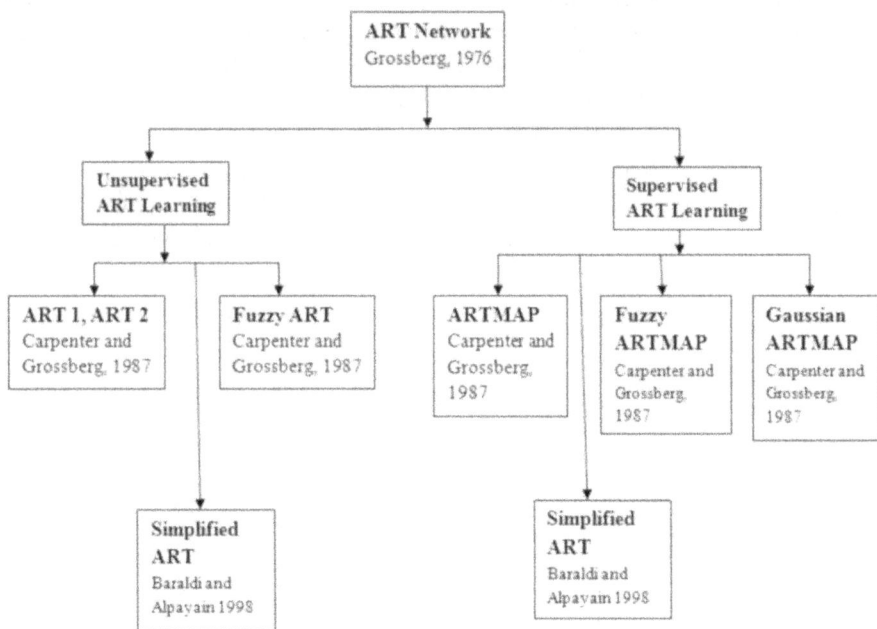

Fig. 3.14: Classification of ART networks

3.3.1. General architecture of ART

A general ART system is shown in figure 3.15, it is based on unsupervised learning model, is comprised of three basic units:

➢ **Field:** a comparison field and a recognition field composed of neurons;
➢ A **vigilance parameter**
➢ A **reset module**

The comparison field accepts an incoming input vector (a one-dimensional array of values) and conveys it to the recognition field to find out its best match. The single neuron whose synaptic weights are most closely matched to the input vector is said to be the best match.

Each **recognition field** neuron produces a negative signal (proportional to that neuron's quality of match to the input vector) to each of the other recognition field neurons and thus inhibits their output. In this way the recognition field exhibits lateral inhibition, allowing each neuron in it to represent a category to which input vectors are classified.

After the input vector is classified, *the reset module* compares the strength of the recognition match to the *vigilance parameter*. If the match level is below the vigilance parameter the winning recognition neuron is inhibited and a search procedure is carried out. In this search procedure, recognition neurons are disabled one by one by the reset function until the vigilance parameter is overcome by a recognition match. At each cycle of the search procedure the most active recognition neuron is selected and then switched off, if its activation is below the vigilance parameter (note that it thus releases the remaining recognition neurons from its inhibition). If no committed recognition neuron's match overcomes the vigilance parameter, then an uncommitted neuron is committed and its weights are adjusted towards matching the input vector. If the vigilance parameter is overcome, training commences: the weights of the winning recognition neuron are adjusted towards the features of the input vector.

F_1 **layer:** an input processing field; also called comparison field.

F_2 **layer:** the cluster units also called the competitive layer or recognition layer.

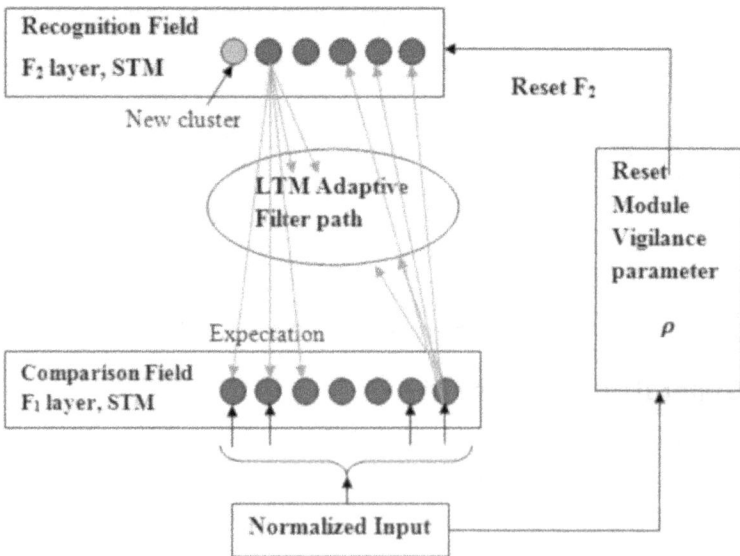

Fig.3.15: General ART architecture

Reset module: The degree of similarity required for patterns to be assigned to the same cluster unit is controlled by a user-defined gain control, known as the *vigilance* *parameter*. The reset mechanism is designed to control the state of each node in the F_2 layer. At any time, an F_2 node is in one of three states:

➢ **Active**

➢ **Inactive**, but available to participate in competition

➢ **Inhibited**, and prevented from participating in competition

There are two sets of connections each with their own weights, called:

➢ Bottom-up weights from each unit of F_1 layer to all the units of F_2 layer.

➢ Top-down weights- from each unit of F_2 layer to all the units of F_1 layer.

3.3.2. ART 1

ART-1 is the first class of ART networks introduced by Carpenter and Grossberg. The network was invented for unsupervised clustering of binary data. It has two major subsystems: *attentional subsystem* and *orienting subsystem*. Figure 3.16 shows the architecture of ART 1 network.

The **attentional subsystem** is a one layer neural network. It consists of: two competitive networks, as Comparison layer F_1 and Recognition layer F_2, fully connected with top-down and bottom-up weights; two control gains, as Gain 1 and Gain 2. The pattern vector is the input to comparison layer F_1. It has D input neurons to learn D - dimensional data and C output neurons to map C maximum clusters. Initially all output neurons are uncommitted 1. Once an output neuron learned from a pattern, it becomes committed. The activation function is computed at all committed output neurons. The input and output is connected by both top-down and bottom-up weights. Baraldi & Parmiggiani have proved mathematically that the bottom-up and top-down attentional module is equivalent to an attentional system with only forward connections. Baraldi and Alpaydin generalize this result to all ART-1 based networks by stating : "the attentional module of all ART 1based systems is functionally equivalent to a feed-forward network featuring no top-down connections.

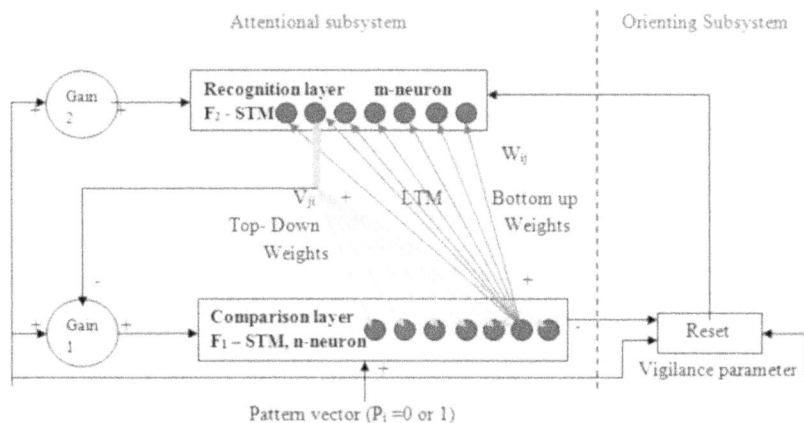

Fig.3.16: architecture of ART-1

The **Orienting-subsystem** consists of: Reset layer for controlling the attentional subsystem overall dynamics based on the vigilance parameter; Vigilance ρ parameter determines the degree of mismatch to be tolerated between the input pattern vectors and the weights connecting F_1 and F_2.

The nodes at F_2 represent the clusters formed. Once the network stabilizes, the top-down weights corresponding to each node in F_2 represent the prototype vector for that node. STM stands for short-term memory and LTM is an acronym for Long Term Memory.

The comparison layer F_1 receives the binary external input, then this external input is passed to the recognition layer F_2, where it is compared to a classification category. The result is passed back to F_1 layer, to determine whether the category matches the input or not. If it matches, then a new input vector is accepted and the cycle is repeated again. If it doesn't matches, then the orienting system inhibits the previous category match in F_2 layer. The two gains, control the activities of F_1 and F_2 layer respectively.

The weight vectors are initialized to 1, for instance, $w_{j1} = 1$, $w_{j2} = 1,..., w_{jD} = 1$, $1 \le j \ge C$. The orienting subsystem is a qualifier, where the match function of the candidate elected by the attentional system is compared against the vigilance parameter ρ. It uses the winner take-all learning strategy. If the condition satisfied, the pattern will be learned by the winning node, otherwise the activation function for the candidate will be set to 0, and a new candidate is elected and tested. The searching procedure keeps on going until either a candidate meets the vigilance constraint or no more candidates are left. If none of the output nodes can encode the pattern, a new node is committed to the pattern.

The goal of the network training is to find a set of templates, which best represent the underlying structure of the samples. Suppose the set of templates $W = \{W_1, W_2,.....W_c\}$ and the number of patterns from X associated with each template $N = \{N1, N2 ,..., NC\}$. It is important to note that the number of output nodes, sets W and N are growing dynamically. The algorithm of ART-1 follows: The three functions, $T()$, $M()$ and $U()$, used in the algorithm shown below are defined as follows:

```
C= 0;                                   Initialize the number of
                                        current templates
W = {ones(D), ones(D),…ones(D)}         Initialize set of templates
while (X not empty)
Learning loop
{
    new = true;                         Set flag "new node needed"
    loop j = 1,C                        Compute activation value for
                                        all templates

    t_J □□ T(x, w_J) ;
    loop i = 1,C                        Search for resonance
    {
        J □□arg max T_j               Find template with highest
                                        activation value
```

```
    if M( x, w_j ) □□P            When resonance occurs
    {
        W_J = U( x, w_J );         Update the template
        new = false;               No new node needed
        break;                     Stop the search for the
                                   resonant node

    }
    else                          If resonance doesn't occur,
    T_J
    Reset W_J
}                                 Continue search for resonant node
NEWNODE(new);                     Create new node if needed
}                                 End of learning loop
```

$T(x,w)$ is called the *choice function* or activation function, which is used to measure the degree of the resemblance of x with w_j and $M(x, w_j)$ is called the *match function*, which is used to qualify how good is the likeness of wj to x. The function is used in conjunction with the *vigilance parameter*, where $M(x\ w_j)$ means a good match (resonance). The vigilance is the most important network parameter that determines its resolution: larger vigilance value normally yields larger number of output nodes and good precision. $U(x, w_j)$ is called the *update function*, which is used to update a template after it resonances with a pattern.

One problem that ART1 runs into is that the final weight values and created clusters depend, to some degree, on the order in which the input vectors are presented. The vigilance parameter helps to solve this: The higher the vigilance is raised, the less dependent the clusters become on the order of input.

3.3.2.1. ART1 Learning: Fast vs. Slow

Fast Learning Mode

In the fast learning mode, it is assumed that weight updates during resonance occur rapidly, relative to the length of time a pattern is presented on any particular trial. The weights reach to the equilibrium on each trial with fast learning. The net is considered stabilized when each pattern chooses the correct cluster unit when it is presented (without causing any unit to reset). For ART1, because the patterns are binary, the weights associated with each cluster unit also stabilize in the fast learning mode. The resulting weight vectors are appropriate for the type of input patterns used in ART1. The equilibrium weights are easy to determine, and the iterative solution of the differential equations that control the weight updates is not necessary (i.e., as it is in the ART2 algorithm).

Slow Learning Mode

In slow learning mode the weight changes occur slowly relative to the duration of a learning trial; the weights do not reach equilibrium on a particular trial. Many more presentations of the patterns are required for slow learning than for fast, but fewer calculations occur on each learning trial in slow learning. Generally, only one weight update, with a relatively small learning rate, takes place on each learning trial in slow learning mode.

ART network has a basic functional **limitation**, namely that this network is only capable of handling binary-valued input signals or, at most, input signals that are basically binary-valued with some limited amount of pattern variance and noise (corrupted binary valued input signals). **ART 2 networks** had been developed to overcome this limitation.

3.4.   Associative Memory

For any sort of pattern recognition task, the core requirement of any system is the feature of pattern storage. This feature can be viewed as a memory function, where the network is required to store the pattern information for future purposes.

Typically an Artificial Neural Network behaves as an associative memory. The reason behind it is memory functioning of human brain. Human memory is based on associations with the memories it contains, for instance, just a snatch of well-known tune is enough to recall the whole thing back to mind, a forgotten joke is suddenly completely remembered when the next-door neighbor starts to tell it again. This type of memory has previously been termed as Content-Addressable Memory (C.A.M.), which means that one small part of the particular memory is linked or associated -with the rest. C.A.M. is a type of memory organization in which the memory is accessed by its contents (as opposed to an explicit address). A content-addressable memory is a type of memory that allows for the recall of data based on the degree of similarity between the input pattern and the patterns stored in memory. It refers to a memory organization in which the memory is accessed by its content, instead of an explicit address in the traditional computer memory system. Therefore, this sort of memory helps in recalling the information based on partial knowledge of its contents, and is suitable in applications where high speed search is required.

Suppose we are given a memory of names of several countries as shown in the figure 3.17 below. If the given memory is content-addressable, using the erroneous string "Bnagaldseh" as key is sufficient to retrieve the correct name "Bangladesh" In this sense, this type of memory is robust and fault-tolerant, as this type of memory exhibits some form of error-correction capability.

There are two classes of associative memory: *autoassociative* and *heteroassociative*; an autoassociative memory is used to retrieve a previously stored pattern that most closely resembles the current pattern, i.e., $X = Y$. On the other hand, in a heteroassociative memory, the retrieved pattern is, in general, different from the input pattern in various aspects like content, type and format etc.

Australia
Srilanka
India
Bangladesh
France
China
Japan
America

Bnagaldseh → (table) Bangladesh →

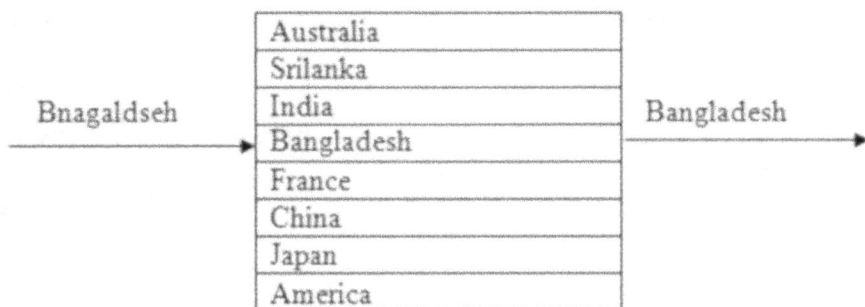

Fig.3.17: an illustration of the working of content addressable memory

Artificial neural networks are comprised of associative memories. One of the simplest artificial neural associative memory is the *linear associator*. The *Hopfield model* and *bidirectional associative memory (BAM)* models are some of the other popular artificial neural network models used as associative memories.

3.4.1.   Linear associator

The linear associator is the first and the simplest model of associative memory. The basic architecture of the linear associator is shown in figure 3.18. It is a *feedforward type network* where the output is produced in a single feedforward computation. In the figure, all the m input units are connected to all the n output units via the connection weight matrix $W = [w_{ij}]_{m \times n}$ where w_{ij} denotes the synaptic strength of the unidirectional connection from the i_{th} input unit to the j_{th} output unit. It is the connection weight matrix that stores the p different associated pattern pairs $\{(X_k, Y_k) \mid k = 1, 2, ..., p\}$ where $X_k \in \{-1, +1\}^m$ and $Y_k \in \{-1, +1\}^n$ in a distributed representation.

Building an associative memory is nothing but constructing the connection weight matrix W such that when an input pattern is presented, the stored pattern associated with the input pattern is retrieved. The process of constructing the connection weight matrix is called *encoding*.

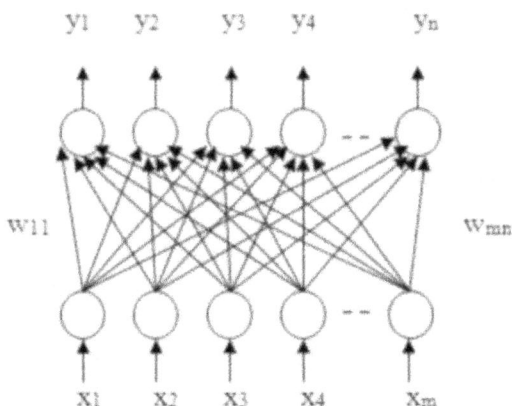

Fig.3.18: architecture of linear associator

During encoding the weight values of the correlation matrix W_k for a particular associated pattern pair (X_k, Y_k) are computed as:

$$(w_{ij})_k = (x_i)_k (y_j)_k \tag{3.40}$$

Where, $(x_i)_k$ represents the ith component of pattern X_k, $(y_j)_k$ represents the jth component of pattern Y_k for $i = 1, 2, ..., m$ and $j = 1, 2, ..., n$. Constructing the connection weight matrix W is then accomplished by summing up the individual correlation matrices, i.e.,

$$w = \alpha \sum_{k=1}^{m} w_k$$

Where, α is the proportionality or normalizing constant. α is usually set to $1/p$ to prevent the synaptic values from going too large when there are a number of associated pattern pairs to be memorized. The connection weight matrix construction above simultaneously stores or remembers p different associated pattern pairs in a distributed manner.

After encoding or memorization, the network can be used for *retrieval*. The process of retrieving a stored pattern given an input pattern is called *decoding*. Given a stimulus input pattern X, decoding or recollection is accomplished by computing the net input to the output units using:

$$\text{Input}_j = \sum_{i=1}^{m} x_i w_{ij} \tag{3.41}$$

Where, *input$_j$* stands for the weighted sum of the input or activation value of node j for $j = 1, 2, ..., n$. Then determine the output of those units using the bipolar output function:

$$y_i = \begin{cases} +1, & \text{if } input\ j \geq \theta \\ -1, & otherwise \end{cases} \tag{3.42}$$

where θ is the threshold value of output neuron j. From the foregoing discussions, it can be seen that the output units behave like the *linear threshold units* (McCulloch and Pitts, 1943) and the *perceptrons*(Rosenblatt, 1958) that compute a weighted sum of the input and produces a (-1 or $+1$) depending whether the weighted sum is below or above a certain threshold value.

However, the input pattern may contain errors and noise, or may be an incomplete version of some previously encoded pattern. Nevertheless, when presented with such a corrupted input pattern, the network will retrieve the stored pattern that is closest to actual input pattern. Therefore, the linear associator (and associative memories in general) is robust and fault tolerant, i.e., the presence of noise or errors results only in a mere decrease rather than total degradation in the performance of the network. Associative memories being robust and fault tolerant are the byproducts of having a number of processing elements performing highly parallel and distributed computations.

Another limitation of associative memories is the presence of *spurious memories*, i.e., meaningless memories or associated pattern pairs other than the original fundamental memories stored. Presence of spurious memories degrades the content-addressability feature of an associative memory. Another characteristic of associative memory is that the storage of the associated pattern pairs $\{(X_k, Y_k) \mid k = 1, 2, ..., p\}$ results in the storage of the associated pattern pairs $\{(X_k^c, Y_k^c) \mid k = 1, 2, ..., p\}$ where c stands for the complement of a vector, i.e., $X_k^c = -X_k$.

3.4.2. Bidirectional Associative memory (BAM)

The architecture of the *Bidirectional Associative Memory* model is similar to that of the model of <u>linear associator</u> we had seen in the previous section; the only dissimilarity is the bidirectional connections, i.e., $w_{ij} = w_{ji}$, for $i = 1, 2, ..., m$ and $j = 1, 2, ..., n$. It can also be viewed as, the units in both the layers serves as both input and output units according to the direction of propagation. If the signals are propagating from the X layer to the Y layer then the units in the X layer behaves as input units however the units in the Y layer act as output units and vice versa, i.e., propagating from the Y layer to the X layer insists the units in the Y layer to behave as input units while the units in the X layer to act as output units. Figure 3.19 is an illustration of the BAM architecture.

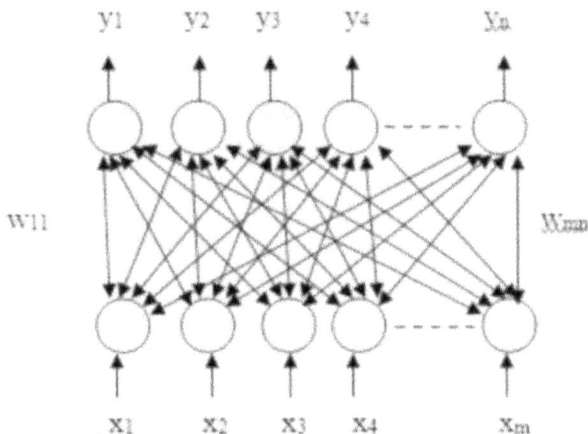

Fig.3.19: architecture of BAM

Just like the linear associator, encoding in BAM can be carried out by using eq. (3.40):

$$(w_{ij})_k = (x_i)_k (y_j)_k$$

to store a single associated pattern pair and to simultaneously store several associated pattern pairs, eq.(3.41) is used,

$$w = \alpha \sum_{k=1}^{m} w_k$$

After encoding, the network can be used for decoding. In BAM, decoding involves reverberating distributed information between the two layers until the network becomes stable. In decoding, an input pattern can be applied either on the X layer or on the *Y* layer. When given an input pattern, the network will propagate the input pattern to the other layer allowing the units in the other layer to compute their output values. The pattern that was produced by the other layer is then propagated back to the original layer and let the units in the original layer compute their output values. The new pattern that was produced by the original layer is again propagated to the other layer. This process is repeated until further propagations and computations do not result in a change in the states of the units in both layers where the final pattern pair is one of the stored associated pattern pairs. The final pattern pair that will be produced by the network depends on the initial pattern pair and the connection weight matrix.

To update the states of the units in either layers various modes can be used namely synchronous, asynchronous, or the combination of the two. In synchronous updating scheme, the states of the units in a layer are updated as a group prior to propagating the output to the other layer. In asynchronous updating, units in both layers are updated in some order and output are propagated to the other layer after each unit update. Lastly, in synchronous-asynchronous updating, there can be subgroups of units in each layer that are updated synchronously while units in each subgroup are updated asynchronously.

3.5.   Hopfield Network

Hopfield, a renowned scientist published two papers in the beginning of the 1980s, which attracted much interest of the artificial intelligence industry. These networks acquires auto-associative properties and are recurrent (fully interconnected), with the exception that no neuron has any connection to itself. This proved to be a milestone in the history of neural networks, which continues today. Hopfield illustrated the fact that physical systems' models could be utilized to untangle several computational problems. Such systems are simple to be implemented in hardware by incorporating standard electronic components such as capacitors and resistors. The concept of Hopfield network derives from a physical system,

"Any physical system whose dynamics in phase is dominated by a substantial number of locally stable states to which it is attracted can therefore be regarded as a content addressable memory. The sequential system will be a potentially useful memory if, in addition any prescribed set of states can readily be made the stable states of the system."

The Hopfield network emphasizes a content-addressable memory and serves as a tool for solving optimization problem.

Although, the prominence of the Hopfield networks in practical applications is limited due to hypothetical limitations of the network structure but, in certain situations, but they might develop fascinating models. The basic operations for which the hopfield networks are thought to be developed are the classification problems with binary pattern vectors. These networks are created by providing input data vectors, or pattern vectors, corresponding to the different classes. These patterns are generally referred to as the *class patterns*. In an *n*-dimensional data space the class patterns must consist of *n* binary components {1,-1}; spatially it can be viewed as, each class pattern corresponds to an edge of a cube in an *n*-dimensional space. The network is then utilized to classify deformed patterns into these classes. When a deformed or imprecise pattern is presented to the network, then it is incorporated with another pattern. If the network works properly, this incorporated pattern is nothing but a class patterns out of several class patterns. In some cases (when the different class patterns are correlated), spurious minima can also appear. This means that some patterns that are not among the pattern vectors are also associated with the pattern.

Hopfield networks are also referred as *associative networks* because of their property of associating a class pattern to each input pattern.

Some of the characteristics of the Hopfield model are quite different from that of the *linear associator model* in that it computes its output and go on performing iterations until the system becomes stable. Figure 3.20 shows a Hopfield model with six units, where each node is connected to every other node in the network.

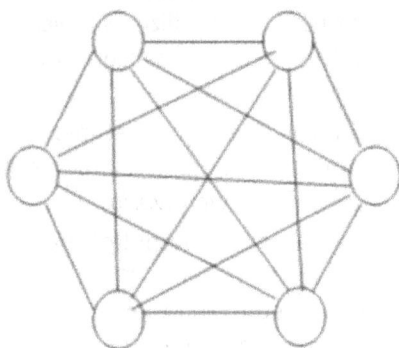

Fig.3.20: a simplified Hopfield Network

Unlike the linear associator model which consists of two layers of processing units, the input layer and the output layer, the Hopfield model is comprised of a single layer of processing elements; each unit is interconnected with all the units present in the model and even with itself. The connection weight matrix **W** of this type of network is square and symmetric, i.e., $w_{ij} = w_{ji}$ for i, j = 1, 2, ..., *m*. Each unit has an extra external input I_j. This extra input leads to a modification in the computation of the net input to the units:

$$\text{Input}_j = \sum_{i=1}^{m} x_i w_{ij} + I_j \qquad (3.43)$$

for *j* = 1, 2, ..., *m*.

Unlike the linear associator, the units in the Hopfield model act as both input and output units. But just like the linear associator, a single associated pattern pair is stored by computing the weight matrix as follows:

$$Wk = X_k^T Y_k \qquad\qquad (3.44)$$
where $Y_k = X_k$

$$w = \alpha \sum_{k=1}^{m} w_k \qquad\qquad (3.45)$$

to store p different associated pattern pairs. As we know that the Hopfield model is an autoassociative memory model, patterns are stored in memory, rather than associated pattern pairs. After encoding, the next step to be done by the network is decoding. Decoding is done in the Hopfield model by a mutual and recursive relaxation search for a saved pattern when the initial stimulus pattern is already available. If X is the input pattern, then by computing the net input to the units and determination of the output of those units by utilizing the output function to yield the pattern X', the decoding is accomplished. This pattern X' is then applied again to the units via feedback, as an input pattern to produce the pattern X''. The pattern X'' is again fed back to the units to produce the pattern X'''. The process is repeated until the network stabilizes on a stored pattern where further computations do not change the output of the units.

If the input pattern X is an incomplete pattern or if it contains some distortions, the stored pattern to which the network stabilizes is typically one that is most similar to X without the distortions. This feature is called *pattern completion* and is very important for image processing applications.

During decoding, several techniques can be employed to update the output of the units such as *synchronous* (or parallel as termed in some literatures), *asynchronous* (or sequential), or a combination of the two (*hybrid*).

In synchronous updating scheme, the output of the units is updated as a group prior to feeding the output back to the network. Whereas, in asynchronous updating scheme, the output of the units are updated in some particular order (e.g. random or sequential) and the output are then fed back to the network after each unit update. Using the hybrid synchronous-asynchronous updating scheme, subgroups of units are updated synchronously while units in each subgroup updated asynchronously. The choice of the updating scheme has an effect on the convergence of the network.

The *Neural Networks* package supports two types of Hopfield networks, a continuous-time version and a binary version. Both network types have a matrix of weights W defined as

$$W = 1/n \sum_{i=1}^{D} \varepsilon_i^T \varepsilon_i \qquad\qquad (3.46)$$

Where, D is the number of class patterns $\{\varepsilon_1, \varepsilon_2.....\}$, vectors consisting of +1/-1 elements, to be stored in the network, and n is the number of components, the dimension, of the class pattern vectors.

3.5.1. Discrete Hopfield networks

In the discrete Hopfield model, the units use a slightly modified bipolar output function where the states of the units, i.e., the output of the units remain the same if the current state is equal to some threshold value:

$$X_i(t+1) = \begin{cases} +1 & if\ input > \theta \\ x(t) & if\ input = \theta \\ -1 & if\ input < \theta \end{cases} \tag{3.47}$$

for $i = 1, 2, ..., m$ and where t is denoting the discrete time. The state of recurrent type networks can be described by an *energy function*. The energy function also proves the stability of recurrent type networks. For the discrete Hopfield model with $w_{ii} = 0$ and $w_{ij} = w_{ji}$ using the asynchronous updating scheme, the energy function E according to Hopfield (1982) is defined as:

$$E = -1/2\sum_{i=1}^{m} \sum_{j=1}^{m} x_i w_{ij} x_j - \sum_{i=1}^{m} x_i I_j + \sum_{i=1}^{m} x_j \theta \tag{3.48}$$

where the energy of the stored patterns is associated to the local minima of the energy function. Hopfield has shown that the energy of the discrete Hopfield model decreases or remains the same after each unit update. Therefore, the network will eventually converge to a local minima corresponding to a stored pattern. The stored pattern to which the network converges depends on the input pattern and the connection weight matrix.

The energy of the discrete Hopfield model is described by:

$$E = -\sum_{i=1}^{m} \sum_{j=1}^{m} w_{ij} - \sum_{i=1}^{m} I_j + \sum_{i=1}^{m} \theta \tag{3.49}$$

for all input patterns X_k, $k = 1, 2, ..., p$. Since the energy is bounded underneath, the network will eventually converge to a local minimum corresponding to a stored pattern.

3.5.2. Continuous Hopfield Networks

The continuous Hopfield model can simply be seen as a generalization of the discrete case. Here, the units use a continuous output function such as the sigmoid or hyperbolic tangent function. In the continuous Hopfield model, each unit has an associated capacitor C_i and resistance r_i that model the capacitance and resistance of real neuron's cell membrane, respectively. Thus the state equation of each unit is now:

$$C_j\ dinput/dt = \sum_{i=1}^{m} x_i w_{ij} - input/R_j\ |\ I_j \tag{3.50}$$

Where, $1/R_j = 1/\rho_j + \sum_{i=1}^{m} w_{ij}$

Just like in the discrete case, there is an energy function characterizing the continuous Hopfield model. The energy function due to Hopfield (1984) is given by:

$$E = -1/2\sum_{i=1}^{m} \sum_{j=1}^{m} x_i w_{ij} x_j - \sum_{i=1}^{m} x_i I_j + \sum_{i=1}^{m} (1/R_j)\int_0^{\pi} f^{-1}(x)dx \tag{3.51}$$

where f is the output function of the units.

It can be shown that $dE/dt \le 0$ when $w_{ij} = w_{ji}$. Therefore, the energy of the continuous Hopfield model decreases or remains the same. The minimum energy of the continuous Hopfield model also exist using analogous computation as that in the discrete Hopfield model.

3.6.   The Boltzmann Machine

Many years of researches on the recall phenomena of memory reveal the fact that, during the recall of stored patterns in a feedback neural network, the probability of error can be considerably minimized if the weights are chosen appropriately. If the probability distribution of the given (desired) patterns, called *pattern environment,* is known, then this information can be utilized directly for the determination of the weights of the network while storing the patterns. The training procedure should try to capture the pattern environment in the network in an optimal way.

3.6.1.   Architecture of a Boltzmann Machine

Suppose set of L patterns are given; each pattern is described by a point in an N-dimensional space, but we actually have no knowledge about the number of processing units required for a feedback network. It may not be possible to store them in a network consisting of N units, if the resulting number of stable states (for a given set of weights) is found lesser than the number of patterns L. That is, the capacity of the network is less than L. Such problems are referred to as the hard problems. In general, we could say that it is quite strenuous to determine whether a given pattern storage problem is a hard problem or not for a given network. The easiest way to cope this problem is to add extra units to the feedback network. These extra units are called hidden units, whereas the remaining N units, to which the input patterns are applied during training, are called visible units (both input and output units). A fully connected system consisting of both hidden and visible units, and operating asynchronously with stochastic update for each unit is, what we called a *Boltzmann machine.* Since the steady state probabilities at thermal equilibrium follow the Boltzmann-Gibb's distribution, the network architecture is called a Boltzmann machine. Since the network architecture is so chosen that the number of stable states is more than the desired number of patterns, the additional stable states become spurious stable states. Existence of the spurious stable states results in a nonzero probability of error in the recall, even though the network is trained to capture the pattern environment in an optimal way. Pattern recall from a Boltzmann machine uses simulated annealing to reduce the effects of these additional stable states, which correspond to local minima in the energy landscape of the network.

The yellow spheres in the figure 3.20 shows input units, blue spheres denotes the hidden units and the green spheres are representing the output units.

A Boltzmann machine can also be used for a pattern association task. This is accomplished by identifying a subset of the visible units with the inputs and the remaining visible units with the outputs of the given pattern pairs. In other words, each input-output pair is considered as a pattern, and these patterns are stored as in the pattern environment storage problem. For recall, the input is presented only to the input subset of the visible units. The output is read out from the output subset of the visible units, after the network reached thermal equilibrium at T = **0** using a simulated annealing schedule to reduce the local minima effects. In general Boltzmann machine architecture can be used for any pattern completion task, in which the stored (input-output) pattern can be recalled by providing partial information about the pattern.

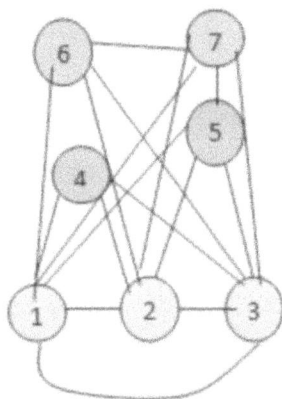

Boltzmann machine is considered to be the Hopfield model with a stochastic nature of learning. The firing rule of the binary network is governed by the following probability function:

Fig.3.21: architecture of Boltzmann machine

Prob $(V_i = 1) = 1 / [1 + \exp(-net_i / Temp)]$

$net_i = \sum_{j \neq i} \sqcap_{ij} V_j - U_i$

Prob $(V_i = 0) = 1 - Prob (V_i = 1),$

Where, Temp is a temperature parameter having an effect on the firing probability.

The Boltzmann machine, as shown in figure 3.20 consists of hidden units, in a way, thus provide weight adjustments by utilizing supervised learning of a stochastic form to minimize the difference between the energies of given states and their desired energies.

Review Questions

1. Explain Counter Propagation Networks.
2. Describe briefly, the architecture of ART, with the help of schematic diagram.
3. Write short notes on:
   (a) Associative Memory
   (b) Boltzmann Machine
   (c) Hopfield Network
4. Explain how, Boltzmann machine can be employed to solve the problems associated with Hopfield network.
5. Explain the architecture of Counter propagation network, how it works in normal and training mode?
6. Explain the significance of hidden layer in pattern recognition.
7. Explain Kohonen Self organizing feature map.

CHAPTER 4

The Fuzzy Logic

"While, traditionally, logic has corrected or avoided it, fuzzy logic compromises with vagueness; it is not just a logic of vagueness, it is- from what Frege"s point of view would have been a contradiction in terms- a vague logic."

- Susan Haack
Professor of Philosophy and Law

"Fuzziness is grayness."

- BartAndrew Kosko
Professor of electrical engineering and Law

"The truth lies in the middle."

- BartAndrew Kosko
Professor of electrical engineering and Law

In this chapter we are going to cover the second most important aspect of soft computing, or we can also call it as the back bone of artificial intelligence- The Fuzzy Logic. The term fuzzy logic was first brought in light by Sir Lotfi A. Zadeh in 1965 when he published the paper "Fuzzy sets" that introduced multivalued set theory and instigated the term fuzzy into the technical literature. Another legend, in the field of Fuzzy Logic is a well known writer and Professor of electrical engineering and law at the university of Southern California- BartAndrew Kosko; also known as the St. Paul of fuzziness, he has contributed major theories and proofs in the development of fuzzy Logic, like fuzzy cognitive maps, fuzzy subsethood, additive fuzzy systems, fuzzy approximation theorems, optimal fuzzy rules, fuzzy associative memories, various neural-based adaptive fuzzy systems, ratio measures of fuzziness, the shape of fuzzy sets, the conditional variance of fuzzy systems, and the spatial view of (finite) fuzzy sets as points in hypercubes and its relationship to the ongoing debate of fuzziness versus probability.

Fuzzy Logic is also known as 'many-valued logic' and deals with approximate rather than exact reasoning. It posits a world in which absolutes, such as those entailed in the words "true" and "false" are of least interest than the range of degree between them. Unlike traditional binary logic (used by traditional computers) which exhibits exact value as either 0 or 1, or either true or false, fuzzy logic variables may have a truth value that ranges in degree between 0 and 1, like may be so, may be not, more or less etc. For example, in case of temperature sensing, a system exhibiting Fuzzy logic will answer slightly warm or fairly cold, rather than just warm and cold. Various principles of Fuzzy Logic such as fuzzy if-then rules have been successfully implemented in various automated machines like motor controllers, surface soil recognition, earthquake prediction, and traffic controlling systems etc, where instead of precise solutions, probabilistic reasoning is of more importance, and henceforth it is also an important tool in soft computing.

The past few years have evidenced a rapid growth in the number and variety of applications of fuzzy logic; in image analyzing applications such as detection of edges, features extraction, classification and clustering. In soft computing, unambiguousness and imprecision tolerance capacities of fuzziness explored new applications in the field of decision making. The tolerance for imprecision and uncertainty contributes in creating the remarkable human ability to understand a slightly noisy speech data, understand defects of natural language, summarize text, and recognize and classify images. With fuzzy logic, we can specify mapping rules in form of vocable rather than numbers.

To make apparent the contribution of fuzzy logic to AI, Many established industries have launched some of the products that display intelligence in more humanlike tasks. Sony has developed a fuzzy based palm top computer that can recognize handwritten Kanji characters. Epson has made a translator that recognizes and translates words in a pencil sized unit. Most interesting was a washing machine that adjusts its washing strategy based on sensed dirt level, fabric type, load size and water level and used a neural network to tune the rules to a user's tastes.

This kind of system is an example of *adaptive* fuzzy logic. With the help of a neural net, it can learn from the data it has collected and adjust its rules. This kind of set up has tremendous possibilities. In literature, the term, Fuzzy logic has been used in two different senses:

(i)   Broadly, it can be viewed as a technique of concepts, principles, and algorithms for dealing with approaches of reasoning that are approximate rather than exact.

(ii) Secondly, it is viewed as a generalization of the various multivalued logics, which have been studied in the area of symbolic logic since the beginning of the twentieth century.

4.1.   Fuzzy Sets

Here in this we will discuss the basic definitions, terminologies and operations for fuzzy sets. Although it is a vast topic and supports numerous applications, it is not possible to cover its all aspects and current developments in the field of artificial intelligence, but we tried our best to summarize the central basic concept of fuzzy sets.

4.1.1.   Classical sets

Classical sets or crisp sets are the sets that are defined by 'crisp' boundaries. Where the boundary of the crisp set is an unambiguous line. It means in a crisp set, an element is the member of the set or not. The whole information about the elements present in the crisp set is defined by the 'universe discourse'. Figure 4.1 shows an abstraction of a universe of discourse, say, X and a crisp set A somewhere is a part of this universe itself.

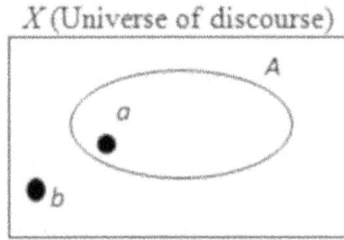

Fig.4.1: Crisp set A

The universe of discourse *X* is a collection of objects having the same characteristics. Each of these objects is called an element or member of *X*. The elements present in *X*, can be discrete, countable or uncountable. For instance,

➢   Set of boys and girls of a particular age group
➢   The clock speeds of computer CPUs
➢   The operating currents of an electronic meter
➢   The Richter magnitude of an earthquake
➢   Integers from 1 to 10 etc.

A classical set A of integers greater than 8 is expressed as,

$$A = \{x \mid x > 8\}; \tag{4.1}$$

Where the unambiguous boundary is set to 8, such that if x is greater than 8, then x belongs to the set A; otherwise not belong to A. Similarly, suppose a classical set A denotes the tall persons, whose heights are greater than 6 ft, the heights are denoted by *x*; in this case the classical set A is expressed as,

$$A = \{x \mid x > 6 \text{ ft}\}; \tag{4.2}$$

If we express equation 4.2 in words, then it would be something like, the persons whose heights are greater than 6 ft. belongs to the category of tall person, and all others does not belong to this category. Yet this is an unnatural and inadequate way of representing out concept of "tall person". For example, what about the person whose height is 5.999 ft? According to the given illustration of equation 4.2, we will not consider him tall; but is this fair? Such of distinction is intuitively unreasonable. The flaw is a result of the sharp transition between inclusion and exclusion in a set i.e. either true or false. This is the limitation of the classical set, because it can-not be considered as the accurate way of expressing human concepts and thoughts. A person feeling cold at 7 degree Celsius of temperature, will also feel the same cold at 6.999 degree Celsius of temperature. Such limitations led for the development of fuzzy sets.

4.1.2.   Fuzzy Sets

Contrasting a classical set, a fuzzy set is considered to be a set without a crisp boundary. Or we could say the boundary is an ambiguous line. Figure 4.2 shows this ambiguous boundary of fuzzy set.

X (Universe of discourse)

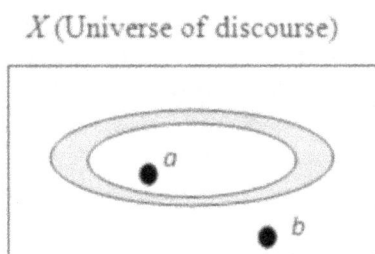

Fig.4.2: Fuzzy set A

In the central un-shaded region of the fuzzy set '*a*' is clearly a member of the set and '*b*' in the outside (un-shaded) region is not considered as a member of the set. But '*c*' which happens to be present on the shaded boundary, is not a clear member of the set. If '*a*' consists of a membership value of 1 and '*b*' has a membership value of 0, then '*c*' should have a membership value between 0 and 1.

The sharp transition from "belong to a set" to "not belong to a set" is converted to "partially belong to a set", and this smooth transition is characterized by membership functions that provide fuzzy sets the essential flexibility that is required for modeling the commonly used linguistic expressions. A membership function can be defined as the correlation between the values of a component and its degree of membership in a set. Let us understand this sharp edge transition and smooth transition with the help of an example:

One of the most common examples of a fuzzy set is comparison of heights and the set of tall people. In this particular example the universe of discourse is the potential heights, let us consider from 3 feet to 9 feet, and the word "tall" represents a curve that defines the degree of tallness of any person. If the set of tall people is defined by the unambiguous boundary of a crisp set, we might say all people taller than six feet would be considered as tall. But this sort of distinction is certainly absurd. In case of the set of all real numbers greater than six, such kind of distinction might make sense, because numbers belong to an abstract plane, but in the case of real people, it is senseless to call one person short and another one tall when they differ in height with a few points, certainly the width of hair.

Fig.4.3: Illustration of crisp boundary of a set of heights of persons

Now the question arises, if the kind of distinction shown above is unreasonable, then how to define the set of tall people, in the right way? The figure 4.4 shows a smoothly varying curve that transits from not-tall to tall.

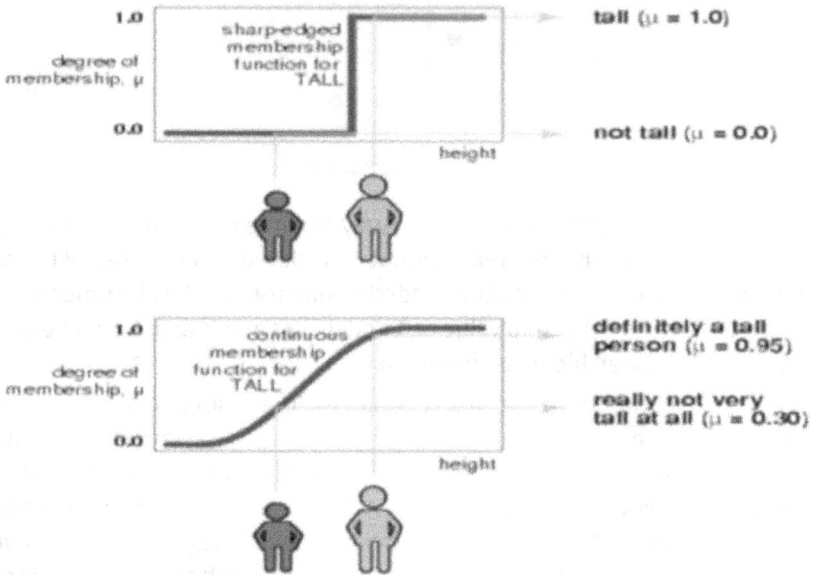

Fig. 4.4: Illustration of smooth transition and sharp edge transition

The output-axis is denoting a number known as the membership value between 0 and 1. The curve represents a membership function and is commonly denoted by μ. This curve is illustrating the transition from not tall to tall. Both people are considered tall to a certain degree, but one is notably less tall than the other.

Subjective interpretations and appropriate units are inbuilt into the fuzzy sets. For example, If we say "She's tall," the membership function "tall" is already taken into account irrespective of the ages of the people, whether it be a six-year-old or a grown woman. Similarly in the case of units, certainly it makes no sense to say "Is she tall in inches or in meters?"

Fuzzy sets were introduced by Zadeh in 1965 in his paper entitled "Fuzzy Sets" to represent/manipulate data and information possessing nonstatistical uncertainties. These were specifically designed to mathematically represent uncertainty and vagueness and to provide techniques for dealing with the imprecision inherent in many practical problems. According to Zadeh a fuzzy set is:

Let X be a set of points, with a general element of X denoted by x. Thus $X = \{x\}$. A fuzzy set A in X is specified by a membership function $fA(x)$ which corresponds to each point in X a real number in the interval $[0, 1]$, with the values of $fA(x)$ at x representing the "grade of membership" of x in the fuzzy set A. Thus, more closer the value of $fA(x)$ to unity, higher the grade of membership of x in A.

This definition of a fuzzy set is similar to that of a superset of a set. The grades of membership of 0 and 1 represents the two possibilities of either truth or false in an ordinary set. The general boolean operations are no longer useful, as the operators that are used to combine sets are not applicable now;

4.2. Some Fundamental Definitions and Nomenclature

4.2.1. Fuzzy Set

A fuzzy set is an extension of a crisp set. Crisp set allow only full membership or no membership at all, where as fuzzy sets allow partial membership.

Definition 1. Suppose X is a collection of objects and is collectively denoted by x [i.e., let $X(x)$ be a non-empty set], then a fuzzy set A in terms of X is defined as set of ordered pairs:

$$A = \{(x), \mu_A\}(x)) : x \varepsilon X \tag{4.1}$$

Where, $\mu_A(x)$ is called the membership function of grade of membership (also known as degree of truth or degree of compatibility) of x collection of objects in the fuzzy set A. This membership function also maps X to the membership space M. Thus we could say that the membership function $\mu_A(x)$ of A, describes a fuzzy set.

The membership function $\mu_A : X \rightarrow [0,1]$, in particular:

$\mu(x) = 1$ implies full membership

$\mu(x) = 0$ implies non-membership

and $0 \leq \mu(x) < 1$ and implies intermediate membership.

Thus, it is clear that the definition of fuzzy set is a simple extension of the definition of a crisp set, in which the characteristic function is authorized to have any values between 0 and 1. If the value the of membership function $\mu_A(x)$ is confined to either 0 or 1, then A is reduced to a classical set and $\mu_A(x)$ represents the characteristic function of A.

Definition 2. A fuzzy set A in a universal set X, is a set defined by the membership function

$$\mu_A : X \rightarrow [0, 1]$$

That assigns a vlaue to each element of X representing its grade of membership in the given fuzzy set.

Suppose A is a fuzzy set in a set X. then, according to definition, $A(x) = \mu_A(x)$ is regarded as the level to which x belongs to A.

The range of the membership function is defined as a subset of the finite collection of non-negative real numbers. Thus a fuzzy set A can be written as:

$$A = \{(x_1, \mu_A(x_1)), (x_2, \mu_A(x_2)), \ldots\ldots, (x_n, \mu_A(x_n))\} \tag{4.2}$$

Or by $\quad A = \{\mu_A(x_1) / x_1, \mu_A(x_2) / x_2, \mu_A(x_3) / x_3, \ldots, \mu_A(x_n) / x_n\}$

Some important points about fuzzy sets which are worth noticed are:

➢   Fuzzy sets represents common sense linguistic labels like fast, slow, large, small, medium, low, high, tall etc.

➢   When M consists of only two points 0 and 1, then A is non-fuzzy set and is similar to the characteristic function of a non-fuzzy set.

➢   The elements of zero degree of membership are usually not listed.

➢   A fuzzy set is wholly represented by stating its membership function.

4.2.2.   Normalized Fuzzy Set

A fuzzy set A is called normal if $\sup_x \mu_A(x) = 1$, i.e. we could say that a non-empty set is always said to be normalized fuzzy set when at least one of its elements attains the maximum possible degree of membership. To make a non-empty fuzzy set A normalized, we have to divide $\mu_A(x)$ by $\sup_x \mu_A(x)$. One point which is worth noticeable here is that it is not necessary that the membership function must be confined to closed interval [0,1], if $\sup_x \mu_A(x) = 1$ then the fuzzy set A is called **normal**.

For example: Let A = {(Sarita,1), (Radha,4), (Sarika,6), (Ritu,10)}.

Here $\sup_A \mu_A(x) = 10$.

Dividing each membership function by 10, the normalized set is,

Normal fuzzy set = {(Sarita,0.1), (Radha,0.4), (Sarika,0.6), (Ritu,1)}.

4.2.3.   Support

The support of a fuzzy set A in X, is the crisp set of all elements $x \in X$, such that $\mu_A(x) > 0$. It is denoted by S(A).

$$S(A) = \{x \in X : \mu_A(x) > 0\} \qquad (4.3)$$

4.2.4.   Crossover points

If A is a fuzzy set, then its crossover point is a point $x \in X$ at which $\mu_A(x) = 0.5$:

Crossover $(A) = \{x \mid \mu_A(x) = 0.5\}$ \qquad (4.4)

Example: Let the universe space $X = \{1,2,3,....,15\}$ and fuzzy set A of X be,

{(2,0), (3,0.1), (4,0.4), (5,0.5), (7,0.2), (8,0.6), (9,1.0), (10,0), (11,0)}

Then, support of fuzzy $S(A) = \{3,4,5,7,8,9\}$.

and Crossover point of A is $x = 5$, since $\mu_A(x) = 0.5$.

4.2.5. Fuzzy Singleton

A fuzzy singleton is a fuzzy set that has a support of a single point in X and have membership function $\mu_A(x) = 1$.

Figure 4.5 illustrates the fuzzy singleton characterizing "45 years old."

Membership Grades

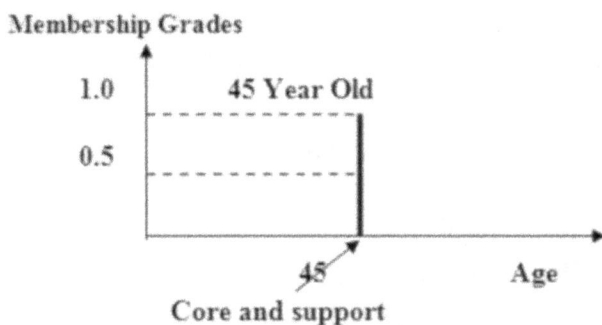

Fig.4.5: the fuzzy singleton "45 years old."

4.2.6.   Core

In a fuzzy set A, the core is defined as, the set of all points x in X such that $\mu_A(x) = 1$:

Core $(A) = \{x \mid \mu_A(x) = 1\}$ (4.5)

4.2.7. α-cut, strong α-cut

The α-cut or α-level set of a fuzzy set A, is nothing but a crisp set defined by,

$A_\alpha = \{x \mid \mu_A(x) \geq \alpha\}, \alpha \in [0,1]$ (4.6)

In words we could say that, an α-cut of a fuzzy set A is A_α that contains all the elements of X that have a membership greater than or equal to the specified value of α

Strong α-cut or strong α-level set are defined similarly,

$A_\alpha^i = \{x \mid \mu_A(x) > \alpha\}, \alpha \in [0, 1]$ (4.7)

4.2.8.   Cardinality of a Finite Fuzzy Set

If A is a finite fuzzy set then its cardinality, denoted by |A|, is defined by,

$$|A| = \sum_{x \in X} \mu_A(x)$$ (4.8)

i.e., summation of the membership functions of all the elements of X in A.

4.2.9.   Convexity

A fuzzy set A is said to be convex if for any $x_1, x_2 \in X$ and any $\lambda \in [0, 1]$,

$\mu_A(\lambda x_1 + (1 - \lambda)x_2) \geq \min \{\mu_A(x_1), \mu_A(x_2)\}$ (4.9)

Alternatively, A is convex if all its α-level sets are convex.

A crisp set C in R^n is convex if and only if for any two points $x_1 \in C$ and $x_2 \in C$, their convex combination $\lambda x_1 + (1 - \lambda)x_2$ is still in C, where, $0 \leq \lambda \leq 1$. Hence the convexity of a crisp level set A_α implies that A_α is composed of a single line segment only.

Note that the definition of convexity of a fuzzy set is not as strict as the common definition of convexity of a function. For comparison, the definition of convexity of function f(x) is,

$$f(\lambda x_1 + (1 - \lambda)x_2) \geq (\lambda f(x_1) + (1 - \lambda)f(x_2), \qquad (4.10)$$

which is a more strict as compared to equation 4.9.

4.2.10. Symmetry

A fuzzy set A is said to be symmetric if its membership function is symmetric around a certain point $x = c$, namely,

$$\mu_A(c + x) = \mu_A(c - x) \text{ for all } x \in X. \qquad (4.11)$$

4.3.   Set- Theoretic Operations

The fuzzy set operations are the generalization of the crisped (classical) operations. Zadeh formulated the fuzzy set theory in the terms of standard operations namely, Complement, Union, Intersection, and Difference. On the basis of these three operations, a number of identities can be established. Before introducing these three basic operations, let us first discuss the concept of containment, which plays a central role in both classical and fuzzy sets.

4.3.1.   Containment or subset

Suppose two Fuzzy sets A and B are given, then Fuzzy set A is said to be the subset of B (or equivalently, contained in the fuzzy set B) if and only if $\mu_A(x) \leq \mu_B(x)$ for all x. Symbolically,

$$A \subseteq B \Leftrightarrow \mu_A(x) \leq \mu_B(x) \qquad (4.12)$$

Figure 4.6 illustrates the concept of $A \subseteq B$.

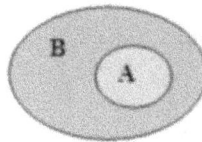

Fig.4.6: Concept of A $\subseteq$ B

4.3.2.   Union

The union of two fuzzy sets A and B is related to each other by,

$$\mu_{A \cup B}(x) = \max(\mu_A(x), \mu_B(x)) \qquad (4.13)$$

As defined by Zadeh, a more precise definition of union is the "smallest" fuzzy set containing both A and B, then it also contains A $\cup$ B. In other words, it is defined as the maximum among the two individual membership functions, therefore it is also called the maximum criterion. Similarly, the intersection is also defined. Figure 4.7 illustrates the concept of union of A and B, the area common to both A and B is the Union of A and B.

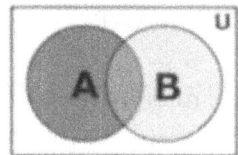

Fig.4.7: Concept of union.

4.3.3. Intersection

In contrast to the case of the union, the intersection of two given fuzzy sets, A and B, is the "largest" fuzzy set which is contained in both A and B

$$\mu_{A \cap B}(x) = \min(\mu_A(x), \mu_B(x)) \qquad (4.14)$$

The membership functions of A and B is related as,

$$\mu_{A \cap B}(x) = \mu_A(x) \wedge \mu_B(x) \qquad (4.15)$$

It can be defined as the minimum of the two individual membership functions. This is called the minimum criterion. The intersection operation in fuzzy set theory is equivalent to the AND operation in the Boolean algebra.

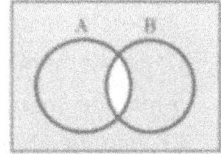

Figure 4.8 illustrates the concept of intersection, in which all the un-common area between A and B is covered (the shaded portion).

Fig.4.8: Concept of intersection

4.3.4. Complement (negation)

The complement of fuzzy set A, denoted by *NOT A*, is defined as,

$$\mu_{not\,A}(x) = 1 - \mu_A(x)) \qquad (4.16)$$

The membership function of the complement of a fuzzy set A with membership function μ_A is defined as the negation of the specified MF. This is also called the negation criterion. In fuzzy set theory the complement operation is equivalent to the NOT operation in Boolean algebra.

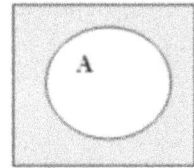

Figure 4.9 shows the concept of complement of A, which covers all the space other then the fuzzy set A.

Fig.4.9: Concept of complement

4.4. Membership Function Formulation and Parameterization

We are already much familiar to the term membership function, here in this section we will discuss it in detail, along with the classes of parameterized functions commonly used to define membership functions of one and two dimensions.

A fuzzy set is completely characterized with its membership function. A *membership function* (MF) is graphically represented by a curve that elucidates the way to map each point in the input space to a membership value (or degree of membership) in the range between 0 and 1. The input space is also called as the *universe of discourse*.

Definition: For a fuzzy set A on the universe of discourse X, a membership function is defined as $\mu_A : X \rightarrow [0, 1]$, where all elements of X are individually mapped to a value in the interval [0, 1]. This specified value is called membership value or degree of membership, calibrates the grade of membership of the element present in X to the fuzzy set A.

Membership function is the crucial component of fuzzy set, which allow us to graphically represent a fuzzy set. The membership function of the element of X denoted as x in the fuzzy set A is also called *grade of membership* or *degree of compatibility* of x in A. The x axis depicts the universe of discourse, whereas the y axis represents the grades of membership in the [0, 1] interval.

Elementary functions are used to build membership functions. There are various membership functions, the most commonly used ones are:

➢ Triangular membership function
➢ Trapezoid membership function
➢ Gaussian membership function
➢ S-membership function
➢ TT- membership function
➢ Exponential membership functions
➢ Generalized bell shaped membership function
➢ Polynomial membership term.

4.4.1. Triangular Membership Functions

Defined by a lower limit *a*, an upper limit *b*, and a value *m*, where *a < m < b*. the tuple {*a, m, b*}, denotes the location of the corresponding corners. The triangular MF is given by:

$$\mu_A(x) = \begin{cases} 0, & x \le a \\ \dfrac{x-a}{m-a}, & a < x \le m \\ \dfrac{b-x}{b-m}, & m < x < b \\ 0, & x \ge b \end{cases}$$

Or triangle (x; a, m, b) = max[min[(x − a) / (m − a), (b − x) / (b − m)], 0] (4.17)

Here *a, m* and *b* are the parameters of the triangular curves, given in figure 4.10.

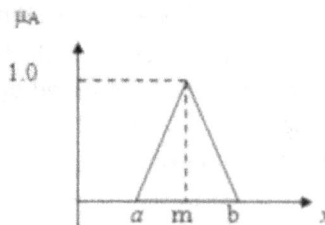

Fig. 4.10: Triangular curve

4.4.2. Trapezoidal Membership Function

Defined by a lower limit *a*, an upper limit *d*, a lower support limit *b*, and an upper support limit *c*, where *a* < *b* < *c* < *d*. variables denoting the location of the corresponding corners.

$$\mu_A(x) = \begin{cases} 0, & (x < a) \text{ or } (x > d) \\ \dfrac{x-a}{b-a}, & a \le x \le b \\ 1, & b \le x \le c \\ \dfrac{d-x}{d-c}, & c \le x \le d \end{cases}$$

Or, trapezoid $(x; a, b, c, d) = max [min [(x-a)/(b-a),1, (d-x)/(d-c)], 0]$ (4.18)

Here, *a*, *b*, c and d are the parameters of the trapezium curve shown in figure 4.11.

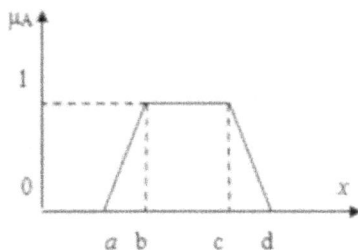

Fig.4.11: Trapezoidal Membership function

Note that a trapezoidal MF with parameter {*a*, *b*, *c*, *d*} can be reduced to a triangular MF, by varying the parameters *b* and *c* such that *b* = *c*.

There are two special categories of a trapezoidal function, called as **R- function** and **L- function**.

➤ R-functions: with parameters $a = b = -\infty$

$$\mu_A(x) = \begin{cases} 0, & x > d \\ \dfrac{d-x}{d-c}, & c \le x \le d \\ 1, & x < c \end{cases}$$

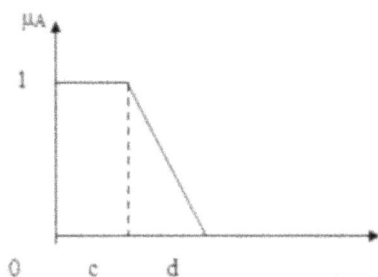

Fig.4.12: R- Membership Function

➤   L-Functions: with parameters c = d = + ∞

$$\mu_A(x) = \begin{cases} 0, & x < a \\ \dfrac{x-a}{b-a}, & a \leq x \leq b \\ 1, & x > b \end{cases}$$

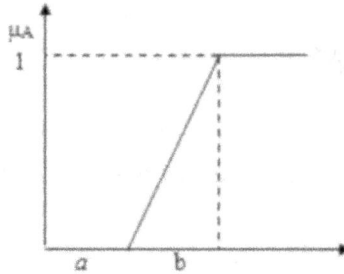

Fig.4.13: L-membership function

Due to their simple formulae and computational efficiency, both triangular and trapezoidal MFs have been extensively used in real time applications. However, because of the presence of straight line segments, they are not smooth at the corner points, due to this other MFs were introduced, in the following section we will discuss them.

4.4.3.   Gaussian Membership Function

Described by a central parameter **m** and a standard deviation denoted by k; **k > 0**. The smaller the value of k is, the narrower the "bell" is,

$$\mu_A(x) = e^{\frac{(x-m)^2}{2k^2}}$$

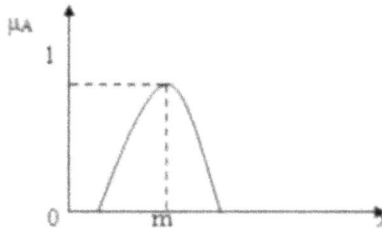

Fig.4.13: Gaussian membership function

4.4.4.   Generalized bell Membership Functions

Defined by three parameters {a, b, c}:

Bell(x; a, b, c) = 1 / 1 + |(x −c)/a|^{2b}

Where, the parameter b is usually positive, in case of negative b, the shape of the Membership Function becomes an upside-down bell). This MF is also called Cauchy

MF, as it is a direct generalization of Cauchy distribution used in probability theory.

4.4.5. S-membership function

$S(x; a, b, c)$ represents a membership function defined as,

$$S(x:a,b,c) = \begin{cases} 0 & \text{for } x < a \\ 2(x-a)^2/(c-a)^2 & \text{for } a \le x < b \\ 1 - 2(x-c)^2/(c-a)^2 & \text{for } b \le x \le c \\ 1 & \text{for } x > c \end{cases} \qquad (4.19)$$

In equation a, b and c are the parameters that are modified to fit the desired membership data. The parameter b is the half width of the curve at the crossover point.

4.4.6. The -shaped membership function

The -shaped membership functions are given by,

$$f(x:b,c) = \begin{cases} S\left(x; c-b, c-\dfrac{b}{2}, c \right) & \text{for } x \le c \\ 1 - S\left(x; c, c \mid \dfrac{b}{2}, c+b \right) & \text{for } x > c \end{cases} \qquad (4.20)$$

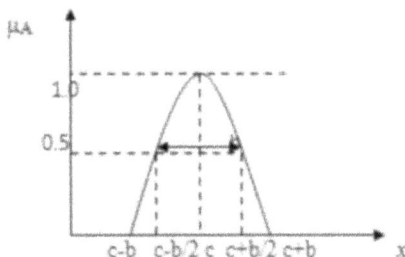

Fig. 4.14 : π - shaped curve

4.4.7. Sigmoidal Membership Functions

A sigmoidal MF is defined by,

$$\text{sig}(x; a, c) = 1 / [1 + \exp\{-a(x - c)\}], \qquad (4.21)$$

where a regulates the slope at the crossover point $x = c$.

As per the sign of the parameter a, a sigmoidal MF is immanently open either from right or left and thus is found suitable for representing notions like "very large" or "very negative." Sigmoidal functions of this kind are extensively used as the activation function of artificial neural networks. Therefore, for a neural network to simulate the behavior of a fuzzy inference system (more on this in later chapters), the first problem we face is to figure out the way to synthesize a close MF through a sigmoidal function.

4.5. Derivatives of Parameterized MFs

Derivatives of Membership functions are important when we need to make the fuzzy systems adaptive, especially for fine-tuning a fuzzy inference system to achieve desired input/output mapping. Here, in this section, the derivatives for the Gaussian and bell MFs are discussed. For the Gaussian MF, let,

$$y = \text{Gaussian } (x; k, m) = e^{-(x-m)^2 / 2k^2} \tag{4.22}$$

Then,
$$\frac{\partial y}{\partial x} = -(x-m)y/k^2 \tag{4.23}$$

$$\frac{\partial y}{\partial x} = -(x-m)^2 y/k^3 \tag{4.24}$$

$$\frac{\partial y}{\partial m} = -(x-m)y/k^2 \tag{4.25}$$

For the bell MF, let,

$$y = \text{bell}(x; a, b, c) = 1 / 1 + |(x-c)/a|^{2b} \tag{4.26}$$

Then,
$$\frac{\partial y}{\partial x} = \begin{cases} -\dfrac{2b}{x-c} y(1-y), & \text{if } x \neq c \\ 0, & \text{if } x = c \end{cases} \tag{4.27}$$

$$\frac{\partial y}{\partial a} = \frac{2b}{a} y(1-y) \tag{4.28}$$

$$\frac{\partial y}{\partial b} = \begin{cases} -2\ln\left|\dfrac{x-c}{a}\right| y(1-y), & \text{if } x \neq c \\ 0, & \text{if } x = c \end{cases} \tag{4.29}$$

$$\frac{\partial y}{\partial x} = \begin{cases} \dfrac{2b}{x-c} y(1-y), & \text{if } x \neq c \\ 0, & \text{if } x = c \end{cases} \tag{4.30}$$

4.6. The Extension Principle

The extension principle was introduced by Zadeh (1975) and later by Yager (1986); provides a mathematical approach for extending classical functions to fuzzy mappings. It has been considered that extension principle is an important tool in the development of fuzzy arithmetic and other areas.

The extension principle is a basic identity that allows the domain of a function to be extended from crisp point in Y to fuzzy sets in X. More specifically, let f: $X \rightarrow Y$ be a function from crisp set X to crisp set Y. Suppose that a fuzzy set A in X is given such as,

$$A = \{\mu_A(x_1) / x_1, \mu_A(x_2) / x_2, \mu_A(x_3) / x_3, \ldots, \mu_A(x_n) / x_n\} \tag{4.31}$$

and we want to determine a fuzzy set $B = f(A)$ in Y that is induced by f, such as,

$$B = f(A) = \{\mu_A(x_1) / y_1, \mu_A(x_2) / y_2, \mu_A(x_3) / y_3, \ldots, \mu_A(x_n) / y_n\} \tag{4.32}$$

Where, $y_i = f(x_i)$, $i = 1, \ldots, n$. In other words, the fuzzy set B can be defined through the values of $f(.)$ in $x_1, \ldots, x_n$.

If f is an one-to-one mapping we can define

$$\mu_B(y) = \mu_A[f^{-1}(y)], y \in Y \tag{4.33}$$

Where $f^{-1}(y)$ is a inverse of f, that is, $f[f^{-1}(y)] = y$. If f is one-to-one, then an ambiguity arises when two or more distinct points in X with different membership values in A are mapped into the same point in Y. For example, we may have $f(x_1) = f(x_2) = y$ but $x_1 \neq x_2$ and $\mu_A(x_1) \neq \mu_A(x_2)$, so the R.H.S. of (A) may take two different values $\mu_A[x_1 = f^{-1}(y)]$ or $\mu_A[x_2 = f^{-1}(y)]$. To resolve this ambiguity, we assign the larger one of the two membership values to $\mu_B(y)$. More generally, the membership function for B is defined as

$$\mu_B(y) = \max \mu_A(x), y \in Y \tag{4.34}$$

The expression of equation 4.32 is called the *extension principle*.

Similarly, if $f(.)$ is a many-to-one mapping, then there exist $x_1, x_2 \mu X, x_1 \neq x_2$, such that $f(x_1) = f(x_2) = y^*, y^* \in Y$. In this case the membership grade of B at $y = y^*$ is the maximum of the membership grades of A at $x = x_1$ and $x = x_2$, since $f(x) = y^*$ may result from either $x = x_1$ or $x = x_2$, since $f(x) = y^*$ may result from either $x = x_1$ or $x = x_2$. More generally, we have,

$$\mu_B(y) = \max \mu_A(x) \tag{4.35}$$
$$x = f^{-1}(y)$$

Example 4.1: Apply the extension principle to fuzzy sets with discrete universes.

Let, $\quad A = 0.1 / -2 + 0.4 / -1 + 0.8 / 0 + 0.9 / 1 + 0.3 / 2$

And, $\quad f(x) = x^2 - 3$

Upon applying the extension principle, we have

$B = 0.1 / 1 + 0.4 / -2 + 0.8 / -3 + 0.9 / -2 + 0.3 / 1$

$\quad = 0.8 / -3 + (0.4 / -2 + (0.1\ 0.3) / 1$

$\quad = 0.8 / -3 + 0.9 / -2 + 0.3 / 1$

Where, represents max. Figure 4.15 illustrates this example.

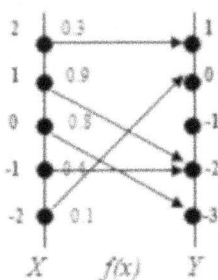

Fig.4.15: Extension principle on fuzzy sets with discrete universe

4.6.1.   Monotonic Functions

Apart for fuzzy logic, a monotonic function is a function which is either entirely non-increasing or non-decreasing. A function is considered monotonic, if its first derivative (which need not be continuous) does not change sign.

Now in terms of Fuzzy set, the term monotonic may also be used to describe set functions which map subsets of the domain to non-decreasing values of the codomain.

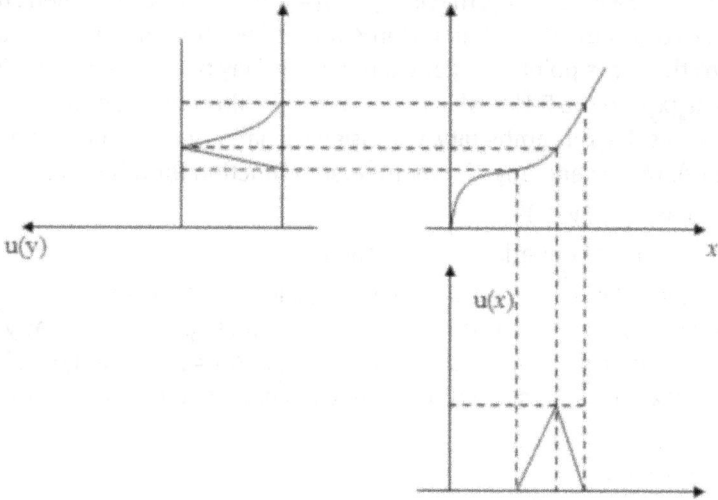

Fig.4.16: A monotonic continuous function

In particular, if $f : X \rightarrow Y$ is a set function from a collection of sets X to an ordered set Y, then f is said to be monotone if whenever $A \subseteq B$ as elements of X, $f(A) \leq f(B)$.

This particular definition comes up frequently in measure theory where many of the families of functions defined (including outer measure, premeasure, and measure) begin by considering monotonic set functions. Mathematically we could describe a completely monotonic function $f(x)$ as,

$$(-1)^{-n} f^{(n)}(x) \geq 0 \tag{4.36}$$

Now, suppose we have to apply extension principle on a monotonic function, the following steps will be involved for each point in the interval:

➢   Compute the image of the interval.

➢   The membership degrees are carried through.

Figure 4.16 shows an entirely non-decreasing monotonic continuous function.

Example 4.2: Apply extension principle to a continuous monotonic function, $y = f(x) = 0.6*x + 4$

Input: Fuzzy number - around-5

Around-5 = 0.3 / 3 + 1.0 / 5 + 0.3 / 7

f(around-5) = 0.3/f(3) + 1/f(5) + 0.3/f(7)

f(around-5) = 0.3/0.6*3 + 4 + 1/ 0.6*5 + 4 + 0.3/0.6*7 + 4

f(around-5) = 0.3/5.8 + 1.0/7 + 0.3/8.2

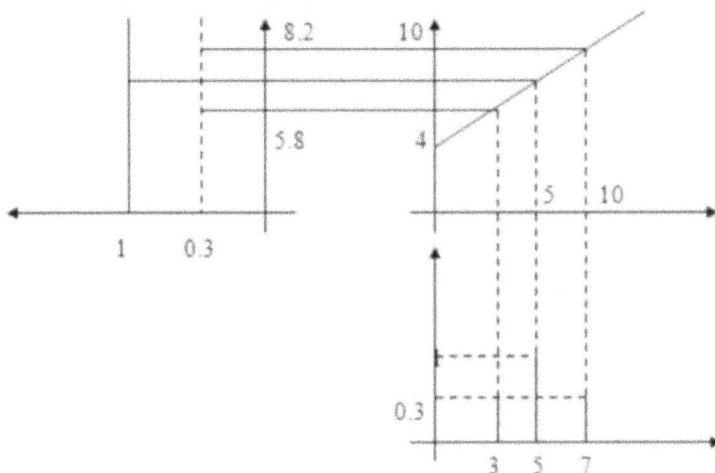

Fig.4.17: illustration of example 4.2

Figure 4.17 illustrates this example.

4.6.2. Non-monotonic Functions

For each point in the interval:

➢ Compute the image of the interval.

➢ The membership degrees are carried through.

➢ When different inputs map to the same value, combine the membership degrees.

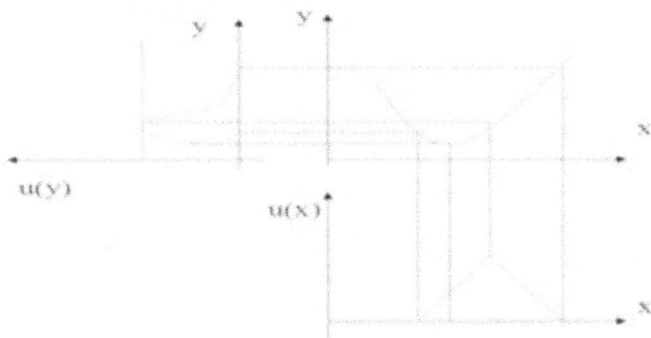

Fig.4.18: a non-monotonic function

Figure 4.18 illustrates a non-monotonic function.

Example 4.3: Apply extension principle to a continuous monotonic function, $y = f(x) = x^2 - 6x + 11$

Input: Fuzzy number - around-4

Around-4 = 0.3 / 2 + 0.6 / 3 + 1 / 4 + 0.6 / 5 + 0.3 / 6

f(around-4) = 0.3 / f(2) + 0.6 / f(3) + 1 / f(4) + 0.6 / f(5) + 0.3 / f(6)

f(around-4) = 0.6 / 3 + 0.6 / 2 + 1/3 + 0.6 / 6 + 0.3 / 11

f(around-4) = 0.6 / 2 + 1 / 3 + 0.6 / 6 + 0.3 / 11

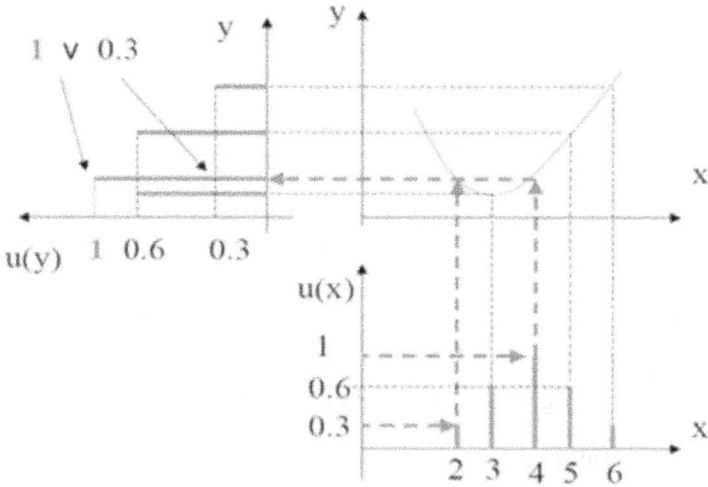

Fig.4.19: Illustration of example 4.3

4.6.3.   Arithmetic Operations

4.6.3.1. Fuzzy Addition

Applying the extension principle to arithmetic operations it is possible to define fuzzy arithmetic operations. Let x and y be the operands, z the result. Let A and B denote the fuzzy sets that represent the operands x and y respectively. Using the extension principle fuzzy addition is defined as,

$$\mu_{A+B}(z) = V(\mu_A(x) \wedge \mu_B(y)) \tag{4.37}$$

x, y

$x + y = z$

Example 4.4: Let, $A = (3^\sim) = 0.3/1 + 0.6/2 + 1/3 + 0.6/4 + 0.3/5$

And $B = (11^\sim) = 0.5/10 + 1/11 + 0.5/12$

Then, $A + B$ = (0.3^0.5)/(1 + 10) + (0.6^0.5)/(2 + 10) + (1^0.5)/(3 + 10) + (0.6^0.5)/(4 + 10) + (0.3^0.5)/(5 + 10) + (0.3^1)/(1 + 11) + (0.6^1)/(2 + 11) + (1^1)/(3 + 11) + (0.6^1)/(4 + 11) + (0.3^1)/(5 + 11) + (0.3^0.5)/(1 + 12) + (0.6^0.5)/(2 + 12) + (1^0.5)/(3 + 12) + (0.6^0.5)/(4 + 12) + (0.3^0.5)/(5 + 12)

$A = (3^\sim) = 0.3/1 + 0.6/2 + 1/3 + 0.6/4 + 0.3/5$

$B = (11^\sim) = 0.5/10 + 1/11 + 0.5/12$

Getting the minimum of the membership values

$A + B = 0.3/11 + 0.5/12 + 0.5/13 + 0.5/14 + 0.3/15 + 0.3/12 + 0.6/13 + 1/14 + 0.6/15 + 0.3/16 + 0.3/13 + 0.5/14 + 0.5/15 + 0.5/16 + 0.3/17$

$A = (3\sim) = 0.3/1 + 0.6/2 + 1/3 + 0.6/4 + 0.3/5$

$B = (11\sim) = 0.5/10 + 1/11 + 0.5/12$

Getting the maximum of the duplicated values

$A + B = 0.3/11 + (0.5 \text{ V } 0.3)/12 + (0.5 \text{ V } 0.6 \text{ V } 0.3)/13 + (0.5 \text{ V } 1 \text{ V } 0.5)/14 + (0.3 \text{ V } 0.6 \text{ V } 0.5)/15 + (0.3 \text{ V } 0.5)/16 + 0.3/17$

$A + B = 0.3 / 11 + 0.5 / 12 + 0.6 / 13 + 1 / 14 + 0.6 / 15 + 0.5 / 16 + 0.3 / 17$

Figure 4.20 illlustrates the graphical representation of the result of example 4.4.

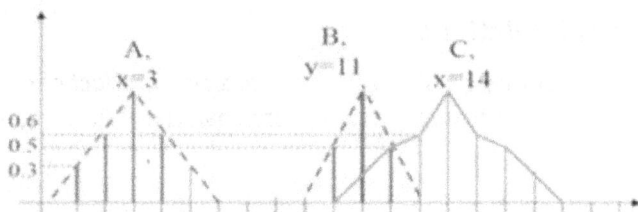

Fig.4.4: graphical representation of example 4.4

4.6.3.2. Fuzzy Product

Let x and y be the operands, z the result. Let A and B denote the fuzzy sets that represent the operands x and y respectively. Using the extension principle fuzzy product operation is defined as,

$$\mu_{A*B}(z) = V(\mu_A(x) \wedge \mu_B(y)) \qquad (4.38)$$

x, y

$x * y = z$

Example 4.5: Let $A = 2 =$ "Approximately 2 = $\{0.6/1 + \frac{1}{2} + 0.8/3\}$

$B = 6 =$ "Approximately 6 = $\{0.8/5 + 1/6 + 0.7/7\}$

Then $A \times B = 12 =$ "Approximately 12 = $\{0.6/1 + \frac{1}{2} + 0.8/3\} \times \{0.8/5 + 1/6 + 0.7/7\}$

$$= \left\{ \frac{\min(0.6, 0.8)}{5} + \frac{\min(0.6, 1)}{6} + \ldots\ldots + \frac{\min(0.8, 1)}{18} + \frac{\min(0.8, 0.7)}{21} \right\}$$

$$= \left\{ \frac{0.6}{5} + \frac{0.6}{6} + \frac{0.6}{7} + \frac{0.8}{10} + \frac{1}{12} + \frac{0.7}{14} + \frac{0.8}{15} + \frac{0.8}{15} + \frac{0.7}{21} \right\}$$

Example 4.6: Let $A = \{0.2/1 + \frac{1}{2} + 0.7/4\}$ and $B = \{0.5/1 + 1/2\}$

If mapping is not one-to-one, we get;

$$\mu_{A \times B}(x, y) = \max \{\min [\mu_A(x), \mu_A(y)]\} \qquad (4.39)$$

$f(A, B) = A \times B$ (arithmetic product)

$\quad = \{0.2/1 + \frac{1}{2} + 0.7/4\} \times \{0.5/1 + 1/2\}$

$$= \left\{ \frac{\min(0.2, 0.5)}{1} + \frac{\max[\min(02, 1), \min(0.5, 1)]}{2} + ... + \right.$$

$$\left. \frac{\max[\min(0.7, 0.5), \min(1.1)]}{4} + \frac{\min(0.7, ,1)}{8} \right\}$$

$\quad = \{0.2/1 + 0.5/2 + \frac{1}{4} + 0.7/8\}$

4.7. Fuzzy Relation

4.7.1. Classical Relations

Let X and Y be two arbitrary classical sets. The **Cartesian product** of crisp sets X and Y, denoted by $X \times Y$, is the nonfuzzy set of all ordered pairs (x, y) such that $x \in X$ and $y \in Y$; that is,

$$X \times Y = \{(x, y) \mid x \in X \text{ and } y \in Y\}. \tag{4.40}$$

The order in which X and Y appears is prominent; i.e., if $X \neq Y$, then $X \times Y \neq Y \times X$. Generally, the Cartesian product of arbitrary n sets $X_1, X_2, ..., X_n$, represented by $X_1 \times X_2 \times ..... \times X_n$, is the non-fuzzy set of all n-tuples $(x_1, x_{2, ...} x_n)$ such that $x_i \in X_i$ for $i \in \{1, 2, ... ,\}$; i.e,

$$X_1 \times X_2 \times .... X_n = x_1, x_{2, ...} x_n) \mid x_1 \in X_1, x_2 \in X_2, ... x_n \in X_n\} \tag{4.41}$$

A **relation** among sets $X_1, X_2, ..., X_n$ is a subset of the Cartesian product $X_1 \times X_2 \times ..... \times X_n$, i.e, if $R(X_1, X_2, ..., X_n)$ is denoting a relation among $X_1, X_2, ..., X_n$, then

$$R(X_1, X_2, ..., X_n) \subset X_1 \times X_2 \times ..... \times X_n. \tag{4.42}$$

Specifically, a **binary relation** between non fuzzy sets X and Y is a subset of the Cartesian product $X \times Y$.

4.7.2. Fuzzy Relation

As we know the importance of membership function on fuzzy sets, before moving towards the core description of fuzzy relation, let us have a look on membership function first.

Since a relation is itself a set, all the basic set operations can be applied to it without modification. Also membership function to represent a relation is given as

$$\mu_R(x_1, x_2, ... x_n) = \begin{cases} 1, if (x_1, x_2, ... x_n) \in R(X_1, X_2 ...... X_n) \\ 0, \qquad\qquad\qquad\qquad otherwise \end{cases} \tag{4.43}$$

Definition 1. A **fuzzy relation** is a fuzzy set defined in the Cartesian product of crisp sets $X_1, X_2, ..., X_n$. with the representation scheme a fuzzy relation R in $X_1 \times X_2 \times ..... \times X_n$ is defined as the fuzzy set

$$R = \{((x_1, x_2, \ldots x_n, \mu_R(x_1, x_2, \ldots x_n)) \mid (x_1, x_2, \ldots x_n) \in X_1 \times X_2 \times \ldots \times X_n\} \tag{4.44}$$

Where, $\mu_R : X_1 \times X_2 \times \ldots \times X_n \to [0,1]$.

Note that an n-array fuzzy relation is a fuzzy subset of the Cartesian product $X_1 \times X_2 \times \ldots \times X_n$

Each tuple $(x_1, x_2, \ldots x_n)$ has a degree of membership. As a special case, a **binary fuzzy relation** is a fuzzy set defined as a Cartesian product of two crisp sets. A binary relation on a finite Cartesian product is usually represented by a fuzzy relational matrix, i.e, a matrix whose elements are the membership values of the corresponding pairs belonging to a fuzzy relation.

Definition 2. A fuzzy binary relation (or simply fuzzy relation) R from X to Y is a fuzzy subset of $X \times Y$

$$R = \{(x, y), \mu_R(x, y) \mid x \in X, y \in Y\} \tag{4.45}$$

$$= \cup\{x, y), \mu_R(x, y)\}$$

Where $\mu_R(x, y)$ is the membership function of R and $\cup_{X \times Y}$ represents the unions of singleton $\{(x, y) \mid \mu_R(x, y)\}$ over $X \times Y$.

When X and Y are finite or discrete, and $|X| = m$ and $|Y| = n$, we may write

$$R = \sum_{i=1}^{m} \sum_{j=1}^{m} (x, y), m_R(x, y)\} \tag{4.46}$$

Definition 3. Fuzzy Relational Matrix : R can also be represented as a rectangular table called a relation matrix by placing $\mu_R(x, y)$ as the matrix elements:

$$R = \begin{Bmatrix} \mu R(x_1, y_1) & \ldots & \mu_R(x_1, y_n) \\ \ldots & \ldots & \ldots \\ \mu_R(x_m, y_1) & \ldots & \mu_R(x_m, y_n) \end{Bmatrix} \tag{4.47}$$

In particular, when $X = Y$, the Cartesian product on X is defined as

$X \times X = \{(x, y \mid x, y \in X\}$

And a fuzzy relation on X is a fuzzy subset of $X \times X$.

4.7.3. Cartesian Product of Fuzzy Sets

Definition 1. Let $A_1, \ldots, A_n$ be fuzzy set in $X_1, X_2, \ldots, X_n$, respectively. The Cartesian product of fuzzy sets $A_1, \ldots, A_n$, denoted by $A_1 \times \ldots \times A_n$, is a fuzzy relation in $X_1 \times X_2 \times \ldots \times X_n$ whose membership function is defined as

$$\mu_{A1} \times \ldots \times A_n (x_1, x_2, \ldots x_n) = \mu_{A1}(x_1) \times _{An}(x_n)$$

Definition 2. If $\mu_{A1}(x), \mu_{A2}(x), \ldots, \mu_{An}(x)$ denotes the membership functions of $A_1, \ldots, A_n$ for $\forall x_1 \in X, x_2 \in X, \ldots, x_n \in X$, then the probability for n-tuple $(x_1, x_2, \ldots x_n)$ to be involved in fuzzy set $A_1 \times \ldots \times A_n$ is,

$$\mu_{A1} \times \ldots \times A_n (x_1, x_2, \ldots x_n) = \text{Min} [\mu_{A1}(x_1), \mu_{A2}(x_2), \ldots, \mu_{An}(x_n)].$$

For $n = 2$, the Cartesian product of two sets A_1 and A_2 in fuzzy set is defined by

$$\mu_{A1} \times A_2 (x_1, x_2) = \text{Min} [\mu_{A1}(x_1), \mu_{A2}(x_2)]$$

Where μ_{A1} and μ_{A2} are the membership functions for A_1 and A_2 and $x_1, x_2 \in X$.

4.7.4. Projections

Because a crisp relation is defined in the product space of two or more sets, the concept of projection were proposed. For example, consider the set $A = \{(x, y) \in R^2 \mid (x-1)^2 + (y-1)^2 \le 1\}$ which is a relation in $X \times Y = R^2$. Then $A_1 = [0, 1] \subset X$, denotes the projection of A on X, and similarly $A_2 = [0, 1] \subset Y$, denotes the projection of A on Y. The cylindrical extension of A_1 to $X \times Y = R^2$ is $A_{1E} = [0, 1] \times (-\infty, \infty)R^2$. These concepts can be extended to fuzzy relations.

Definition. Let R be a fuzzy relation in $X_1 \times X_2 \times \ldots \times X_n$ and $\{i_1, \ldots, i_k\}$ be a subsequence of $\{1, 2, \ldots, n\}$, then the projection of R on $X_{i1} \times \ldots \times X_{ik}$ is a fuzzy relation R_p in $X_{i1} \times \ldots \times X_{ik}$ defined by the membership function

$$\mu_{RI} (x_{i1}, x_{i2}, \ldots x_{ik}) = \max \mu_R (x_1, x_2, \ldots x_k) \tag{4.48}$$

4.7.5. Operations on Fuzzy Relations

Suppose R and S are fuzzy relations on Cartesian space $X \times Y$, then the following operations applies (Similar to operations on Fuzzy sets):

Union: $\mu_{R^* \cup S}(x, y) = \max\{\mu_R(x, y), \mu_s(x, y)\}$

Intersection: $\mu_{R \cap S}(x, y) = \min\{\mu_R(x, y), \mu_s(x, y)\}$

Complement: $\mu_{\text{not } R}(x, y) = 1 - \mu_R(x, y)$

Containment or (inclusive): $R \subset S = \mu_{\text{not } R}(x, y) \le \mu_s(x, y)$

4.7.6. Compositions of Fuzzy Relations

Let $P(X, Y)$ and $Q(Y, Z)$ be two binary relations that share a common set Y. The *composition* of P and Q, denoted by $P \circ Q$, is defined as a fuzzy relation in $X \times Z$ such that $(x, z) \in P \circ Q$ if and only if there exists at least one $y \in Y$ such that $(x, y) \in P$ and $(y, z) \in Q$. Using the membership function representation of relations, its membership function is given by

$$\mu_{P \circ Q}(x, z) = \max t[\mu_p(x, y), \in_Q(y, z)] \tag{4.49}$$

For any $(x, z) \in X \times Z$, where t is any t- norm, i.e., $R(X, Z) = P(X, Y) \circ Q(Y, Z)$ is composition of relation if following conditions hold:

$(x, y) \in R$ if exists $y \in Y$ such that $(x, y) \in P$ and $(y, z) \in Q$.

The two most commonly used compositions are max-min composition and max-product composition, which are defined as follows:

➤ The max-min composition of fuzzy relations $P(X, Y)$ and $Q(Y, Z)$ is a fuzzy relation $P \circ Q$ in $X \times Z$ defined by the membership function

$$\mu_{P \circ Q} (x, z) = \max \min [\mu_p(x, y), \mu_Q(y, z)] \tag{4.50}$$

where $(x, z) \in X \times Z$.

➤ The max-product composition of fuzzy relations $P(X, Y)$ and $Q(Y, Z)$ is a fuzzy relation $P \circ Q$ in $X \times Z$ defined by the membership function

$$\mu_{P \circ Q}(x, z) = \max [\mu_P(x, y) . \mu_Q(y, z)] \tag{4.51}$$

here $(x, z) \in X \times Z$.

4.7.7. Properties of Fuzzy Relations

Associativity: $P \circ (Q \circ R) = (P \circ Q) \circ R$.

Distributivity over union: $P \circ (Q \cup R) = (P \circ Q) (P \circ R)$

Weak Distributivity over intersection: $P \circ (Q \cap R) \subseteq (P \circ Q) \cap (P \circ R)$

Monotonicity: $S \subseteq T \rightarrow (R \circ S) \subseteq (R \circ T)$.

4.7.8. Fuzzy relations on the same universe

(i)   A fuzzy relation $R_{(A, A)}$ is said to be **reflexive** if
$\mu_R(a, a) = 1$ for all $a \in A$.

(ii) A fuzzy relation $R_{(A, A)}$ is said to be **symmetric** if
$\mu_R(a, b) = \mu_R(b, a)$ for all $a, b \in A$.

(iii) A fuzzy relation $R_{(A, A)}$ is referred as **antisymmetric** if

$$a \neq b \rightarrow \begin{cases} \mu R(a,b) \neq \mu R(b,a) \\ or\, \mu R(a,b) = \mu R(b,a)\, \text{for all } a,b \in A; \end{cases}$$

and perfectly antisymmetric if
$a \neq b \rightarrow (\mu_R(a, b) > 0 \rightarrow \mu_R(b, a) = 0)$ for all $a, b, \in A$.

(iv) A fuzzy relation $R_{(A, A)}$ is said to be **transitive** if
$\mu_{R \circ R}(a, b) \leq \mu_R(a, b)$ for all $a, b \in A$.

Definitions:

(a) R is an *equivalence relation*, if it is *reflexive, symmetric* and *transitive*.

(b) R is a *partial order relation*, if it is *reflexive, antisymmetric* and *transitive*.

(c) R is a *total order relation*, if R is a *partial order relation*, and $\forall u, v \in U$ either (u, v) or $(v, u) \in R$.

4.7.9. Fuzzy Implication

Let A and B be two fuzzy sets in X, Y respectively. The implication $I: A \rightarrow B \in X \times Y$ is defined as,

$$I = A \times B = \int_{X \times Y} \mu_A(X) \cap \mu_B(Y) / (X, Y) \tag{4.52}$$

The rule "if the error is negative big *then* control output is positive big" is an implication: error x implies control action y.

Let there be two discrete fuzzy sets $A = \{(x_i, \mu_A(x_i), i = 1,....., n\}$ defined on X and $B = \{(v_{j}, _B(v_j)), j = 1, ..., m\}$ defined on V. Then the implication $A \rightarrow B$ is a fuzzy relation R:

$$R = \{((x_i, v_j), \mu_R(x_i, v_j)), i = 1,...,n, j = 1....,m\} \tag{4.53}$$

Defined on $X \times Y$, whose membership function $\mu_R(x_i, v_j)$ is given by,

$$\left\{ \begin{matrix} \mu A(x1) \\ \mu A(x2) \\ \mu A(x3) \end{matrix} \right\} \times [\mu_B(v_1)\mu_B(v_2)........\mu_B(v_m)]$$

$$= \begin{matrix} \mu A(x1) \wedge \mu B(v1) & \mu A(x1) \wedge \mu B(v2) & \mu A(x1) \wedge \mu B(vm) \\ \mu A(x2) \wedge \mu B(v1) & \mu A(x2) \wedge \mu B(v2) & \mu A(x2) \wedge \mu B(vm) \\ \mu A(xn) \wedge \mu B(v1) & \mu A(xn) \wedge \mu B(v2) & \mu A(xn) \wedge \mu B(vm) \end{matrix}$$

4.8.   Fuzzy If- Then Rules

Fuzzy If-Then rule or fuzzy rule or fuzzy implication or fuzzy conditional statements are expressions of the form "If A Then B", where A and B are labels of **fuzzy** sets characterized by appropriate membership functions. Due to their concise form, **fuzzy If-Then rules** are often employed to capture the imprecise modes of reasoning that play an essential role in the human ability to make decision in an environment of uncertainty and imprecision. The set of **If-Then rules** relate to a fuzzy logic system that are stored together is called a **Fuzzy Rule Base**.

Fuzzy sets and fuzzy operators are the subjects and verbs of fuzzy logic. These if-then rule statements are used to formulate the conditional statements that comprise fuzzy logic.

A single fuzzy if-then rule assumes the form

➢   if x is A then y is B

where A and B are linguistic values defined by fuzzy sets on the ranges (universes of discourse) X and Y, respectively. The if-part of the rule "x is A" is called the *antecedent* or premise, while the then-part of the rule "y is B" is called the *consequent* or conclusion. Before we could move further on the grounds of fuzzy if-then rules to model and analyze a system, let us first formalize the expression "if x is A then y is B", which is sometimes abbreviated as $A \to B$. In essence, the expression describes a relation between two variables x and y; this suggests that a fuzzy if-then rule be defined as a binary fuzzy relation R on the product space $X \times Y$. Generally, there are two ways to interpret the fuzzy rule $A \to B$, if we interpret $A \to B$ as A coupled with B then,

$$R = A \to B = A \times B = \int_{X \times Y} \mu_A(x) * \mu_B(y)/(x, y) \qquad (4.54)$$

Where, * is a t-norm operator and $A \to B$ is used again to represent the fuzzy relation R. On the other hand, if $A \to B$ is interpreted as A leads to (entails) B, then it can be written as four different formulas:

● Material implication:

$$R = A \to B = \neg A \cup B \qquad (4.55)$$

● Propositional calculus:

$$R = A \rightarrow B = \neg A \cup (A \cup B) \tag{4.56}$$

- Extended propositional calculus:

$$R = A \rightarrow B = \neg(A \cup \neg B) \cup B \tag{4.57}$$

- Generalization of modus ponens:

$$\mu_R(x, y) = \sup\{c \mid \mu_A(x)^* \, c \leq \mu_B(y) \text{ and } 0 \leq c \leq 1\} \tag{4.58}$$

where * is a t-norm operator.

Although these four formulae are different in appearance, they all reduce to the familiar identity $A \rightarrow B = \neg A \cup B$ when A and B are apparently the propositions following the two valued logic.

Another linguistic example of fuzzy if-then rule might be

➢ *If service is good then tip is average*

Note that *good* is represented as a number between 0 and 1, and so the antecedent is an interpretation that returns a single number between 0 and 1. On the other hand, *average* is represented as a fuzzy set, and so the consequent is an assignment that assigns the entire fuzzy set B to the output variable y. In the if-then rule, the word "is" gets used in two entirely different ways depending on whether it appears in the antecedent or the consequent. In MATLAB terms, this is the distinction between a relational test using "==" and a variable assignment using the "=" symbol. A less confusing way of writing the rule would be

➢ *If service == good then tip = average*

In general, the input to an if-then rule is the current value for the input variable (in this case, *service*) and the output is an entire fuzzy set (in this case, *average*). This set will later be *defuzzified,* assigning one value to the output.

Interpreting an if-then rule involves distinct parts: first evaluating the antecedent (which involves *fuzzifying* the input and applying any necessary *fuzzy operators*) and second applying that result to the consequent (known as *implication*). In the case of two-valued or binary logic, if-then rules don't present much difficulty. If the premise is true, then the conclusion is true. If we relax the restrictions of two-valued logic and let the antecedent be a fuzzy statement, how does this reflect on the conclusion? The answer is a simple one. If the antecedent is true to some degree of membership, then the consequent is also true to that same degree. In other words,

➢ in binary logic: $p \rightarrow q$ (p and q are either both true or both false)

in fuzzy logic: $0.5 \, p \rightarrow 0.5 \, q$ (partial antecedents provide partial implication)

The antecedent of a rule can have multiple parts.

➢ *if sky is gray and wind is strong and barometer is falling, then ...*

in which case all parts of the antecedent are calculated simultaneously and resolved to a single number using the logical operators described in the preceding section. The consequent of a rule can also have multiple parts.

> ➢ *if temperature is cold then open the hot water valve and eventually shut the cold water valve*

in which case all consequents are affected equivalently by the result of the antecedent. How is the consequent affected by the antecedent? The consequent specifies a fuzzy set be assigned to the output. The *implication function* then modifies that fuzzy set to the degree specified by the antecedent. The most common ways to modify the output fuzzy set are truncation using the min function (where the fuzzy set is "chopped off" as shown below) or scaling using the prod function (where the output fuzzy set is "squashed").

The whole interpretation process is illustrated in below figure 4.5.

4.8.1.   Summary of interpretation of Fuzzy If-Then Rules

Fuzzy if-then rules can be interpreted as a three-part process.

1.   *Fuzzify inputs*: Set all fuzzy statements present in the antecedent to a degree of membership in the interval [0, 1]. The fuzzification task is over at this point if the antecedent is comprised of only one part. But if multiple parts are present, go to second step.

2.   *Apply fuzzy operator to multiple part antecedents*: If the antecedents consists multiple parts, further apply fuzzy logic operators and set the antecedent to a value between 0 and 1.

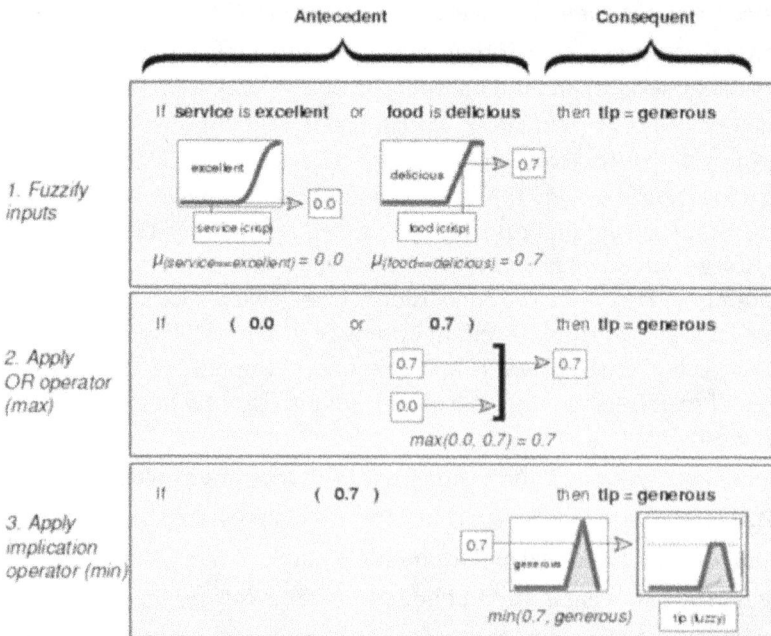

Fig.4.5: Interpretation of fuzzy if-then rule

3. *Apply implication method*: Lastly our objective is to produce the output fuzzy set using the entire rule. Consequently the fuzzy rule assigns an entire fuzzy set to the output. This fuzzy set is represented by a membership function that is chosen to indicate the qualities of the consequent. If the antecedent is only partially true, (i.e., is assigned a value less than 1), then the output fuzzy set is truncated according to the implication method.

4.9. Fuzzy Reasoning

Fuzzy reasoning or approximate reasoning is an inference procedure that derives conclusions from a set of fuzzy if-then rules and known facts. The basic rule of inference in traditional two-valued logic is *modus ponens,* according to which we can infer the truth of a proposition *B* from the truth of *A* and the implication $A \rightarrow B$. For instance, if *A* is identified with "Ram is clever" and *B* with "Ram will pass the exam", then if it is true that "Ram is clever", it is also true that "Ram will pass the exam." The concept is illustrated as follows:

Premise 1 (fact):	*x* is *A*,
Premise 2 (rule):	if *x* is *A* then *y* is *B*,
Consequence (conclusion):	*y* is *B*

However, in most of the cases of human reasoning, modus ponens is employed in an approximate manner. For example, if we have the same implication rule "if Ram is clever, then he will pass the exam" and we know that "Ram is more or less clever", then we may infer that "Ram will pass exam with good marks or boundary marks." This can be written as,

Premise 1 (fact):	*x* is A^1,
Premise 2 (rule):	if *x* is *A* then *y* is *B*,
Consequence (conclusion):	*y* is B^1,

Where A^1 is close to *A* and B^1 is close to *B*. When *A*, *B*, A^1 and B^1 are fuzzy sets of appropriate universes, the foregoing inference procedure is called **approximate reasoning** or **fuzzy reasoning**; it is also called **generalized modus ponens (GMP)**, for having modus ponens as a special case.

Definition 1: *Fuzzy reasoning*

Let *A*, A^1 and *B* be fuzzy sets of *X*, X^1 and Y respectively. Let the fuzzy implication $A \rightarrow B$ is expressed as fuzzy relation *R* on $X \times Y$. Then the fuzzy set B produced by "*x* is *A*" and the fuzzy rule "if *x* is *A* then *y* is *B*" is defined by,

$$\mu_B^1(y) = \max_x \min[\mu_A^1(x), \mu_R(x, y)] \tag{4.59}$$

$$= C_x[\mu_A^1(x) \wedge \mu_R(x, y)],$$

Or equivalently,

$$B^1 = A^1 R = A^1 (A \rightarrow B) \tag{4.60}$$

Now we can use the inference procedure of fuzzy reasoning to derive conclusions, provided that the fuzzy implication $A \rightarrow B$ is defined as an appropriate binary fuzzy relation.

Now we will discuss the computational aspects of the fuzzy reasoning.

4.9.1.   Single Rule with Single Antecedent

This is the simplest case, described by equation (4.59). Further simplifying the equation yields,

$$\mu_B^1(y) = V_x[\mu_A^1(x) \wedge \mu_A(x)] \wedge \mu_B(y)$$

$$= w \wedge \mu_B(y)$$

In other words, first we find the degree of match w as the maximum of $\mu_A^1(x) \wedge \mu_A(x)$ (the shaded area in the antecedent part of figure 4.6); then the MF of the resulting B^1 is equivalent to the MF of B clipped by w, a shown in the shaded area of the consequent part of figure 4.6. Intuitively, w represents a measure of degree of belief for the antecedent part of a rule; this measure gets propagated by the if-then rules and the resulting degree of belief or MF for the consequent part (B^1 in figure 4.6) should be greater than w.

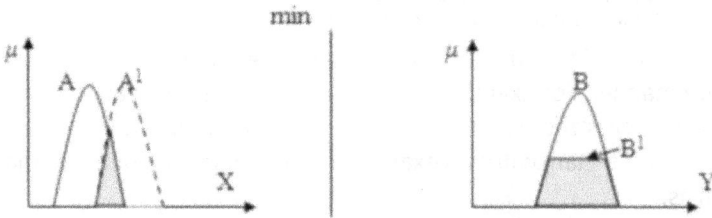

Fig.4.6: Graphical interpretation of GMP using Mamdani's fuzzy implication and the max-min composition.

4.9.2.   Single Rule with Multiple Antecedents

A fuzzy if-then rule with two antecedents is usually written as "if x is A and y is B then z is C." The corresponding problem for GMP is expressed as:

Premise 1 (fact):	x is A^1 and y is B^1,
Premise 2 (rule):	if x is A and y is B then z is C,
Consequence (conclusion):	z is C^1.

The fuzzy rule in premise 2 can be put into the simpler form "$A \times B \rightarrow C$."Intuitively, this fuzzy rule can be transformed into a ternary fuzzy relation R_m based on Mamdani's fuzzy implication function, as follows:

$$R_m(A,B,C) = (A \times B) \times C = \int_{X \times Y \times Z} \mu_A(x) \wedge \mu_B(y) \wedge \mu_C(z)/(x,y,z) \qquad (4.61)$$

The resulting C^1 is expressed as,

$C^1 = (A^1 \times B^1)(A \times B \rightarrow C)$

Thus,

$$\mu_C^1(z) = V_{x,y}[\mu_A^1(x) \wedge \mu_B^1(y)] \wedge [\mu_A(x) \wedge \mu_B(y) \wedge \mu_C(z)]$$

$$= V_{x,y}\{[\mu_A^1(x) \wedge \mu_B^1(y) \wedge \mu_A(x) \wedge \mu_B(y)]\} \wedge \mu_c(z)$$

$$= \underbrace{\{V_x[\mu_A^1(x) \wedge \mu_A(x)]\}}_{w_1} \wedge \underbrace{\{V_y[\mu_B^1(y) \wedge \mu_B(y)]\}}_{w_2} \wedge \mu_C(z)$$

$$= \underbrace{(w_1 \wedge w_2)}_{\text{Firing Strengh}} \wedge \mu_C(z),$$

(4.62)

Where w_1 and w_2 are the maxima of the MFs of $A \cap A^1$ and $B \cup B^1$, respectively. In general w_1 denotes the degree of compatibility between A and A^1; similarly w_2 denotes the degree of compatibility between B and B^1. Since the antecedent part of the fuzzy rule is constructed by the connective "and," $w_1 \wedge w_2$ is called the firing strength or degree of fulfillment of the fuzzy rule, which represents the degree to which the antecedent part of the rule is satisfied. A graphic interpretation is shown in figure 4.7, where the MF of the resulting C^1 is equal to the MF of C clipped by the firing strength w, $w = w_1 \wedge w_2$.

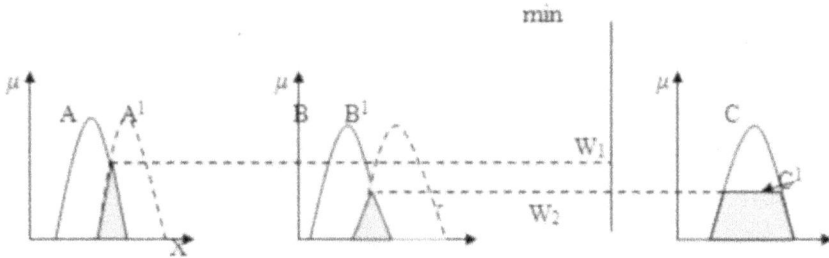

Fig.4.7: Approximate reasoning for multiple antecedents

4.9.3. Multiple Rules with Multiple Antecedents

The interpretation of the multiple rules is usually taken as the union of the fuzzy relations corresponding to the fuzzy rules. Therefore, for a GMP problem written as,

Premise 1 (fact):	x is A^1 and y is B^1,
Premise 2 (rule1):	if x is A_1 and y is B_1 then z is C_1,
Premise 3 (rule2):	if x is A_2 and y is B_2 then z is C_2,
Consequence (conclusion):	z is C^1,

We can employ the fuzzy reasoning shown in figure 4.8 as an inference procedure to derive the resulting output fuzzy set C^1.

To verify this inference procedure, let $R_1 = A_1 \times B_1 \rightarrow C_1$ and $R_2 = A_2 \times B_2 \rightarrow C_2$. Since the max-min composition operator is distributive over the operator, it follows that,

$$C^1 = (A^1 \times B^1) \ o \ (R_1 \times R_2)$$
$$= [(A^1 \times B^1) \ R_1] \ [(A^1 \times B^1) \ o \ R_2]$$

(4.63)

$$= C_1^1 \cup C_2^1,$$

Where, C_1^1 and C_2^1 are the inferred fuzzy sets for rules 1 and 2, respectively. Figure 4.8 shows graphically the operation of fuzzy reasoning for multiple rules with multiple antecedents. When a given fuzzy rule assumes the form "if x is A or y is B then z is C", then firing strength is given as the maximum of degree of match on the antecedent part for a given condition. This fuzzy rule is equivalent to the union of the two fuzzy rules "if x is A then z is C" and "if y is B then z is C."

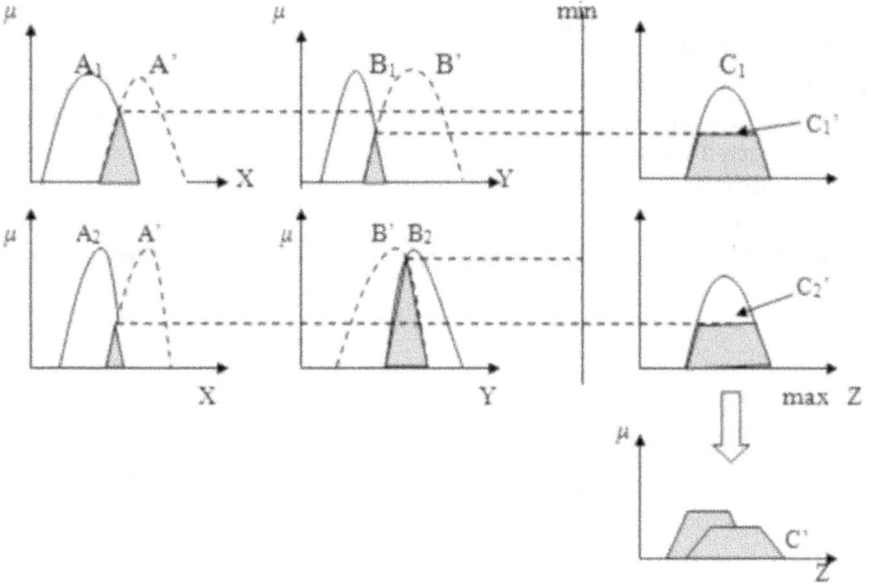

Fig.4.8: Fuzzy reasoning for multiple rules with multiple antecedents

In summary, the process of fuzzy reasoning or approximate reasoning can be divided into four steps:

Degrees of compatibility: Compare the known facts with the antecedents of fuzzy rules to find the degree of compatibility with respect to each antecedent MF.

Firing Strength: Combine degrees of compatibility with respect to antecedent MFs in a rule using fuzzy AND or OR operators to form a firing strength that indicates the degree to which the antecedent part of the rule is satisfied.

Qualified (induced) consequent MFs: Apply the firing strength to the consequent MF. (The qualified consequent MFs represent how the firing strength gets propagated and used in a fuzzy implication statement.)

Overall output MF: Aggregate all the qualified consequent MFs to obtain an overall output MF.

4.10. Fuzzy Inference Systems

Fuzzy inference is the process of formulating the mapping from a given input to an output using fuzzy logic. The mapping then provides a basis from which decisions can be made, or patterns discerned. A fuzzy inference system (FIS) essentially defines a nonlinear mapping of the input data vector into a scalar output, using fuzzy rules. i.e., It is the actual process of mapping from a given input to an output using fuzzy logic or fuzzy rules. The mapping process involves input/output membership functions, FL operators, fuzzy if – then rules, aggregation of output sets, and defuzzification.

Fuzzy inference systems systems have been successfully applied in fields such as automatic control, data classification, decision analysis, expert systems, and computer vision. Because of its multi-disciplinary nature, the fuzzy inference system is known by a number of names, such as *fuzzy-rule based system, fuzzy expert system, fuzzy model, fuzzy associative memory, fuzzy logic controller,* and *simply fuzzy system.*

A general model of a fuzzy inference system (FIS) is shown in below figure. The FIS maps crisp inputs into crisp output. FIS consists of four components: **the fuzzifier, inference engine, rule base,** and **defuzzifier.**

The **rule base** contains linguistic rules that are provided by the experts. Once the rules have been established, the FIS can be viewed as a system that maps an input vector into an output vector.

The **fuzzifier** maps input numbers into corresponding fuzzy memberships. This is required in order to activate rules that are in terms of linguistic variables. The fuzzifier takes input values and determines the degree to which they belong to each of the fuzzy sets via membership functions.

The **inference engine** defines mapping from input fuzzy sets into output fuzzy sets. It determines the degree to which the antecedent is satisfied for each rule. Outputs for each rule are then aggregated. during aggregation, fuzzy sets that represent the output of each rule are combined into a single fuzzy set. Fuzzy rules are fired in parallel, which is an important aspect of FIS.

The **defuzzifier** maps the output fuzzy sets into a crisp number. A general schematic of an FIS is shown in below figure 4.9

The step of fuzzy reasoning (inference operations upon fuzzy IF-THEN rules) performed by FISs are:

➢ Compare the input variables with the membership functions on the antecedent part to obtain the membership values of each linguistic label. (this step is often called fuzzification).

➢ Combine (usually multiplication or min) the membership values on the premise part to get firing strength (degree of fulfillment) of each rule. (Rule Base).

➢ Generate the qualified consequents (either fuzzy or crisp) or each rule depending on the firing strength.

➢ Aggregate the qualified consequents to produce a crisp output. (This step is called defuzzification).

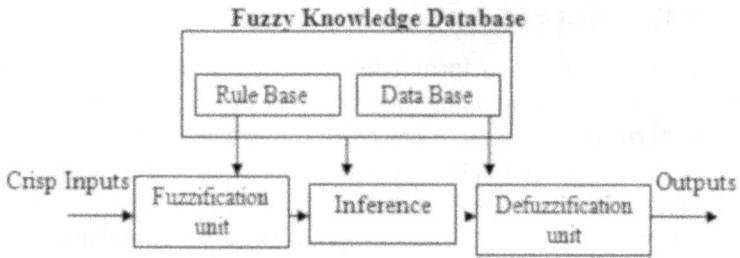

Fig.4.9: Block diagram of a fuzzy inference system or fuzzy controller system

4.10.1. Types of Fuzzy Inference systems

There are two types of fuzzy inference systems: Mamdani-type and Sugeno-type. These two inference systems vary somewhat in the way outputs are determined.

4.10.1.1. Mamdani-type FIS

Mamdani's fuzzy inference method is the most commonly seen fuzzy methodology. Mamdani's method was among the first control systems built using fuzzy set theory. It was proposed in 1975 by Ebrahim Mamdani as an attempt to control a steam engine and boiler combination by synthesizing a set of linguistic control rules obtained from experienced human operators. Mamdani's research was based on Lotfi Zadeh's 1973 paper on fuzzy algorithms for complex systems and decision processes. Although the inference process we are about to describe in the next few sections is somewhat different from the methods described in the original paper, however the basic notion is identical.

An example of a Mamdani inference system is given in figure 4.10. To compute the output of this FIS given the inputs, one must go through six steps:

➢ determining a set of fuzzy rules

➢ fuzzifying the inputs using the input membership functions,

➢ combining the fuzzified inputs according to the fuzzy rules to establish a rule strength,

➢ finding the consequence of the rule by combining the rule strength and the output membership function,

➢ combining the consequences to get an output distribution, and

➢ defuzzifying the output distribution (this step is only if a crisp output (class) is needed).

The following graphical representations illustrate this process.

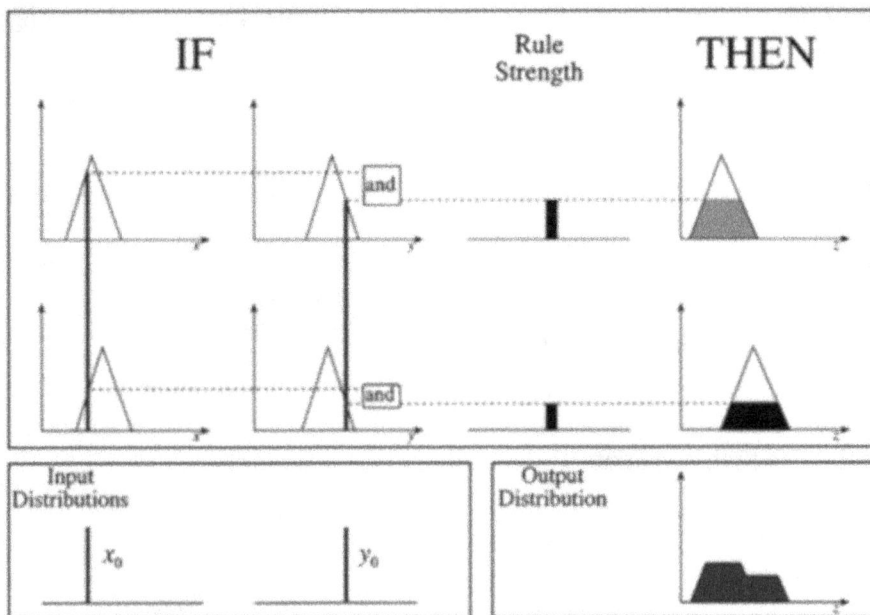

Fig.4.10: A two input, two rule Mamdani FIS with crisp inputs

4.10.1.1.1. Creating fuzzy rules

Fuzzy rules are a collection of linguistic statements that describe the methodology for FIS in making decision regarding classification of an input or control of an output. Fuzzy rules always exists in the following form:

if (input1 is membership function1) **and/or** *(input2 is membership function2)* **and/or ?. then** *(output$_n$ is output membership function$_n$).*

For example, one could make up a rule that says:

if temperature is high **and** *humidity is high* **then** *room is hot.*

So, there are membership functions that define our interpretation for high temperature (input1), high humidity (input2) and a hot room (output1). This process of accepting an input such as temperature and handle it through a membership function to determine what we actually interpret by "high" temperature is called fuzzification and is discussed in the next section. Furthermore, we must define what we interpret by "and" / "or" in the fuzzy rule. This interpretation is referred as fuzzy combination and will be discussed in the section 4.11.1.1.3.

4.10.1.1.2. Fuzzification

The objective of fuzzification is to map the inputs from a set of sensors (or features of those sensors such as amplitude or spectrum) to values from 0 to 1, by processing them through input membership functions. In the example shown in figure 4.10, there are two inputs, x_0 and y_0. These inputs are mapped into fuzzy numbers by drawing a line up from the inputs to the input membership functions above and marking the intersection point.

These input membership functions, as previously discussed, can represent fuzzy concepts such as "large" or "small", "old" or "young", "hot" or "cold", etc. For instance, x_0 could be the EMG energy coming from the front of the forearm and y_0 could be the EMG energy emitting from the back of the forearm. The membership functions could then depict "large" amounts of tension coming from a muscle or "small" amounts of tension. When choosing the input membership functions, the definition of what we interpret by "large" and "small" may vary for each input.

4.10.1.1.3. Fuzzy combinations (T-norms)

In making a fuzzy rule, we use the concept of "and", "or", and sometimes "not". The sections below describe the most common definitions of these "fuzzy combination" operators. Fuzzy combinations are also referred to as "T-norms".

(i) **Fuzzy "AND" :**

The fuzzy "and" is written as:

$$u_{A \cap B} = T(u_A(x), u_B(x)) \tag{4.64}$$

where μ_A is read as "the membership in class A" and μ_B is read as "the membership in class B". There are many ways to compute "and". The two most common are:

1. Zadeh - $\min(u_A(x), u_B(x))$ This technique, named after the inventor of fuzzy set theory simply computes the "and" by taking the minimum of the two (or more) membership values. This is the most common definition of the fuzzy "and".

2. Product - $u_a(x)$ times $u_b(x)$) This techniques computes the fuzzy "and" by multiplying the two membership values.

Both techniques have the following two properties:

$T(0, 0) = T(a, 0) = T(0, a) = 0$

$T(a, 1) = T(1, a) = a$

One of the most interesting things about both definitions is that they can also be used to compute the Boolean "and". Table 4.1 shows the Boolean "and" operation. Notice that both fuzzy "and" definitions also work for these numbers.

Input1 (*A*)	Input2 (*B*)	Output (*A* "and" *B*)
0	0	0
0	1	0
1	0	0
1	1	1

Table 4.1: The Boolean "and"

The fuzzy "and" is an extension of the Boolean "and" to numbers that are not just 0 or 1, but between 0 and 1.

(ii) **Fuzzy "OR" :**

The fuzzy "or" is written as:

$$u_{AUB} = T(u_A(x), u_B(x)) \tag{4.65}$$

Like the fuzzy "and", there are two techniques for computing the fuzzy "or":

1. Zadeh - $\max(u_A(x), u_B(x))$ This technique computes the fuzzy "or" by taking in account the maximum among the two (or more) membership values. This is the most common method of computing the fuzzy "or".

2. Product - $u_A(x) + u_B(x) - u_A(x) u_B(x)$ This technique uses the difference between the sum of the two (or more) membership values and the product of the membership values.

Both techniques have the following properties:

$$T(a, 0) = T(0, a) = a$$

$$T(a, 1) = T(1, a) = 1$$

Similar to the fuzzy "and", both definitions of the fuzzy "or" also can be used to compute the Boolean "or". Table 4.2 shows the Boolean "or" operation. Notice that both fuzzy "or" definitions also work for these numbers. The fuzzy "or" is an extension of the Boolean "or" to numbers that are not just 0 or 1, but between 0 and 1.

Input1 (A)	Input2 (B)	Output (A "or" B)
0	0	0
0	1	1
1	0	1
1	1	1

Table4.2: The Boolean "or"

4.10.1.1.4. Consequence

The consequence of a fuzzy rule is computed using two steps:

➢ Computing the rule strength by combining the fuzzified inputs using the fuzzy combination process discussed in section 4.11.1.1.3. This is shown in Figure 4.10. Notice in this example, the fuzzy "and" is used to combine the membership functions to compute the rule strength.

➢ Clipping the output membership function at the rule strength. Once again, refer to Figure 4.10 to see how this is done for a two input, two rule Mamdani FIS.

4.10.1.1.5. Combining Outputs into an Output Distribution

The outputs of all of the fuzzy rules must now be combined to obtain one fuzzy output distribution. This is usually, but not always, done by using the fuzzy "or". Figure 4.10 shows an example of this. The output membership functions shown on the right hand side of the figure are united using the fuzzy "or" to obtain the output distribution shown on the lower right corner of the figure.

4.10.1.1.6. Defuzzification of Output Distribution

In many instances, it is desired to come up with a single crisp output from a FIS. For instance, if one was trying to interpret an alphabet drawn by hand on a drawing tablet, ultimately the FIS would have to come up with a crisp number to tell the computer which letter was drawn. This crisp number is obtained in a process known as defuzzification. Popularly, there are two known techniques for defuzzifying:

1. Center of mass – Under this technique the output distribution found in section 4.7.1.1.5 is taken and its center of mass is determined, to come up with one crisp number. This is computed as follows:

$$z = \frac{\sum_{j=1}^{q} Z_j u_C(Z_j)}{\sum_{j=1}^{q} u_C(Z_j)}$$

where z is the center of mass and u_c is the membership in class c at value z_j. An example outcome of this computation is shown in figure 4.11.

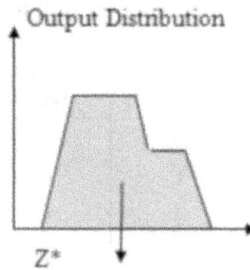

Fig.4.11: Defuzzification Using the Center of Mass

2. Mean of maximum –

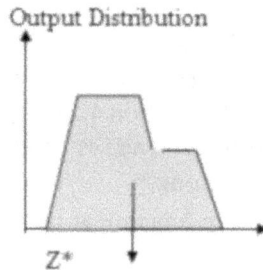

Fig.4.12: Defuzzification Using the Mean of Maximum

This technique takes the output distribution found in section 4.7.1.1.5 and finds its mean of maxima to come up with one crisp number. This is computed as follows:

$$Z = \sum_{j=1}^{l} z_j / l$$

where z is the mean of maximum, z_j is the point at which the membership function is maximum, and I is the number of times the output distribution reaches the maximum level. An example outcome of this computation is shown in figure 4.12.

4.10.1.1.7. Fuzzy Inputs

In summary, figure 4.10 shows a two input Mamdani FIS. It fuzzifies the two inputs by determining the intersection of the crisp input value with the input membership function. The minimum operator is used to compute the fuzzy "and" for uniting the two fuzzified inputs to obtain a rule strength. The output membership function is clipped at the rule strength. At the final step, the maximum operator is employed to compute the fuzzy "or" for summing the outputs of the two rules.

Figure 4.13 shows a modification of the Mamdani FIS where the input y_0 is fuzzy, not crisp. This can be used to handle the inaccuracies in the measurement. For instance, suppose we have to calculate the output of a pressure sensor; Even when exactly same pressure is applied, the sensor may have slightly different voltages. This uncertainty is modeled by the fuzzy input membership function. The fuzzy input function is united with the rule input membership function by employing the fuzzy "and" as illustrated in Figure 4.13.

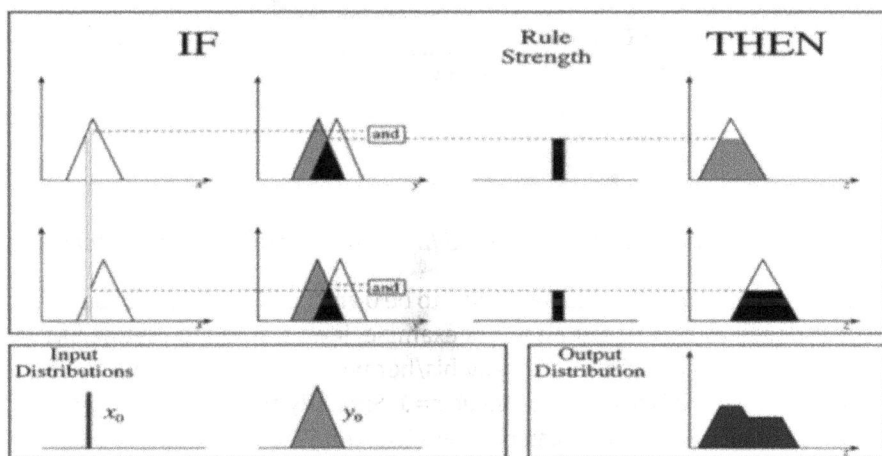

Fig.4.13: A two Input, two rule Mamdani FIS with a fuzzy input

4.10.1.2. Sugeno type FIS

The Sugeno FIS is quite similar to the Mamdani FIS discussed in section 4.11.1.1. The most basic difference is that the output result is not computed by adjusting the rule strength of an output membership function. Actually, in the Sugeno FIS no output membership function is present, instead the output is generated by multiplying each input by a constant and then summing up the results. The process is illustrated in Figure 4.14. "Rule strength" in this example is referred to as "degree of applicability" and the output is referred to as the "action". Also notice that there is no output distribution, only a "resulting action" which is the mathematical combination of the rule strengths (degree of applicability) and the outputs (actions).

One of the major limitations of the Sugeno FIS is that there is no genuine method for determining the coefficients, p, q, and r. Furthermore, the Sugeno produces only crisp outputs which may not be suitable for many applications, like HCI application. Here, the question arises; then how could we utilize a Sugeno FIS for such applications which requires fuzzy outputs? The reason is that there are algorithms which can be used to automatically optimize the Sugeno FIS.

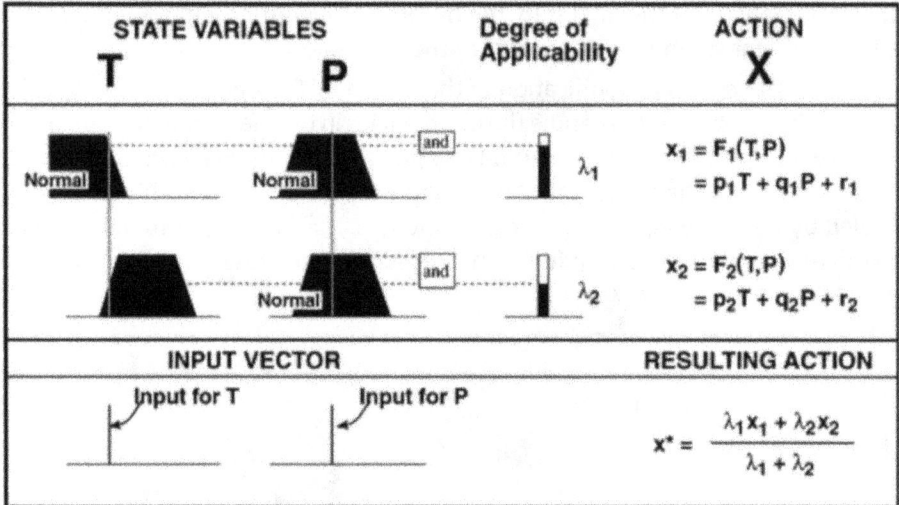

Fig.4.14: A two input, two rule Sugeno FIS (p_n, q_n, and r_n are user-defined constants)

In classification, p and q can be chosen to be 0 and r can be chosen to be a number that corresponds to a particular class. For example, if we wanted to use the EMG from a person's forearm to classify which way his/her wrist was bending, we could assign the class "bend inward" to obtain the value $r = 1$. Similarly, the class "bend outward" to obtain $r = 0$. Finally, we could assign the class "no bend" to obtain the value $r = 0.5$.

4.10.2. Mamdani Vs Sugeno method

The following are some final considerations about the two different methods.

Advantages of the Sugeno Method

➢   It is computationally efficient.

➢   It works well with linear techniques (e.g., PID control).

➢   It works well with optimization and adaptive techniques.

➢   It has guaranteed continuity of the output surface.

➢   It is well suited to mathematical analysis.

Advantages of the Mamdani Method

➤ It is intuitive.

➤ It has widespread acceptance.

➤ It is well suited to human input.

4.11. Hybrid Systems

A hybrid system or more precisely a hybrid intelligent system is one that combines at least two intelligent technologies. For example, combining a neural network with a fuzzy system results in a hybrid neuro-fuzzy system. The hybridization of fuzzy logic, neural networks and evolutionary computation forms the core of soft computing, an emerging approach to building hybrid intelligent systems capable of reasoning and learning in an uncertain and imprecise environment. Neural Networks mimic our ability to learn from past experiences and adapt according to circumstances; Fuzzy Logic addresses to imprecision and vagueness in input and output; Genetic algorithms are inspired by biological evolution, can systemize random search and reach to optimum characteristics.

Although words are less precise than numbers, precision carries a high cost. We use words when there is a tolerance for imprecision. Soft computing exploits the tolerance for uncertainty and imprecision to achieve greater tractability and robustness, and lower the cost of solutions. We also use words when the available data is not precise enough to use numbers. This is often the case with complex problems, and while "hard" computing fails to produce any solution, soft computing is still capable of finding good solutions.

Each of the above mentioned technologies have provided efficient solutions to many problems belonging to different domains. However, each of these technologies have their own advantages and disadvantages, it is upto us, to hybridize them in the right way so as to overcome the weakness of one with the strength of other.

Lotfi Zadeh is reputed to have said that a good hybrid would be "British Police, German Mechanics, French Cuisine, Swiss Banking and Italian Love". But "British Cuisine, German Police, French Mechanics, Italian Banking and Swiss Love" would be a bad one. Likewise, a hybrid intelligent system can be good or bad – it depends on which components constitute the hybrid. So our goal is to select the right components for building a good hybrid system.

Typically, a hybrid system is classified into three:

➤ **Sequential hybrid system:** the technologies are used in pipelining fashion.

➤ **Auxiliary hybrid system:** the one technology acts as the subroutine for other technology.

➤ **Embedded hybrid system:** All the participating technologies are totally linked with each other.

4.11.1. Sequential Hybrid System

In sequential hybrid system, the participating technologies are used in pipelined fashion, i.e. output of one technology becomes the input of another and so on. However, since an integrated combination of technologies is not present, this type of hybridization is referred to as the weakest of all hybridization techniques.

Example: A Genetic algorithm preprocessor obtains the optimal parameters for different instances of a problem and hands over the preprocessed data to a neural network for further processing.

4.11.2. Auxiliary Hybrid System

In Auxiliary hybrid system, one technology acts as the subroutine of other technology, and this subroutine process or manipulate the required information. The second technology processes the information provided by the first and hands it over for further use. This techniques, seems to be better than the sequential hybridization.

Example: A Neuro-Genetic system in which a neural network employs the genetic algorithm to optimize its structural parameters that defines its architecture.

4.11.3. Embedded Hybrid System

The participating technologies are integrated in such a manner that they appear intertwind. The technologies are so closely linked to each other that it would appear that the technologies can-not be used individually for solving any problem.

Example: A Neuro-fuzzy hybrid system, may have a neural network that receives fuzzy inputs, processes on it and produce fuzzy outputs.

4.11.4. Neural Expert Systems

The objective of *Expert systems* is to model human reasoning, and they employ logical inferences and decision trees for the same task. Neural network depends on parallel data processing and emphasize on modelling a human brain.

Expert systems view the brain as a mystery-box. Neural network tries to mimic its ability to learn by looking at its structure and functions. In a *rule-based* expert system knowledge is represented by *IF-THEN* production rules. Knowledge in neural networks is stored as synaptic weights among neurons.

In **expert systems,** knowledge can be distributed into individual rules and the user can easily observe and interpret the piece of knowledge applied by the system. In neural networks, we cannot consider a particular synaptic weight as an individual piece of knowledge. The knowledge is lodged in the entire network; it cannot be separated into individual pieces, and any change in the synaptic weight may lead to imprecise results. A neural network is, actually, a **mystery-box** for its user.

A hybrid system that integrates a neural network and a rule-based expert system is referred to as a **neural expert system** (or a **connectionist expert system**). Below figure 4.15 shows the basic block diagram of a neural expert system.

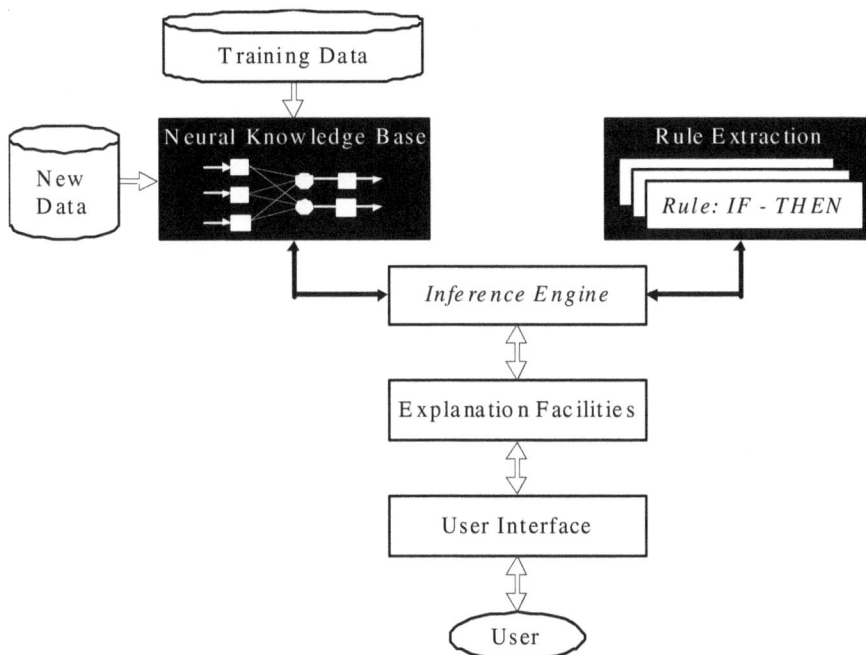

Fig.4.15: Basic structure of a neural expert system

Inference engine is the core of a neural expert system. Its function is to control the information flow in the system and to initiate the deduction over the neural knowledge base, ensuring **approximate reasoning**.

4.11.4.1. Approximate reasoning

In a rule-based expert system, the function of the inference engine is to compare the condition part of each rule with the data given in the database. If the IF part of the rule matches the data present in the database, the rule is fired and the antecedents part i.e., THEN part is executed. Precise matching is essential for inference engine as it cannot deal with noisy or incomplete data.

Instead of the knowledge base, the neural expert system utilizes a trained neural network. Because, in case of a NN, the input data is not required to match accurately to the data that was used in network training. This ability is what we called as approximate reasoning.

4.11.4.2. Rule extraction

Neurons in the network are interconnected through links, each of which exhibits a synaptic weight attached to it. Each synaptic weight in a trained neural network determine the strength or prominence of the associated neuron inputs.

4.11.4.3. The neural knowledge base

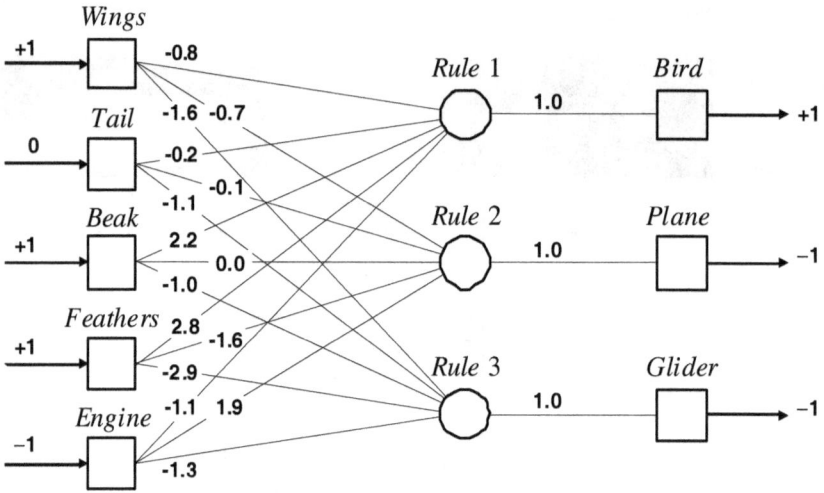

Fig.4.16: An example for explaining the neural knowledge base

If we set each input of the input layer to either +1 (true), −1 (false), or 0 (unknown), we can provide a semantic interpretation for the activation of any output neuron. For instance, if the object has *Wings* (+1), *Beak* (+1) and *Feathers* (+1), but does not have *Engine* (−1), then we could say that the given object is *Bird* (+1):

$$X_{Rule1} = 1.(-0.8) + 0.(-0.2) + 1.2 \cdot 2 + 1.2 \cdot 8 + (-1).(-1.1) = 5.3 > 0$$

$$Y_{Rule1} = Y_{Bird} = +1$$

We can similarly conclude that this object is not *Plane*:

$$X_{Rule2} = 1.(-0.7) + 0.(-0.1) + 1.0 \cdot 0 + 1.(-1.6) + (-1).1.9 = -4.2 < 0$$

$$Y_{Rule2} = Y_{Plane} = -1$$

and not *Glider*:

$$X_{Rule3} = 1.(-0.6) + 0.(-1.1) + 1.(-1.0) + 1.(-2.9) + (-1).(-1.3) = -4.2 < 0$$

$$Y_{Rule3} = Y_{Glider} = -1$$

By associating a corresponding question with each input neuron, we could enable the system to prompt the user for initial values of the input variables:

Neuron: Wings

Question: Does the object exhibits wings?

Neuron: Tail

Question: Does the object exhibits a tail?

Neuron: Beak

Question: Does the object exhibits a beak?

Neuron: Feathers

Question: Does the object exhibits feathers?

Neuron: Engine

Question: Does the object exhibits an engine?

An inference can be made if the known net weighted input to a neuron is greater than the sum of the absolute values of the weights of the unknown inputs.

$$\sum_{i=1}^{n} x_i w_i > \sum_{j=1}^{n} |w_j| \qquad (4.66)$$

where $i \in$ known, $j \notin$ known and n is the number of neuron inputs.

4.11.5. Neuro-fuzzy systems

Neuro-fuzzy hybrid systems are the combination of Neural Networks along with Fuzzy systems. *Fuzzy logic* and neural networks are natural complementary tools in building intelligent systems. While neural networks are low-level computational structures that perform well when dealing with raw data, fuzzy logic deals with reasoning on a higher level, using linguistic information acquired from domain experts.

Merit of Neural Networks

➢ Can model complex non-linear relationships and are suitable for classification phenomenon in predetermined classes.

Demerit of Neural Networks

➢ Neural networks output precision is often limited to least square errors; the training time required is quite large; the training data has to be chosen over entire range where the variables are expected to change.

Merit of Fuzzy Logic

➢ Fuzzy logic systems are efficient at handling imprecise inputs and outputs defined by fuzzy sets, and thus provide greater flexibility in formulating detail system description.

Integrated neuro-fuzzy systems have the potential to extend the capability of system beyond either of these technologies applied individually. They can combine the parallel computation and learning abilities of neural networks with the human-like knowledge representation and explanation abilities of fuzzy systems. As a result, neural networks become more transparent, while fuzzy systems become capable of learning.

A *neuro-fuzzy system* is a neural network which is functionally equivalent to a fuzzy inference model. It can be trained to develop IF-THEN fuzzy rules and determine membership functions for input and output variables of the system. Expert knowledge can be incorporated into the structure of the neuro-fuzzy system. At the same time, the connectionist structure avoids fuzzy inference, which entails a substantial computational burden. The integrated system found useful in:

➢ Accomplishing mathematical relationships among many variables in a complex dynamic process,

➢ Performing mapping with some degree of imprecision.

➢ Controlling non-linear systems to an extent non possible with conventional linear control systems.

There are specifically two methods to perform Neuro-Fuzzy hybridization:

➢ One is to provide NNs with fuzzy capabilities, thereby increasing the network's expressiveness and flexibility to adapt to uncertain environments.

➢ Second, is to apply neuronal learning capabilities to fuzzy systems so that the fuzzy systems become more adaptive to changing environments. This method is called NN driven fuzzy reasoning.

The structure of a neuro-fuzzy system is similar to a multi-layer neural network. In general, a neuro-fuzzy system has input and output layers, and three hidden layers that represent membership functions and fuzzy rules.

Each layer in the neuro-fuzzy system is associated with a specific step in the fuzzy inference process.

Layer 1 represents the **input layer**. Each neuron present in this layer conveys external crisp signals directly to the next layer. That is,

$$y_i^{(1)} = x_i^{(1)} \qquad\qquad\qquad (4.67)$$

Layer 2 is the **fuzzification layer**. Neurons in this layer represent fuzzy sets used in the antecedents of fuzzy rules. A fuzzification neuron receives a crisp input and determines the degree to which this input belongs to the neuron's fuzzy set.

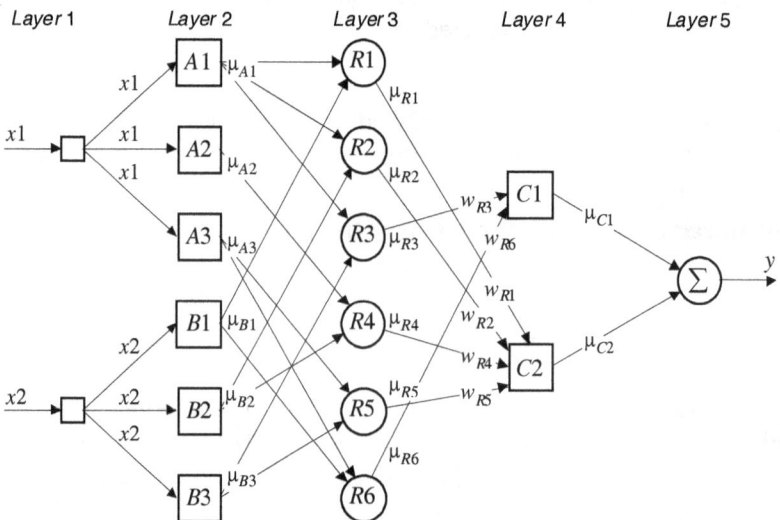

Fig.4.17: a neuro-fuzzy system

The activation function of a membership neuron is set to the function that specifies the neuron's fuzzy set. We use triangular sets, and therefore, the activation functions for the neurons in *Layer 2* are set to the **triangular membership functions**. A triangular membership function can be specified by two parameters $\{a, b\}$ as follows:

$$
y_i^{(2)} = \begin{cases}
0, & \text{if } x_i^{(2)} \le a - \dfrac{b}{2} \\[2mm]
1 - \dfrac{2\left|x_i^{(2)} - a\right|}{b} & \text{if } a - \dfrac{b}{2} < x_i^{(2)} < a + \dfrac{b}{2} \\[2mm]
0, & \text{if } x_i^{(2)} \ge a + \dfrac{b}{2}
\end{cases}
$$

**Layer 3** is the **fuzzy rule layer**. Each neuron in this layer corresponds to a single fuzzy rule. A fuzzy rule neuron receives inputs from the fuzzification neurons that represent fuzzy sets in the rule antecedents. For instance, neuron *R1*, which corresponds to *Rule* 1, receives inputs from neurons *A1* and *B1*.

In a neuro-fuzzy system, intersection can be implemented by the **product operator**. Thus, the output of neuron *i* in *Layer 3* is obtained as:

$$
Y_i^{(3)} = X_{1i}^{(3)} \times x_{2i}^{(3)} \times \ldots \times x_{ki}^{(3)}
$$

$$
y_{R1}^{(3)} = \mu_{A1} \times \mu_{B1} = \mu_{R1}
$$

Triangular activation functions

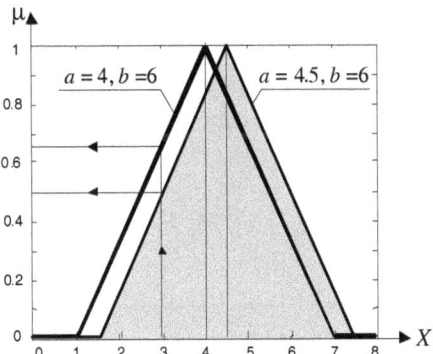

(a) Effect of parameter a.   (b) Effect of parameter b.

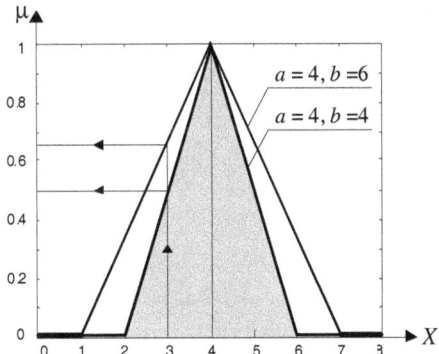

Fig.4.18: Triangular activation functions

**Layer 4** is the **output membership layer**. Neurons in this layer represent fuzzy sets used in the consequent of fuzzy rules.

An output membership neuron combines all its inputs by using the fuzzy operation **union**. This operation can be implemented by the **probabilistic OR**. That is, the value of μ_{C1} represents the integrated firing strength of fuzzy rule neurons *R3* and *R6*.

$$y_i^{(4)} = x_{1i}^{(4)} \oplus x_{2i}^{(4)} \oplus \ldots \oplus x_{ki}^{(4)}$$

$$y_{C1}^{(3)} = \mu_{R1} \oplus \mu_{R1} = \mu_{C1}$$

Layer 5 is the **defuzzification layer**. Each neuron in this layer represents a single output of the neuro-fuzzy system. It takes the output fuzzy sets clipped by the respective integrated firing strengths and combines them into a single fuzzy set.

Neuro-fuzzy systems can apply standard defuzzification methods, including the centroid technique. We will use the **sum-product composition** method.

The sum-product composition calculates the crisp output as the weighted average of the centroids of all output membership functions. For example, the weighted average of the centroids of the clipped fuzzy sets C1 and C2 is calculated as,

$$y = [(\mu_{C1} \times a_{C1} \times b_{C1}) + (\mu_{C2} \times a_{C2} \times b_{C2})] / [(\mu_{C1} \times b_{C1}) + (\mu_{C2} \times b_{C2})]$$

4.11.5.1. Learning

A neuro-fuzzy system is a multi-layer neural network, and thus standard learning algorithms to develop neural networks are applicable to it, including the back-propagation algorithm.

When a training input-output example is applied to the system, the back-propagation algorithm determines the system output response and compares it with the desired or target output of the training example. As the name suggests, the error is propagated backwards along the network; from the output layer towards the input layer. As the error is propagated, the neuron activation functions are modified. Necessary modifications are determined be differentiating the activation functions of the neurons.

Here is a demonstration of how a neuro-fuzzy system handles a simple example. The five-rule neuro-fuzzy system is trained by the dataset as shown below.

Five-rule neuro-fuzzy system

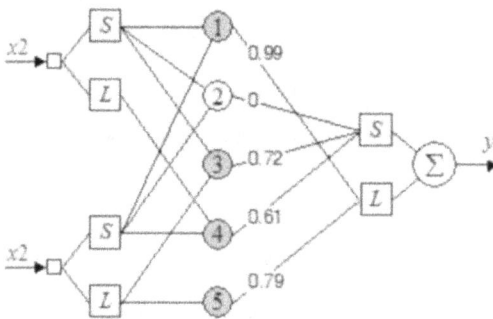

(a) Five-rule system.   (b) Training for 50 epochs.

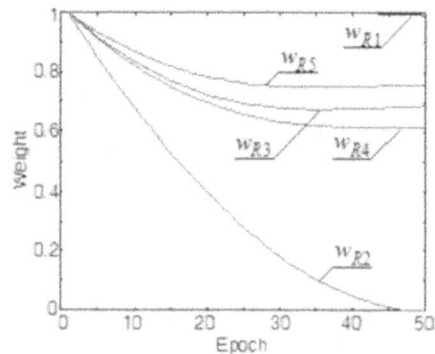

Fig.4.19: Illustration of five-rule neuro-fuzzy system

Suppose that fuzzy IF-THEN rules are applied to the system structure. *Past* or existing knowledge can dramatically accelerate the system training.

Besides, if the quality of training data is poor, the only solution comes with the expert knowledge. However, probabilities of experts making mistakes can-not be neglected, and this results in false or redundant rules used in a neuro-fuzzy system. Therefore, it is highly recommended that a neuro-fuzzy system should also be capable of identifying redundant rules.

Given input and output linguistic values, a neuro-fuzzy system can automatically generate a complete set of fuzzy IF-THEN rules.

Let us construct a system for the XOR example. This system consists of $2^2 \times 2 = 8$ rules. As expert knowledge is not incorporated in the system this time, we set all initial weights between *Layer* 3 and *Layer* 4 to 0.5. After training we could eliminate all rules whose certainty factors are less than a sufficiently small number, say 0.1. As a result, we obtain the same set of four fuzzy IF-THEN rules that represents the XOR operation.

Eight-rule neuro-fuzzy system

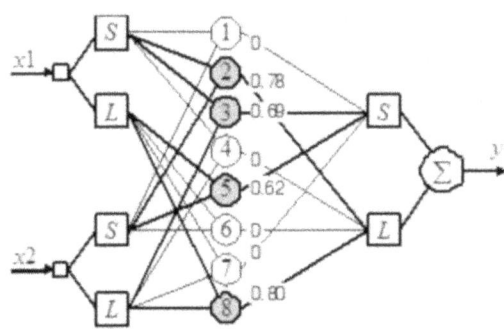

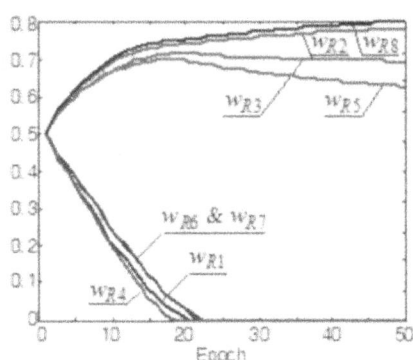

(*a*) Eight-rule system. (*b*) Training for 50 epochs.

Fig.4.20: Illustration of eight-rule neuro-fuzzy system

4.11.5.2. Summary

➢ The hybridization of fuzzy logic and neural networks constitutes a formidable means for designing intelligent systems.

➢ Domain knowledge can be applied to a neuro-fuzzy system by human experts in the form of linguistic variables and fuzzy rules.

➢ When a representative set of examples is available, a neuro-fuzzy system can automatically modify it into well defined fuzzy IF-THEN rules, and thus reduce our dependency on expert knowledge when building intelligent systems.

4.11.6. Neuro-Genetic Hybrid

The Neural Networks and Genetic Algorithms represent two distinct methodologies.

➢ **Neural Networks:** can learn various tasks from examples, classify phenomena and model nonlinear relationships.

➢ **Genetic Algorithms:** have offered themselves as potential candidates for the optimization of parameters of NN.

➢ **Integration of GAs and NNs** has turned out to be useful.

- Genetically evolved nets have reported comparable results against their conventional counterparts.

- The gradient descent learning algorithms have reported difficulties in learning the topology of the networks whose weights they optimize.

- GA based algorithms have provided encouraging results especially with regard to face recognition, animal control, and others.

- Genetic algorithms encode the parameters of NNs as a string of properties of the network, i.e. chromosomes. A large population of chromosomes representing many possible parameters sets, for the given NN, is generated.

- GA-NN is also known as GANN have the ability to locate the neighborhood of the optimal solution quicker than other conventional search strategies.

- The drawbacks of GANN algorithms are : large amount of memory required to handle and manipulate chromosomes for a given network; the question is whether this problem scales as the size of the networks become large.

One of the examples of neuro-genetic hybridization is GA based Back Propagation Network, which we will discuss in detail in the upcoming chapter-5, because prior to it a basic understanding of GA is essential.

4.11.7. Fuzzy-Genetic Hybrid

Fuzzy systems have been integrated with GAs. The fuzzy systems like NNs (feed forward) are universal approximators in the sense that they exhibit the capability to approximate general nonlinear functions to any desired degree of accuracy. The adjustments of system parameters called for in the process, so that the system output matches the training data, have been tackled using GAs. Several parameters which a fuzzy system is involved with like input/output variables and the membership function that define the fuzzy systems, have been optimized using GAs.

An example of Fuzzy-Genetic Hybrid is the Fuzzy logic controlled GAs, which we will discuss in the upcoming sections, but before switching to this core topic, let us first learn about fuzzy logic controllers.

4.12. Fuzzy Logic Controllers

The assumption that all engineering system modeling can be reduced to an exact set of algebraic and differential equations has been challenged by research that recognizes that measurements process modeling and control can never be exact for real complex problems. There is a necessity to reach advanced control technologies that are capable of:

> Managing uncertainty and expert knowledge
> Accommodating significant changes in the plant and its environment.
> Incorporating techniques for learning either uncertain information, or an adaptive environment, and techniques of combining existing knowledge with a learning process.

The main problem is to represent and compute processes that are imprecisely described and are controlled by humans without recourse to mathematical models, algorithms or a deep knowledge of the physical knowledge involved. Fuzzy Logic plays an effective conceptual frame work for dealing with the problem of knowledge representation in an environment of uncertainty and vagueness. One of the most successful applications of FL are the Fuzzy Logic Controllers (FLCs) or Fuzzy Inference Systems (FIS). FLCs implement an expert operator's approximate reasoning process in the selection of a control action.

Another problem is to handle the adaptive environment, i.e. to develop such systems that can efficiently involve themselves in learning even with the continually adaptive process parameters. FL is a powerful tool for knowledge representation in computational intelligence. Whereas, adaptive control, learning and self organization are better handled by employing Genetic Algorithms (GAs). GAs are search algorithms that use operations found in natural genetics to guide the trek through a search space. These are theoretically proven to provide robust search in complex spaces, offering a valid approach to problems requiring efficient and valid search.

FL and GAs are two important tools for modeling and managing intelligent and automatic control systems, which are able of supporting above mentioned features. Each of them have their own strengths, as in the case of FL the ability to handle non-linearity and explicit knowledge expression; on the other hand the learning capability and global and local search approach of GAs. The integration between both of them may provide useful results. Here we will discuss their integration in Fuzzy Logic Controllers.

4.12.1. Description of Fuzzy Logic Controllers

The purpose of any controller is to look periodically the values of the state variables of the controlled system and to obtain the values associated to their control variables by means of the relationships existing between them. If those relationships can be expressed in a mathematical way, it is not too much difficult to design the controller. The problem exists, as it happens in a lot of real world nonlinear systems with complex dynamics; there is not a mathematical model to represent their existing relationships.

In the early 40's and 50's, differential equations were used to mathematically model many dynamic systems. This method was found to be the foundation of Control Theory, which in addition with Transform Theory provided an extremely powerful means of analyzing and designing control systems. Unfortunately, in too many instances this approach could not be sustained because many systems have unknown parameters and highly complex and non-linear characteristics that make them not to be amenable to the full force of mathematical analysis as dictated by the Control Theory.

Over the last few years the application of Artificial Intelligence techniques has become a research topic in the domain of processes control, to overcome the previous drawbacks and to obtain efficient controllers which utilizes the human experience in a more related form than the conventional mathematical approach. This new field of process control is called Expert Control, and Fuzzy Logic Control is its main topic. FLCs were introduced by Mamdani and Assilian, and are now considered as one of the most important applications of the Fuzzy Set Theory suggested by Zadeh in 1965, introducing the concept of Fuzzy set. FLCs are knowledge based controllers that are usually derived from a knowledge acquisition process or are automatically synthesized from a self organizing control architecture.

While conventional linear controllers can be viewed as a hyperplane in a N+1 dimensional space, mapping an Nth dimensional state vector to a control action, FLCs, on the other hand, typically define a non linear mapping from the system's state space to the control space. Thus, we could visualize the results of a FLC as a nonlinear control surface reflecting the process operator's prior knowledge.

A FLC is comprised of four major components:

➢ Knowledge Base, comprises the information given by the process operator in form of linguistic control rules.

➢ Fuzzification Interface, for transforming the crisp data into fuzzy sets.

➢ Inference System, defines mapping from input fuzzy sets into output fuzzy sets.

➢ Defuzzification interface, that translates the fuzzy control action so obtained to a real control action using a defuzzification method.

For more detailed description of FLC, refer section 4.11.

4.12.2. Description of the Genetic Algorithm

GAs are general purpose search algorithms that use principles inspired by natural population genetics to evolve solutions to problems. The basic idea is to maintain a population of knowledge structures that evolves over time through a process of competition and controlled variation. Each structure in the population represents a candidate solution to the concrete problem and has an associated fitness to determine in the process of competition which structures are used to form new ones. The new ones are created using genetic operators such as crossover and mutation. GAs have had a great measures of success in search and optimization problems. The reason of great part of its success is their ability to exploit accumulating information about an initially unknown search space in order to bias subsequent search into useful subspaces, i.e., their robustness. This is their key feature, overcoat in large, complex and poorly understood search spaces, where the classical search tools are inappropriate, offering a valid tool to problems requiring efficient and effective search.

A GA starts with a population of randomly generated solutions, chromosomes and advances toward better solutions by applying genetic operators, modeled on the genetic processes occurring in nature. In these algorithms we maintain a population of solutions for a given problem; this population undergoes evolution in a form of natural selection. In each generation, relatively good solutions reproduce to give offsprings that replace the relatively bad solutions which die. An evolution or fitness function plays the role of the environment to distinguish between good and bad solutions. The process of going from the current population to the next population constitutes one generation in the execution of a genetic algorithm.

Although there are many possible variants of the basic GA, the fundamental underlying operates on a population of chromosomes or individuals (representing possible solutions to the problem) and consists of three operations:

1.   Evaluation of individual fitness,
2.   Formation of a gene pool (intermediate population) and
3.   Recombination and mutation.

Genetic Algorithms will be discussed in more details in the upcoming chapters.

4.13.   Design of Fuzzy Logic Controllers using Genetic Algorithms

When we try to design a FLC, two problems arise: first, how to establish the structure of the controller and, second, how to set numerical values of the controller parameters. The GAs have been successfully applied in these problems, learning controller structure as well as tuning controller parameters. In fact, the GAs search the fuzzy control rules (FCR) base that verify the optimality conditions specified by their fitness function according to the required features. In the following section some proposals according the above settled aspects are discussed.

4.13.1.   Tuning controller parameters

A FLC contains a number of sets of parameters that can be altered to modify the controller performance. They are:

➢   The scaling factors for each variable,
➢   the fuzzy sets representing the meaning of linguistic values,
➢   the if-then rules.

Each of these sets of parameters has been used as the controller parameters to be adapted in different adaptive FLCs.

GAs have been used to modify the fuzzy set definitions, to alter the shapes of the fuzzy sets defining the meaning of the linguistic terms, to determine the membership functions that produce maximum control performance according to the inference system (fuzzy implication and conjunctive operator) and the defuzzification strategy used. That is, to tune the FCR set, in order to make the FLC behaves as closely as possible to the operator or expert behavior. This method relies on having a set of training data against which the controller is tuned.

The tuning method using GAs fits the membership functions of the fuzzy rules dealing with the parameters of the membership functions, minimizing a square error function defined by means of an input-output data set for evaluation.

Recent works have been centered on the use of GAs altering the set definitions so that the FLC matches a suitable set of reference data as closely as possible.

A chromosome represents one possible solution to the problem, that is, one possible FCR base . The fitness function itself depends on the task of the FLC, usually the square error can be considered, then the chromosome is tested by evaluating the training data set.

4.13.2. Learning controller structure

For learning the controller structure different hypotheses can be considered, either to work with a determined variables domain or to manage rules with a free structure. According to these two possible models, different GA learning processes have been proposed.

4.13.2.1. Determined variables domain

We assume that each universe, U, contains a number of referential sets having their linguistic meaning which form a finite set of fuzzy sets on U. Membership functions are defined to represent the developer's conception of the linguistic variables. For instance if X is a variable on U for temperature, then one may define A_1 as "low temperature", A_i $(1 < i < r)$ as "medium temperature" and A_r as "high temperature". These referential fuzzy sets are characterized by their membership functions $A_i(u) : U \rightarrow [0; 1]$; $i = 1, \ldots\ldots,$ r. To ensure the performance of the fuzzy model and provide an uniform basis for further study it is required that all referential sets should be normal convex and satisfy the following completeness condition:

$$\forall u \in U \; \exists j, \; 0 \leq r, \text{ such that } A_j(u) \geq \delta$$

δ where is a fixed threshold, the completeness degree of the universes.

4.13.2.2. Free variables structure

Rules with a free structure, without an initial fuzzy set referential, can be also considered.

The rules have the form

R_i : IF x_1 is A_i and ... and x_n is A_{in} THEN y_1 is B_i and ... and y_m is B_{im}

where $x_1 \ldots\ldots\ldots, x_n$ and $y_1, \ldots.., y_m$ are the process state variables and the control variables

respectively, and $A_1, \ldots.., A_{in}, B_i, \ldots.., B_{im}$ are fuzzy sets in the universes of discourse $U_1, \ldots., U_n, V_1, \ldots.. V_m$.

These fuzzy sets are characterized by their membership functions

$A_{ij}(B_{ih}) : U_j(V_h) \rightarrow [0; 1]$; $j = 1, \ldots. n$; $h = 1, \ldots.. m$

We can consider every fuzzy set associated to a normalized trapezoidal membership function. Next we describe two of the GA learning processes proposed in the literature for each one of the variables structure.

4.13.3. GA learning processes with determined variables domain

The method proposed by Karr

The rule set is formed as follows. Membership functions were defined to represent the developer's conception of the linguistic variables (fuzzy sets) and these variables made the formation of the rule set a straightforward task. The selection of the decision variables and the fuzzy sets describing required a number of rules n. From all combination of antecedent labels, one action must be found via GAs. Considering seven fuzzy sets describing the control variables, the entire set of possible actions for one rule was represented as a three-bit string (000 represented action 1, 001 represented action 2, and so on). Because n rules were possible, a string of length 3n represents every possible rule set for the FLC.

Once an acceptable rule set was learned with a GA, the selection of high-performance membership functions with the rule set is carried out using the above described tuning process.

The method proposed by Thrift

The method proposed by Thrift is similar to the above proposed by Karr, except that Thrift introduced a new possible value for the consequent of rules, the label " ". The " " symbol indicates that there is no fuzzy set entry at a position that it appears. A chromosome is formed from the decision table by going row wise and producing a string of numbers from the code set.

In this way, during the learning process it is determined the number of rules necessary in the control process because the rules with the consequent label " " can be eliminated.

The codification of the solutions is different of the above proposal. Each rule has assigned a gene taking integer numbers. There exist as many genes as possible combinations of the state variable labels. The range of the genes from 0 to m includes a code for the label " " as possible value of a gene. There are particular features of the GA based on the coding strategy described above. A mutation operator changes a fuzzy code either up or down a level, or to the blank code (if it is already blank, then it chooses a non-blank code at random). The crossover operator is the standard two-point crossover.

4.13.4. GA learning processes with free rules structure

The Method proposed by Cooper and Vidal [Coo93]

In contrast to prior genetic fuzzy systems which require every input-output combination to be enumerated, they propose a novel encoding scheme which maintains only those rules necessary to control the target system.

They defined a special GA where mutations include inversion of the copied bit and the addition or deletion of an entire rule. These latter two mutations permit the size of a system's FCR base to evolve. The cycle of evaluation and reproduction continues for a predetermined number of generations or until an acceptable performance level is achieved.

The membership function for each variable is a triangle characterized by the location of its center and the half-length of its base. A single rule, therefore, consists of the concatenation of the one-byte unsigned characters (assuming values from 0 to 255) specifying the centers and half-lengths of the membership functions. The rule descriptions for a single fuzzy system are then concatenated into a single bit string where the number of rules is not restricted.

To be meaningful, the genetic paradigm requires that the rules in the two strings be aligned so that similar rules are combined with each other. Simply by combining the strings in the order they appear it does not preserve much information about either system and produces nearly random results, rather as a child system that performs in a manner similar to its parents.

Therefore, before reproduction, both strings must be aligned so that the centers of the input variables match as closely as possible. The most closely matching rules are combined first, followed by the next most closely matching rules from those that remain and so on. Any rules forming a longer string that is not matched are added at the end.

The method proposed by Herrera et al.

The proposed learning fuzzy control rules process is based on the use of GAs under the following hypotheses:

➤ There is some linguistic information from the experience of the human controller but linguistic rules alone are usually not enough for designing a successful control system or could not be available.

➤ There is some numerical information from sampled input-output (state-control) pairs that are recorded experimentally.

➤ There is some numerical information from sampled input-output (state-control) pairs that are recorded experimentally.

➤ The combination of these two kinds of information may be sufficient for a successful design of a FCR base. v· We include the possibility of not having any linguistic information and having complete numerical information.

According to the aforementioned hypothesis a learning process is designed according to the following goals:

➤ to develop a generating FCR process from numerical data pairs; and

➤ to develop a general approach combining both kinds of information, linguistic information and fuzzy control rules obtained by the generating process, into a common framework using both simultaneously and cooperatively to solve the control design problem.

In order to reach these goals, it is proposed a methodology based on the design of the three following components:

(a)   a generating fuzzy rules process of desirable fuzzy rules able to include the complete knowledge of the set of examples,

(b)   a combining information and simplifying rules process, which finds the final set of fuzzy rules able to approximate the input-output behavior of a real system,

(c)   a tuning process of the final set of rules, all of them developed by means of GAs As it is possible to have some linguistic IF THEN rules given by an expert, it is used a linguistic fuzzy rules structure to represent them. On other hand, there are sampled input-output pairs and to generate the fuzzy rules covering these examples is used a free fuzzy rules structure. Then both types of rules are combined, applying a simplified method based on a GA, and generally a tuning method is applied over the simplified set of rules.

The generating fuzzy rules process consists of a generating method of desirable fuzzy rules from examples using GAs together with a covering method of the set of examples.

➢   The generating method of fuzzy rules is developed by means of a real coded GA (RCGA) where a chromosome represents a fuzzy rule and it is evaluated by means of a frequency method. The RCGA finds the best rule in every running over the set of examples according to the following features which will be included in the fitness function of the GA.

➢   The covering method is developed as an iterative process. It permits to obtain a set of fuzzy rules covering the set of examples. In each iteration, it runs the generating method, it chooses the best chromosome (rule), assigns to every example the relative covering value and removes the examples with a covering value greater than predefined value.

Because we can obtain two similar rules in the generating process or one rule similar to another given by an expert, it is necessary to combine and simplify the complete set of rules for obtaining the final set of rules. Finally, the tuning method presented in Her95a] is applied over the simplified set of rules.

4.14.   Applications of Fuzzy logic

During the past several years, many applications of FLCs have been developed successfully. FLCs have been proved to superior in performance to conventional systems in many applications. It should be noted that the first industrial application was the cement kiln controller developed by the Danish cement plant manufacturer F.L. Smith in 1979. Some of other more recent applications are water treatment, combustion control system for a refuse incineration plant, Japanese sake fermentation control, elevator control, highway tunnel ventilation control system, automatic train operation system, container crane operation system, fully automatic washing machine, vacuum cleaner, video equipment, recuperative turbo-shaft engine control, locomotive wheel slip control, steam turbine cycling, power electronics control, heat exchange, warm water process control, activated sludge waste water treatment, traffic junction, aircraft flight control, turning process, robot control, model-car parking and turning, automobile speed control, nuclear reactor control, fuzzy memory devices, fuzzy computer, water purification process control, control of a liquid level rig, automobile transmission control, gasoline refinery catalytic reformer control etc.

Review Questions

1. Write a short note on Fuzzy Logic and its consequences in artificial intelligence.
2. Explain Fuzzy sets, and highlight the points, how these are different from the classical sets.
3. Describe briefly the set-theoretic operations and various membership functions.
4. Write a short note on Extension principle, along with the monotonic and non-monotonic functions.
5. What do you mean my Fuzzy – relations? Explain operations on fuzzy relations and properties.
6. Briefly explain Fuzzy if-then rules, and summarize the procedure of interpretation using them, also explain Fuzzy reasoning.
7. Describe Fuzzy inference systems, along with Mamdani type and Sugeno type FIS,
8. What are hybrid systems, explain different types of hybridization, and how it is useful in artificial intelligence.
9. Explain Fuzzy Logic controlled genetic algorithm.

CHAPTER 5

The Evolutionary Computation

"Some people would claim that things like love, joy and beauty belong to a different category from science and can't be described in scientific terms, but I think they can now be explained by the theory of evolution."

-Stephen Hawking
Theoretical, physicist, cosmologist and author

"It is not the strongest or the most intelligent who will survive but those who can best manage change."

-Leon C. Megginson
Professor Emeritus

"There's almost no food that isn't genetically modified. Genetic modification is the basis of all evolution. Things change because our planet is subjected to a lot of radiation, which causes DNA damage, which gets repaired, but results in mutations, which create a ready mixture of plants that people can choose from to improve agriculture."

-Nina Fedoroff
Professor of life sciences and biotechnology

The third most important aspect of soft computing is Evolutionary Computation. As we know that, today's intelligence of humans is not just a one night process, rather it is a journey of millions of years from apes to homo-sapiens, which passed through millions of adaptations in the environment and living conditions. In chase of building human like intelligence in the world of artificial intelligence, scientists tried to inbuilt this natural evolution in artificial intelligence too, and this lead to the development of evolutionary computation. Evolutionary computation, offers practical advantages to the researcher facing difficult optimization problems. These advantages are multi-fold, including the simplicity of the approach, its robust response to changing circumstance, its flexibility, and many other facets. The evolutionary approach can be applied to problems where heuristic solutions are not available or generally lead to unsatisfactory results. As a result, evolutionary computation has received increased interest, particularly with regards to the manner in which they maybe applied for practical problem solving.

In this chapter, we review the development of the field of evolutionary computations from standard genetic algorithms to genetic programming, passing by evolution strategies and evolutionary programming. For each of these orientations, we identify the main differences from the others. In nature, evolution is mostly determined by natural selection or different individuals competing for resources in the environment. Those individuals that are better are more likely to survive and propagate their genetic material. The genetic information (genome) encoding is done in a way that admits asexual reproduction which results in offspring that are genetically identical to the parent. Sexual reproduction allows some exchange and re-ordering of chromosomes, producing offspring that contain a combination of information from each parent. This is the recombination operation, which is often referred to as crossover because of the way strands of chromosomes cross over during the exchange. The diversity in the population is achieved by mutation.

5.1. Evolutionary Algorithm

Evolutionary algorithms are worldwide nowadays, have proved its caliber and successfully applied to numerous application, and handling problems from different domains, including optimization, automatic programming, machine learning, operations research, bioinformatics, and social systems. In many cases the mathematical function, which describes the problem is not known and the values at certain parameters are obtained from simulations. Contrary to many other optimization techniques an important advantage of evolutionary algorithms is they can efficiently handle multimodal functions.

Usually grouped under the term evolutionary computation or evolutionary algorithms, we find the domains of genetic algorithms, evolution strategies, evolutionary programming and genetic programming; these are also known as the basic constituents of EA, as illustrated in figure 5.2. They all share a common conceptual base of simulating the evolution of individual structures via processes of selection, mutation, and reproduction.

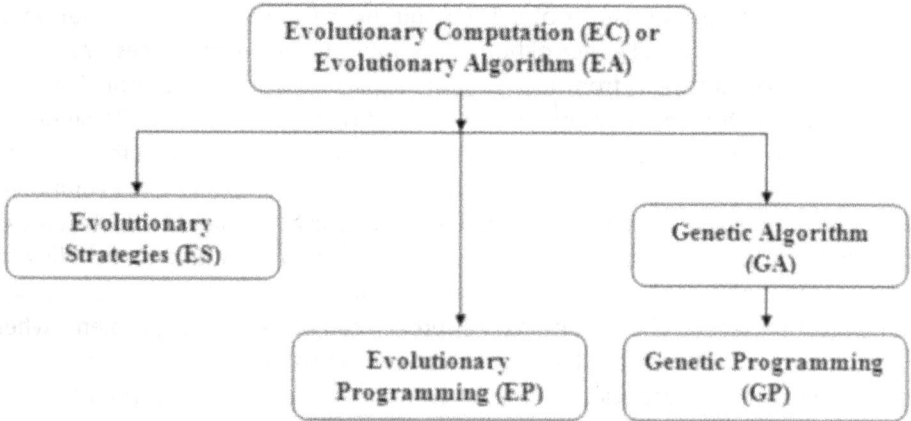

```
                  ┌─────────────────────────────────┐
                  │  Evolutionary Computation (EC) or │
                  │  Evolutionary Algorithm (EA)      │
                  └─────────────────────────────────┘

  ┌──────────────────┐     ┌──────────────────┐     ┌──────────────────┐
  │  Evolutionary    │     │  Evolutionary    │     │  Genetic Algorithm│
  │  Strategies (ES) │     │  Programming (EP)│     │  (GA)            │
  └──────────────────┘     └──────────────────┘     └──────────────────┘
                                                     ┌──────────────────┐
                                                     │ Genetic Programming│
                                                     │  (GP)            │
                                                     └──────────────────┘
```

Fig.5.1: Classification of EC as per its basic constituents

The evolution process of artificial neural networks is what we call evolutionary algorithms. The processes depend on the perceived performance of the individual structures as defined by the problem. A population of candidate solutions (for the optimization task to be solved) is initialized. New solutions are created by applying reproduction operators (mutation and/or crossover). The fitness (how good the solutions are) of the resulting solutions are evaluated and suitable selection strategy is then applied to determine which solutions will be maintained into the next generation. An initial population of different artificial genotype, each encoding the free parameters (e.g. the connection strengths and/or the architecture of the network and/or the learning rules) of a corresponding neural network, is created randomly. The population of networks is evaluated in order to determine the fitness of each individual network. The fittest networks are allowed to reproduce (sexually or a-sexually) by generating copies of their genotypes with the addition of changes introduced by some genetic operators (e.g., mutations, crossover, and duplication). This process is repeated for a number of generations until a network that satisfies the performance criterion (fitness function) set by the researcher is obtained. All the free parameters might be encoded by the genotype. This procedure is then iterated and is illustrated in figure 5.2.

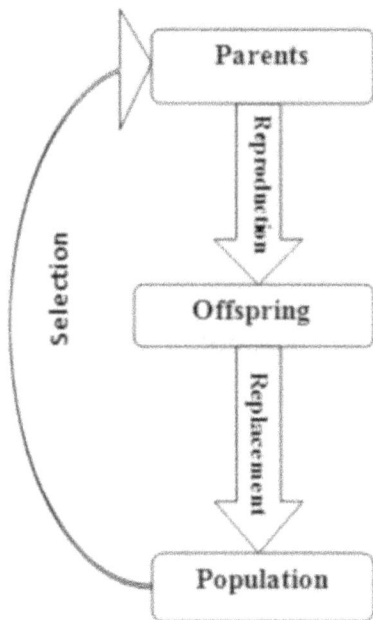

Fig.5.2: Flow chart of an evolutionary algorithm

A more detailed step wise process cycle of Evolutionary Algorithms is shown in figure 5.3.

➢ Generate a random population of individuals
➢ Select parents, generate offspring with cross-over and/or mutation operator(s)
➢ Evaluate and score all individuals in population by using the fitness function
➢ Select new individuals on the basis of their fitness

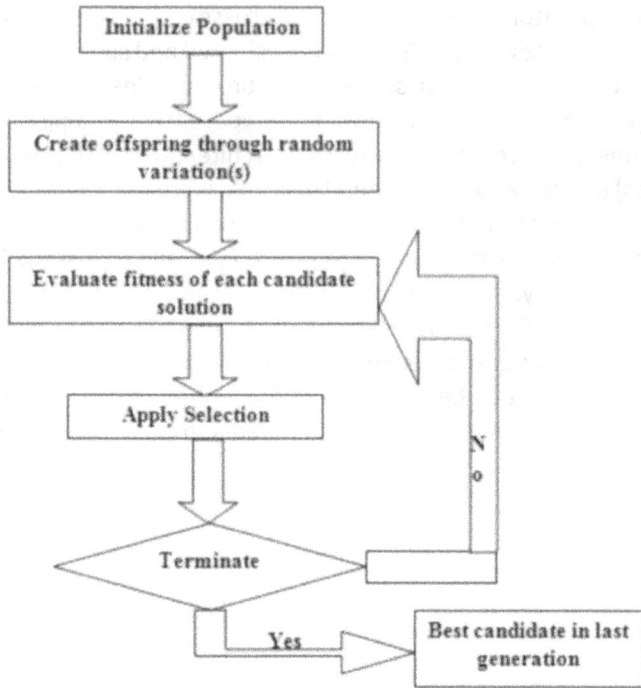

Fig.5.3: Process cycle of EA

5.1.1.   Advantages of Evolutionary Algorithms

A primary advantage of evolutionary computation is that it is conceptually simple. The procedure may be written as difference equation:

$$x[t + 1] = s(v(x[t])) \tag{5.1}$$

where $x[t]$ is the population at time t under a representation x, v is a random variation operator, and s is the selection operator.

Other advantages can be listed as follows:

➢   Evolutionary algorithm performance is representation independent, in contrast with other numerical techniques, which might be applicable for only continuous values or other constrained sets.

➢   Evolutionary algorithms offer a framework such that it is comparably easy to integrate prior knowledge about the problem. Incorporating prior information concentrates the evolutionary search, providing a more efficient investigation of the state space of possible solutions.

➢   Evolutionary algorithms can also be combined with more traditional optimization techniques. This might be as easy as the gradient minimization technique used after primary search with an evolutionary algorithm (for example fine tuning of weights of a evolutionary neural network), or it may involve simultaneous application of other algorithms (e.g., hybridizing with simulated annealing or tabu search to improve the efficiency of basic evolutionary search).

➢ The evaluation of each solution can be dealt in parallel and only selection (which requires at least pair wise competition) requires some serial processing. Absolute parallelism is not possible in many global optimization algorithms like simulated annealing and Tabu search.

➢ Traditional methods of optimization are not robust to dynamic changes in problem the environment and often require a complete restart in order to provide a solution (e.g., dynamic programming). In contrast, evolutionary algorithms can be used to adapt solutions to changing circumstance.

➢ Perhaps the greatest advantage of evolutionary algorithms comes from the ability to address problems for which there are no human experts. Although human expertise should be used when it is available, it often proves less than adequate for automating problem-solving routines.

5.2. Genetic Algorithms

GAs are stochastic search algorithms based on the mechanism of natural selection and natural genetics. The basic GA is very generic and there are many aspects that can be implemented differently according to the problem (For instance, representation of solution or chromosomes, type of encoding, selection strategy, type of crossover and mutation operators, etc.) In practice, GAs are implemented by having arrays of bits or characters to represent the chromosomes. The individuals present in the population then pass through a process of simulated evolution. Simple bit manipulation operations permit the implementation of crossover, mutation and other genetic operations. For every gene (parameter) the number of bits and the decimal range in which they decode are usually the same but nothing precludes the utilization of a different number of bits or range for every gene.

GA, contrary to conventional search techniques, begins with an initial set of random solutions called population satisfying boundary and/or system constraints to the problem. Each individual in the population is referred to as a chromosome, depicting the best solution to the problem at hand. Usually chromosome is a string of symbols, but not essentially, a binary bit string. The chromosomes evolve along successive iterations called generations. In each generation, the chromosomes are evaluated, by setting some measures of fitness. To build the next generation, new chromosomes, called offspring, are created by either merging two chromosomes from current generation using a crossover operator or modifying a chromosome using a mutation operator. A new generation is formed by selection, according to the fitness values, some of the parents and offspring, and rejecting the unfitted ones in order to retain the population size constant. Fitter chromosomes have higher probabilities of being selected. After several generations, the algorithms converge to the best chromosome, which possibly represents the best or suboptimal solution to the problem. When compared to other evolutionary algorithms, one of the most important GA feature is its focus on fixed-length character strings although variable-length strings and other structures have been used. A typical flow chart of genetic algorithm is depicted in figure 5.4.

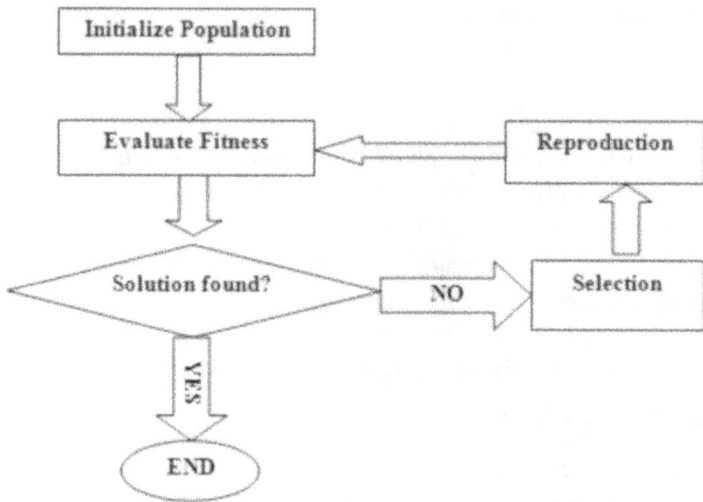

Fig.5.4: Flow chart of Genetic Algorithm

A basic program of genetic algorithm is depicted in figure 5.5

Procedure: Basic Genetic Algorithm

Input: problem data, GA parameters
Output: the best solution
Begin
$t \bullet \leftarrow 0$;
nitialize $P(t)$ by encoding routine; evaluate $P(t)$ by decoding routine; **while** (**not** terminating condition) **do**
create $C(t)$ from $P(t)$ by crossover routine;
create $C(t)$ from $P(t)$ by mutation routine; evaluate $C(t)$ by decoding routine;
select $P(t+1)$ from $P(t)$ and $C(t)$ by selection routine;
$t \bullet \leftarrow t+1$;
end
output the best solution
end

Fig.5.5: Pseudo Code of basic genetic algorithms

5.2.1. Implementation of Genetic Algorithm

Several components are taken into account, in the implementation of GA. First, a genetic representation of solutions should be decided (i.e., encoding); second, a fitness function for evaluating solutions should be given. (i.e., decoding); third, genetic operators such as crossover operator, mutation operator and selection methods should be designed; last, a necessary component for applying GA to the constrained optimization is how to handle constraints because genetic operators used to manipulate the chromosomes often yield infeasible offspring.

5.2.1.1. GA Vocabulary

Because GA is rooted in both natural genetics and computer science, the terminologies used in GA literatures are a concoction of the natural and the artificial. In a biological organism, the structure that encodes the prescription that specifies how organism is to be constructed is called a chromosome. One or more chromosomes may be required to specify the complete organism. The complete set of chromosomes is called a genotype, and the resulting organism is called a phenotype. Each chromosome comprises a number of individual structures called genes. Each gene encodes a particular feature of the organism, and the location, or locus, of the gene within the chromosome structure, determines what particular characteristic the gene represents. At a particular locus, a gene may encode one of several different values of the particular characteristic it represents. The different values of a gene are called alleles. The correspondence of GA terms and optimization terms is summarized in Table 5.1.

Genetic algorithms	Explanation
Chromosomes (string, individual)	Solution (coding)
Genes (bits)	Part of solution
Locus	Position of gene
Alleles	Values of gene
Phenotype	Decoded solution
Genotype	Encoded solution

Table 5.1: Explanation of GA terms

How to encode a solution of a given problem into a chromosome is a key issue for the GA. This issue has been investigated from many aspects, such as mapping characters from a genotype space to a phenotype space when individuals are decoded into solutions and the metamorphosis properties when individuals are manipulated by genetic operators.

5.2.1.2. Classification of Encoding

In Holland's work, encoding is carried out using binary strings. The binary encoding for function optimization problems is known to have severe drawbacks due to the existence of Hamming cliffs, which describes the phenomenon that a pair of encodings with a large Hamming distance belongs to points with minimal distances in the phenotype space. For example, the pair 01111111111 and 10000000000 belongs to neighboring points in the phenotype space (points of the minimal Euclidean distances) but have the maximum Hamming distance in the genotype space. To cross the Hamming cliff, all bits have to be changed at once. The probability that crossover and mutation will occur to cross it can be very small. In this sense, the binary code does not preserve locality of points in the phenotype space. For many real-world applications, it is nearly impossible to represent their solutions with the binary encoding. Various encoding methods have been created for particular problems in order to have an effective implementation of the GA. According to what kind of symbols is used as the alleles of a gene, the encoding methods can be classified as follows:

➢ Binary encoding
➢ Real number encoding
➢ Integer/literal permutation encoding
➢ A general data structure encoding

The real number encoding is best for function optimization problems. It has been widely confirmed that the real number encoding has higher performance than the binary or Gray encoding for function optimizations and constrained optimizations. Since the topological structure of the genotype space for the real number encoding method is identical to that of the phenotype space, it is easy for us to create some effective genetic operators by borrowing some useful techniques from conventional methods. The integer or literal permutation encoding is suitable for combinatorial optimization problems. Since the essence of combinatorial optimization problems is to search for a best permutation or combination of some items subject to some constraints, the literal permutation encoding may be the most reasonable way to deal with this kind of issue. For more complex real-world problems, an appropriate data structure is suggested as the allele of a gene in order to capture the nature of the problem. In such cases, a gene may be an array or a more complex data structure. According to the structure of encodings, the encoding methods also can be classified into the following two types:

➢ One-dimensional encoding
➢ Multi-dimensional encoding

In most practices, the one-dimensional encoding method is adopted. However, many real-world problems have solutions of multi-dimensional structures. It is natural to adopt a multi-dimensional encoding method to represent those solutions. According to what kinds of contents are encoded into the encodings, the encoding methods can also be divided as follows:

Solution only

➢ Solution + parameters

In the GA practice, the first way is widely adopted to conceive a suitable encoding to a given problem. An individual consists of two parts: the first part is the solution to a given problem and the second part, called strategy parameters, contains variances and covariance of the normal distribution for mutation. The purpose for incorporating the strategy parameters into the representation of individuals is to facilitate the evolutionary self-adaptation of these parameters by applying evolutionary operators to them. Then the search will be performed in the space of solutions and the strategy parameters together. In this way a suitable adjustment and diversity of mutation parameters should be provided under arbitrary circumstances.

5.2.1.3. Properties of Encodings

Given a new encoding method, it is usually necessary to examine whether it can build an effective genetic search with the encoding. Several principles have been proposed to evaluate an encoding:

Property 1 (*Space*): Chromosomes should not require extravagant amounts of memory.

Property 2 (*Time*): The time complexity of executing evaluation, recombination and mutation on chromosomes should not be a higher order.

Property 3 (*Feasibility*): A chromosome corresponds to a feasible solution.

Property 4 (*Legality*): Any permutation of a chromosome corresponds to a solution.

Property 5 (*Completeness*): Any solution has a corresponding chromosome.

Property 6 (*Uniqueness*): The mapping from chromosomes to solutions (decoding) may belong to one of the following three cases

Property 7 (*Heritability*): Offspring of simple crossover (*i.e.*, one-cut point crossover) should correspond to solutions which combine the basic feature of their parents.

Property 8 (*Locality*): A small change in chromosome should imply a small change in its corresponding solution.

In a typical application of GA's, the given problem is transformed into a set of genetic characteristics (parameters to be optimized) that will survive in the best possible manner in the environment. Example, if the task is to optimize the function given in equation 5.2.

$$\min f(x1, x2) = (x1 - 5)2 + (x2 - 2)2, \, -3 \le x1 \le 3, \, -8 \le x\,2 \le 8 \tag{5.2}$$

The parameters of the search are identified as $x1$ and $x2$, which are called the phenotypes in evolutionary algorithms. In genetic algorithms, the phenotypes (parameters) are usually converted to genotypes by using a coding procedure. Knowing the ranges of $x1$ and $x2$ each variable is to be represented using a suitable binary string. This representation using binary coding helps in making the parametric space independent of the type of variables used. The genotype (chromosome) in some way should contain information about solution, which is also known as encoding. GAs utilizes a binary string encoding as shown below.

Chromosome A: 110110111110100110110

Chromosome B: 110111101010100011110

Each bit of the chromosome string represents some characteristic of the solution. There are several types of encoding (example, direct integer or real numbers encoding). The encoding depends directly on the problem. Permutation encoding can be used in ordering problems, such as Travelling Salesman Problem (TSP) or task ordering problem. In permutation encoding, every chromosome is a string of numbers, which represents number in a sequence. A chromosome using permutation encoding for a 9 city TSP problem will look like as follows:

Chromosome A: 4 5 3 2 6 1 7 8 9

Chromosome B: 8 5 6 7 2 3 1 4 9

Chromosome represents order of cities, in which salesman will visit them. Special care is to taken to ensure that the strings represent real sequences after crossover and mutation. Floating-point representation is very useful for numeric optimization (example: for encoding the weights of a neural network). It should be noted that in many recent applications more sophisticated genotypes are appearing (example: chromosome can be a tree of symbols, or is a combination of a string and a tree, some parts of the chromosome are not allowed to evolve etc.)

5.2.1.4. Reproduction Operators

For producing offspring the individuals are chosen using a selection strategy after evaluating the fitness value of each individual in the selection pool. In the selection pool each individual receives a reproduction probability depending on its own fitness value and the fitness value of all other individuals present in the selection pool. In genetic algorithm **selection** is the stage in which individual genomes are selected from a population for later breeding (recombination or crossover).

A basic selection procedure may be implemented as follows:

1. A fitness function is evaluated for each individual, yielding fitness values, which are then normalized. Normalization refers to dividing the fitness value of each individual by the sum of all fitness values, resulting the aggregation of all resulting fitness values equal to unity.

2. The population is categorized by descending fitness values.

3. Computation of accumulated normalized fitness values are done (the accumulated fitness value of an individual is the aggregation of its own fitness value along with the fitness values of all the previous individuals). The last individual's accumulated fitness should be equal to 1 (otherwise something went wrong in the normalization step!).

4. Randomly a number R between 0 and 1 is selected.

5. The selected individual's accumulated normalized value is higher than R.

If this procedure is iterated until here are enough selected individuals, the selection method is referred as fitness proportionate selection or roulette-wheel selection. If instead of a single pointer spun multiple times equally spaced pointers on a wheel that spin once, is called stochastic universal sampling. Repeatedly choosing the most optimum individual out of a randomly selected subset is what we meant by, tournament selection. Truncation selection is taking into account the optimum half, third or any another proportion of the individuals.

Other selection algorithms do not consider all individuals for selection; rather only those whose fitness value is more prominent than a given (arbitrary) constant are selected. Other algorithms select from a confined pool where only a definite percentage of the individuals are allowed, based on fitness value. Retaining the best individuals in a generation unaltered in the next generation is referred as *elitism* or *elitist selection*. It is considered as a successful (slight) alternative of the basic process of building a new population.

During the past two decades, many selection methods have been proposed, examined, and compared. Common selection methods are as follows:

➢ Roulette wheel selection
➢ Tournament selection
➢ Truncation selection
➢ Ranking and scaling
➢ Sharing
➢ Elitist selection

Roulette wheel selection, proposed by Holland, is the best and the simplest known selection type. The basic idea is to determine selection probability or probability of survival for each chromosome that is proportional to the fitness value. This technique is similar to a roulette wheel with each slice proportional in size to the fitness. The selection process is based on spinning the wheel the number of times equal to population size, each selecting a single chromosome for the new procedure. The individuals are plotted to contiguous segments of a line, such that segment of each individual is equal in size to its fitness. A random number is produced and the individual whose segment spreads the random number is selected. The process is iterated until the desired number of individuals is obtained. As illustrated in Fig. 5.5, chromosome1 conceives the highest fitness and hence has the highest probability for being selected.

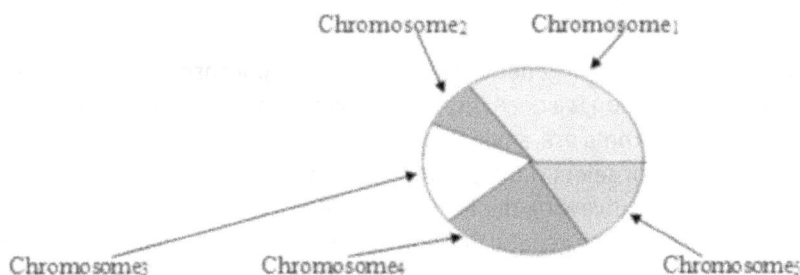

Fig.5.5 Roulette wheel selection

Tournament selection runs a tournament" among a few individuals chosen at random from the population and selects the winner (the one with the best fitness). Selection pressure can be easily adjusted by changing the tournament size. If the tournament size is larger, weak individuals have a smaller chance to be selected. A number of individuals are chosen randomly from the population and the best individual from this group is selected as parent. This process is repeated as often as individuals to choose. These selected parents produce uniform at random offspring. The tournament size will often depend on the problem, population size etc. The parameter for tournament selection is the tournament size. Tournament size takes values ranging from 2 –number of individuals in population.

Truncation selection is said to be a deterministic procedure that provides ranks to all individuals according to their fitness and selects the best individual among them as parents. *Elitist selection* is generally used as supplementary to the proportional selection process.

Ranking and Scaling mechanisms are introduced to deal with these problems. The scaling method plots crude objective function values to positive real values, and the probability of survival for each chromosome is evaluated according to these values. Fitness scaling has a bifold objective: (1) to maintain a reasonable differential between relative fitness ratings of chromosomes, and (2) to prevent too-rapid takeover by some super-chromosomes to meet the requirement to limit competition early but to stimulate it later.

Sharing selection is employed to maintain the diversity of population for multi-model function optimization. A sharing function optimization is used to maintain the diversity of population. A sharing function is a method of evaluating the degradation of the fitness of an individual due to a neighbor at some distance. With the degradation, the reproduction probability of individuals in a crowd peak is restrained while other individuals are encouraged to give offspring.

Elitism, When creating new population by crossover and mutation, we have a big chance that we will lose the best chromosome. Elitism is name of the method that first copies the best chromosome (or a few best chromosomes) to new population. The rest is done in conventional way. Elitism can very efficiently increase the performance of GA, because it prevents losing the optimal solution.

5.2.1.5. Genetic Operators

A Genetic Operator is used in genetic algorithms for the purpose of maintaining genetic diversity. Genetic variation is a necessity for the process of evolution. Genetic operators used in genetic algorithms are analogous to those which occur in the natural world: survival of the fittest, or selection; reproduction (crossover, also called recombination); and mutation. Genetic diversity, the level of biodiversity, refers to the total number of genetic characteristics in the genetic makeup of a species. It is distinguished from genetic variability, which describes the tendency of genetic characteristics to vary. The academic field of population genetics includes several hypotheses and theories regarding genetic diversity. The neutral theory of evolution proposes that diversity is the result of the accumulation of neutral substitutions.

Diversifying selection is the hypothesis that two subpopulations of a species live in different environments that select for different alleles at a particular locus. This may occur, for instance, if a species has a large range relative to the mobility of individuals within it. Frequency-dependent selection is the hypothesis that as alleles become more generic, higher their vulnerability. This is often invoked in host-pathogen interactions, where a high frequency of a defensive allele among the host means that it is more likely that a pathogen will spread if it is able to overcome that allele. When GA proceeds, both the search direction to optimal solution and the search speed should be considered as important factors, in order to keep a balance between exploration and exploitation in search space. In general, the exploitation of the accumulated information resulting from GA search is done by the selection mechanism, while the exploration to new regions of the search space is accounted for by genetic operators. The genetic operators mimic the process of heredity of genes to create new offspring at each generation. The operators are used to alter the genetic composition of individuals during representation. In essence, the operators perform a random search, and cannot guarantee to yield an improved offspring. Crossover and mutation are two primary operators of GA. Performance of GA very much depends on the genetic operators. The implementation of operators and their types depends on encoding and the problem to be solved. There are many methods to perform crossover and mutation. In this section we will demonstrate some of the popular methods with some examples and suggestions how to do it for different encoding schemes.

Crossover: Crossover is the most prominent genetic operator. It operates on two chromosomes at a time and generates offspring by combining both chromosomes' features. A simple way to achieve crossover would be to choose a random cut-point and generate the offspring by combining the segment of one parent to the left of the cut-point with the segment of the other parent to the right of the cut-point. This method works well with bit string representation. The performance of GA depends to a great extent, on the performance of the crossover operator used.

The crossover probability (denoted by P_c) of each generation is defined as the probability of the number of offspring produced to the population size (usually denoted by popSize). This probability controls the expected number $P_c \times$ pop Size of chromosomes to undergo the crossover operation. A higher crossover probability allows exploration of more of the solution space, and reduces the chances of settling for a false optimum; but if this probability is too high, it results in the wastage of a lot of computation time in exploring unpromising regions of the solution space. Up to now, several crossover operators have been proposed for the real numbers encoding, which can roughly be put into four classes: conventional, arithmetical, direction-based, and stochastic. The conventional operators are made by extending the operators for binary representation into the real-coding case. The conventional crossover operators can be broadly divided by two kinds of crossover:

> ➤ Simple crossover: one-cut point, two-cut point, multi-cut point or uniform
> ➤ Random crossover: flat crossover, blend crossover

The arithmetical operators are constructed by borrowing the concept of linear combination of vectors from the area of convex set theory. Operated on the floating point genetic representation, the arithmetical crossover operators, such as convex, affine, linear, average, intermediate, extended intermediate crossover, are usually adopted. The direction-based operators are formed by introducing the approximate gradient direction into genetic operators. The direction-based crossover operator uses the value of objective function in determining the direction of genetic search. The stochastic operators give offspring by altering parents by random numbers with some distribution.

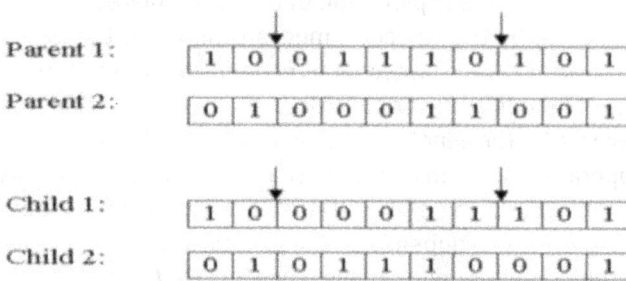

Fig.5.6: Crossover.

It selects genes from parent chromosomes and creates a new offspring. The simplest way to do this is to choose randomly some crossover point and everything before this point is copied from the first parent and then everything after a crossover point is copied from the second parent. A single point crossover is illustrated as follows (/ is the crossover point):

Chromosome A: **11111** / **00100110110**

Chromosome B: 10011 / 11000011110

Offspring A: **11111** / 11000011110

Offspring B: 10011 / **00100110110**

As illustrated in Fig. 5.6, there are several crossover techniques. In a uniform crossover bits are randomly copied from the first or from the second.

Mutation: Mutation is referred to as a background operator which generates spontaneous random changes in various chromosomes. A simple way to achieve mutation would be to alter one or more genes. In GA, mutation serves the crucial role of either (a) replacing the genes lost from the population during the selection process so that they can be tried in a new context or (b) providing the genes that were not present in the initial population. The mutation probability (denoted by P_m) is defined as the percentage of the total number of genes in the population. The mutation probability controls the probability with which new genes are introduced into the population for trial. If it is too low, many genes that would have been useful are never tried out, while if it is too high, there will be much random perturbation, the offspring will start losing their resemblance to the parents, and the algorithm will lose the ability to learn from the history of the search. Up to now, several mutation operators have been proposed for real numbers encoding, which can roughly be put into four classes as crossover can be classified. Random mutation operators such as uniform mutation, boundary mutation, and plain mutation, belong to the conventional mutation operators, which simply replace a gene with a randomly selected real number with a specified range. Dynamic mutation (non uniform mutation) is designed for fine-tuning capabilities aimed at achieving high precision, which is classified as the arithmetical mutation operator. Directional mutation operator is a kind of direction-based mutation, which uses the gradient expansion of objective function. The direction can be provided randomly in the form of free direction to avoid the jamming of chromosomes into a corner. If the chromosome is near the boundary, the mutation direction given by some criteria might point toward the close boundary, and then jamming could occur. Several mutation operators for integer encoding have been proposed.

➢ Inversion mutation selects two positions within a chromosome at random and then inverts the substring between these two positions.

➢ Insertion mutation randomly selects a gene and inserts it in a random position.

➢ Displacement mutation randomly selects a substring of genes and inserts it in a random position. Therefore, insertion can be understood as a special case of displacement. Reciprocal exchange mutation randomly selects two positions and then swaps the genes on the positions.

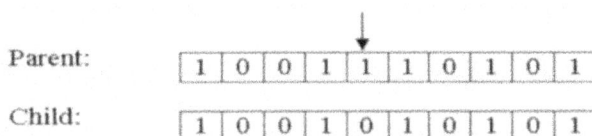

Fig.5.7: Mutation

5.3. Evolutionary Programming

Fogel, Owens and Walsh's book is the landmark publication for Evolutionary Programming (EP). In the book, Finite state automata are evolved to predict symbol strings generated from Markov processes and non-stationary time series. The basic evolutionary programming method involves the following steps:

1. Choose an initial population (possible solutions at random). The number of solutions in a population is highly relevant to the speed of optimization, but no definite answers are available as to how many solutions are appropriate (other than > 1) and how many solutions are just wasteful.

2. New offspring's are created by mutation. Each offspring solution is assessed by computing its fitness. Typically, a stochastic tournament is held to determine N

solutions to be retained for the population of solutions. It should be noted that evolutionary programming method typically does not use any crossover as a genetic operator.

When comparing evolutionary programming to genetic algorithm, one can identify the following differences:

➤ GA is implemented by having arrays of bits or characters to represent the chromosomes. In EP there are no such restrictions for the representation. In most cases the representation follows from the problem.

➤ EP typically uses an adaptive mutation operator in which the severity of mutations is often reduced as the global optimum is approached while GA's use a pre-fixed mutation operator. Among the schemes to adapt the mutation step size, the most widely studied being the "meta-evolutionary" technique in which the variance of the mutation distribution is subject to mutation by a fixed variance mutation operator that evolves along with the solution.

On the other hand, when comparing evolutionary programming to evolution strategies, one can identify the following differences:

➤ When implemented to solve real-valued function optimization problems, both typically operate on the real values themselves and use adaptive reproduction operators.

➤ EP typically uses stochastic tournament selection while ES typically uses deterministic selection.

➤ EP does not use crossover operators while ES (P/R,C and P/R+C strategies) uses crossover. However the effectiveness of the crossover operators depends on the problem at hand.

5.3.1. Genetic Programming

Genetic Programming (GP) technique provides a framework for automatically developing an efficient computer program from a high-level problem statement of the problem. Genetic programming achieves this goal of automatic programming by genetically breeding a population of computer programs using the principles of Darwinian natural selection and biologically inspired operations. The operations include most of the techniques discussed in the previous sections. The main difference between genetic programming and genetic algorithm is the representation of the solution. Genetic programming creates computer programs in the LISP or scheme computer languages as the solution. LISP is an acronym for LISt Processor and was developed by John McCarthy in the late 1950s. Unlike most languages, LISP is usually used as an interpreted language. This means that, unlike compiled languages, an interpreter can process and respond directly to programs written in LISP. The main reason behind choosing LISP for the implementation of GP is due to the advantage of having the same structures of programs and data, which could provide easy means for manipulation and evaluation. Genetic programming is the extension of evolutionary learning into the space of computer programs. In GP the individual population members are not fixed length character strings that encode possible solutions to the problem at hand, they are programs that, when executed, are the candidate solutions to the problem. These programs are expressed in genetic programming as parse trees, rather than as lines of code. For example, the simple program "$a + b * f(4, a, c)$" would be represented as shown in Figure 5.8. The terminal and function sets are also important components of genetic programming. The terminal and function sets are the alphabet of the programs to be made. The terminal set consists of the variables (example, a, b and c in Figure 5.8) and constants (example, 4 in Fig. 5.8). The most common way of writing down a function with two arguments is the infix notation. That is, the two arguments are connected with the operation symbol between them as $a + b$ or $a * b$. A different method is the prefix notation. Here the operation symbol is written down first, followed by its required arguments as $+ab$ or $*ab$. While this may be a bit more difficult or just unusual for human eyes, it opens some advantages for computational uses. The computer language LISP uses symbolic expressions (or S-expressions) composed in prefix notation. Then a simple S-expression could be (*operator, argument*) where *operator* is the name of a function and *argument* can be either a constant or a variable or either another symbolic expression as (*operator, argument* (*operator, argument*) (*operator, argument*)).

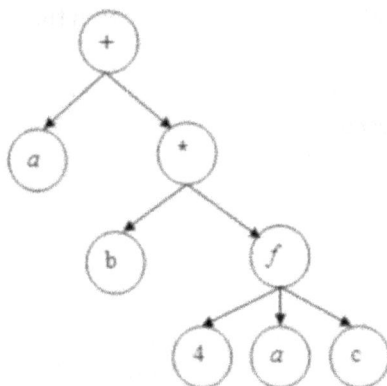

Fig.5.8: A simple tree structure

Generally speaking, GP procedure could be summarized as follows:

➤ Generate an initial population of random compositions of the functions and terminals of the problem;

➤ Compute the fitness values of each individual in the population;

➤ Using some selection strategy and suitable reproduction operators produce two offspring;

➤ Procedure is iterated until the required solution is found or the termination conditions have reached (specified number of generations).

5.3.1.1. Computer Program Encoding

A parse tree is a structure that grasps the interpretation of a computer program.

Functions are written down as nodes, their arguments as leaves. A subtree is the part of a tree that is under an inner node of this tree. If this tree is cut out from its parent, the inner node becomes a root node and the subtree is a valid tree of its own. There is a close relationship between these parse trees and S-expression; in fact these trees are just another way of writing down expressions. While functions will be the nodes of the trees (or the operators in the S-expressions) and can have other functions as their arguments, the leaves will be formed by terminals, that is symbols that may not be further expanded. Terminals can be variables, constants or specific actions that are to be performed. The process of selecting the functions and terminals that are needed or useful for finding a solution to a given problem is one of the key steps in GP. Evaluation of these structures is straightforward. Beginning at the root node, the values of all sub expressions (or subtrees) are computed, descending the tree down to the leaves.

5.3.1.2. Reproduction of Computer Programs

The creation of an offspring from the crossover operation is accomplished by deleting the crossover fragment of the first parent and then incorporating the crossover fragment of the next parent. The second offspring is produced in a symmetrically. A simple crossover operation is illustrated in Figure 5.9. In GP the crossover operation is implemented by taking randomly selected sub trees in the individuals and exchanging them.

Mutation is another important feature of genetic programming. Two types of mutations are commonly used. The simplest type is to replace a function or a terminal by a function or a terminal respectively. In the second kind an entire subtree can replace another subtree. Figure 5.10 explains the concept of mutation. GP requires data structures that are easy to handle and evaluate and robust to structural manipulations. These are among the reasons why the class of S-expressions was chosen to implement GP. The set of functions and terminals that will be used in a specific problem has to be chosen carefully. If the set of functions is not powerful enough, a solution may be very complex or not to be found at all. Like in any evolutionary computation technique, the generation of first population of individuals is important for successful implementation of GP. Some of the other factors that influence the performance of the algorithm are the size of the population, percentage of individuals that participate in the crossover/ mutation, maximum depth for the initial individuals and the maximum allowed depth for the generated offspring etc. Some specific advantages of genetic programming are that no analytical knowledge is needed and still could get accurate results. GP approach does scale with the problem size. GP does impose restrictions on how the structure of solutions should be formulated.

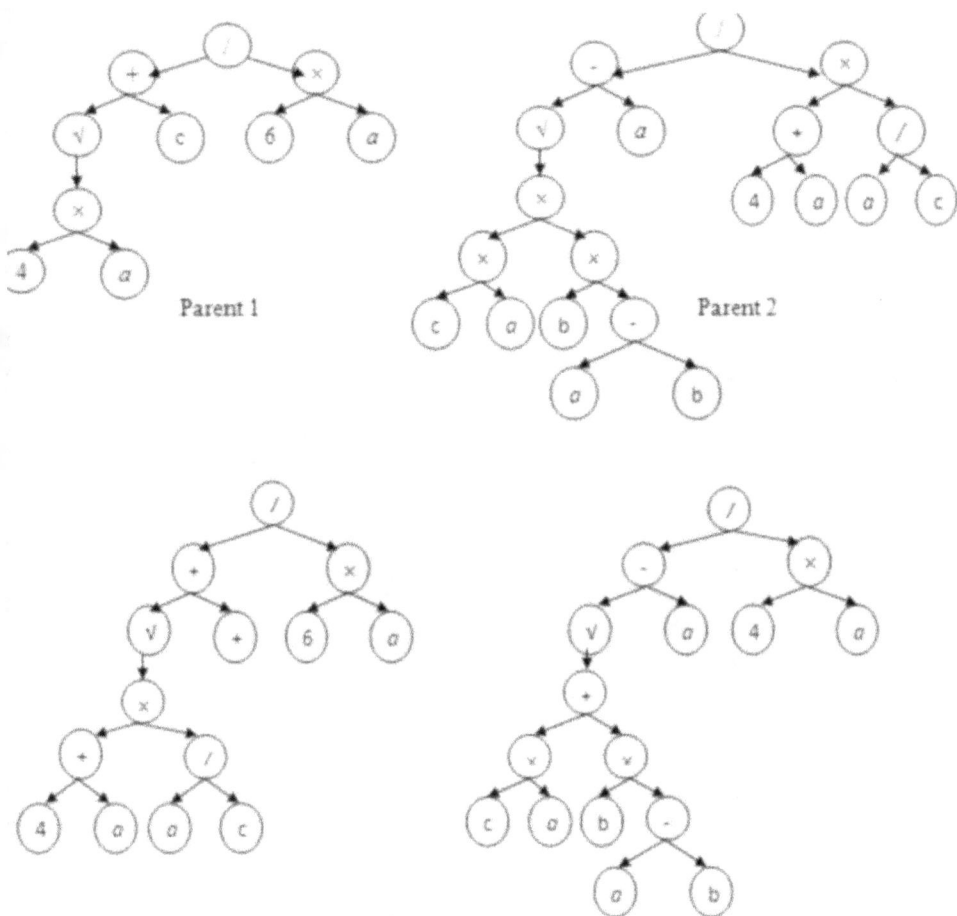

Fig.5.9: Illustration of crossover operator

5.4.   Variants of Genetic Programming

Several variants of GP could be seen in the literature. Some of them are Linear Genetic Programming (LGP), Gene Expression Programming (GEP), Multi Expression Programming (MEP), Cartesian Genetic Programming (CGP), Traceless Genetic Programming (TGP) and Genetic Algorithm for Deriving Software (GADS).

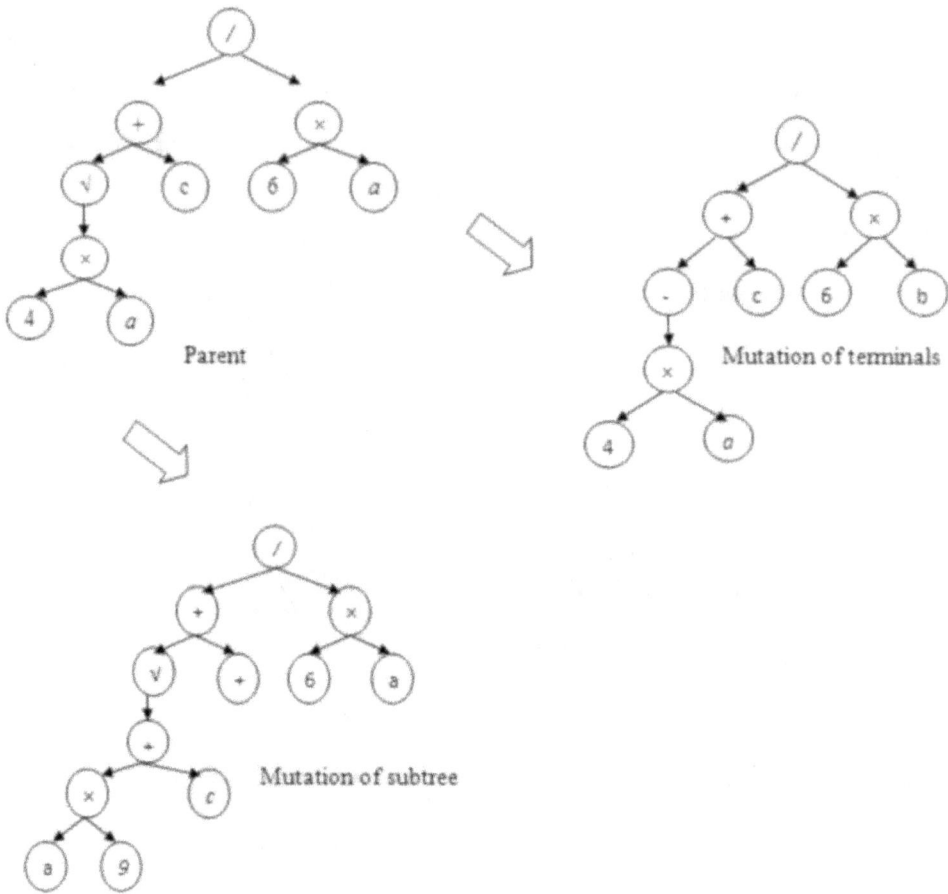

Fig.5.9: Illustration of mutation operator in GP

5.4.1. Linear Genetic Programming

Linear genetic programming is a variant of the GP technique that acts on linear genomes. Its main characteristics in comparison to tree-based GP lies in that the evolvable units are not the expressions of a functional programming language (like LISP), but the programs of an imperative language (like c/c⁺⁺). This can tremendously hasten the evolution process as, no matter how an individual is initially represented, finally it always has to be represented as a piece of machine code, as fitness evaluation requires physical execution of the individuals. The basic unit of evolution here is a native machine code instruction that runs on the floating-point processor unit (FPU). Since different instructions may have different sizes, here instructions are clubbed up together to form instruction blocks of 32 bits each. The instruction blocks hold one or more native machine code instructions, depending on the sizes of the instructions. A crossover point can occur only between instructions and is prohibited from occurring within an instruction. However the mutation operation does not have any such restriction. LGP uses a specific linear representation of computer programs. A LGP individual is represented by a variable length sequence of simple C language instructions. Instructions operate on one or two indexed variables (registers) r, or on constants c from predefined sets.

An important LGP parameter is the number of registers used by a chromosome. The number of registers is usually equal to the number of attributes of the problem. If the problem has only one attribute, it is impossible to obtain a complex expression such as the quartic polynomial. In that case we have to use several supplementary registers. The number of supplementary registers depends on the complexity of the expression being discovered. An inappropriate choice can have disastrous effects on the program being evolved. LGP uses a modified steady-state algorithm. The initial population is randomly generated. The settings of various linear genetic programming system parameters are of utmost importance for successful performance of the system. The population space has been subdivided into multiple subpopulation or demes. Migration of individuals among the subpopulations causes evolution of the entire population. It helps to maintain diversity in the population, as migration is restricted among the demes. Moreover, the tendency towards a bad local minimum in one deme can be countered by other demes with better search directions. The various LGP search parameters are the mutation frequency, crossover frequency and the reproduction frequency: The crossover operator acts by exchanging sequences of instructions between two tournament winners. Steady state genetic programming approach was used to manage the memory more effectively.

5.4.2. Gene Expression Programming

The individuals of gene expression programming are encoded in linear chromosomes which are expressed or translated into expression trees (branched entities). Thus, in GEP, the genotype (the linear chromosomes) and the phenotype (the expression trees) are different entities (both structurally and functionally) that, nevertheless, work together forming an indivisible whole. In contrast to its analogous cellular gene expression, GEP is rather simple. The main players in GEP are only two: the chromosomes and the Expression Trees (ETs), being the latter the expression of the genetic information encoded in the chromosomes. As in nature, the process of information decoding is called translation. And this translation implies obviously a kind of code and a set of rules. The genetic code is very simple: a one-to-one relationship between the symbols of the chromosome and the functions or terminals they represent. The rules are also very simple: they determine the spatial organization of the functions and terminals in the ETs and the type of interaction between sub-ETs. GEP uses linear chromosomes that store expressions in breadth-first form. A GEP gene is a string of terminal and function symbols. GEP genes are composed of a *head* and a *tail*. The head contains both function and terminal symbols. The tail may contain terminal symbols only. For each problem the head length (denoted *h*) is chosen by the user. The tail length (denoted by *t*) is evaluated by

$t = (n - 1)h + 1,$ (5.3)

where n is the number of arguments of the function with more arguments. GEP genes may be linked by a function symbol in order to obtain a fully functional chromosome. GEP uses mutation, recombination and transposition. GEP uses a generational algorithm. The initial population is randomly generated. The following steps are repeated until a termination criterion is reached: A fixed number of the best individuals enter the next generation (elitism). The mating pool is filled by using binary tournament selection. The individuals from the mating pool are randomly paired and recombined. Two offspring are obtained by recombining two parents. The offspring are mutated and they enter the next generation.

5.4.3.   Multi Expression Programming

A GP chromosome generally encodes a single expression (computer program). A Multi Expression Programming (MEP) chromosome encodes several expressions. The best of the encoded solution is chosen to represent the chromosome. The MEP chromosome has some advantages over the single-expression chromosome especially when the complexity of the target expression is not known. This feature also acts as a provider of variable-length expressions. MEP genes are represented by substrings of a variable length. The number of genes per chromosome is constant. This number defines the length of the chromosome. Each gene encodes a terminal or a function symbol. A gene that encodes a function includes pointers towards the function arguments. Function arguments always have indices of lower values than the position of the function itself in the chromosome. The proposed representation ensures that no cycle arises while the chromosome is decoded (phenotypically transcripted). According to the proposed representation scheme, the first symbol of the chromosome must be a terminal symbol. In this way, only syntactically correct programs (MEP individuals) are obtained. The maximum number of symbols in MEP chromosome is given by the formula:

Number of Symbols = $(n + 1) \times$ (*Number of Genes* $- 1) + 1,$ (5.4)

where n is the number of arguments of the function with the greatest number of arguments. The translation of a MEP chromosome into a computer program represents the phenotypic transcription of the MEP chromosomes. Phenotypic translation is obtained by parsing the chromosome top-down. A terminal symbol specifies a simple expression. A function symbol specifies a complex expression obtained by connecting the operands specified by the argument positions with the current function symbol. Due to its multi expression representation, each MEP chromosome may be viewed as a forest of trees rather than as a single tree, which is the case of Genetic Programming.

5.4.4.   Cartesian Genetic Programming

Cartesian Genetic Programming (CGP) uses a network of nodes (indexed graph) to achieve an input to output mapping. Each node consists of a number of inputs, these being used as parameters in a determined mathematical or logical function to create the node output. The functionality and connectivity of the nodes are stored as a string of numbers (the genotype) and evolved to achieve the optimum mapping. The genotype is then mapped to an indexed graph that can be executed as a program. In CGP there are very large number of genotypes that map to identical genotypes due to the presence of a large amount of redundancy. Firstly there is node redundancy that is caused by genes associated with nodes that are not part of the connected graph representing the program. Another form of redundancy in CGP, also present in all other forms of GP is, functional redundancy.

5.4.5.　Traceless Genetic Programming (TGP)

The main difference between Traceless Genetic Programming and GP is that TGP does not explicitly store the evolved computer programs. TGP is useful when the trace (the way in which the results are obtained) between the input and output is not important. TGP uses two genetic operators: crossover and insertion. The insertion operator is useful when the population contains individuals representing very complex expressions that cannot improve the search.

5.4.6.　Grammatical Evolution

Grammatical evolution is a grammar-based, linear genome system. In grammatical evolution, the Backus Naur Form (BNF) specification of a language is used to describe the output produced by the system (a compilable code fragment). Different BNF grammars can be used to produce code automatically in any language. The genotype is a string of eight-bit binary numbers generated at random and treated as integer values from 0 to 255. The phenotype is a running computer program generated by a genotype-phenotype mapping process. The genotype-phenotype mapping in grammatical evolution is deterministic because each individual is always mapped to the same phenotype. In grammatical evolution, standard genetic algorithms are applied to the different genotypes in a population using the typical crossover and mutation operators.

5.4.7.　Genetic Algorithm for Deriving Software (GADS)

Genetic algorithm for deriving software is a GP technique where the genotype is distinct from the phenotype. The GADS genotype is a list of integers representing productions in a syntax. This is used to generate the phenotype, which is a program in the language defined by the syntax. Syntactically invalid phenotypes cannot be generated, though there may be phenotypes with residual nonterminals.

5.5.　Schema Theorem

From the early stages of development of Genetic Algorithm (GA) theory, the Schema Theorem and the Building Block Hypothesis have been the dominant explanation for the working process of GA.

5.5.1. Schema Theorem and its contribution towards understanding GA behavior

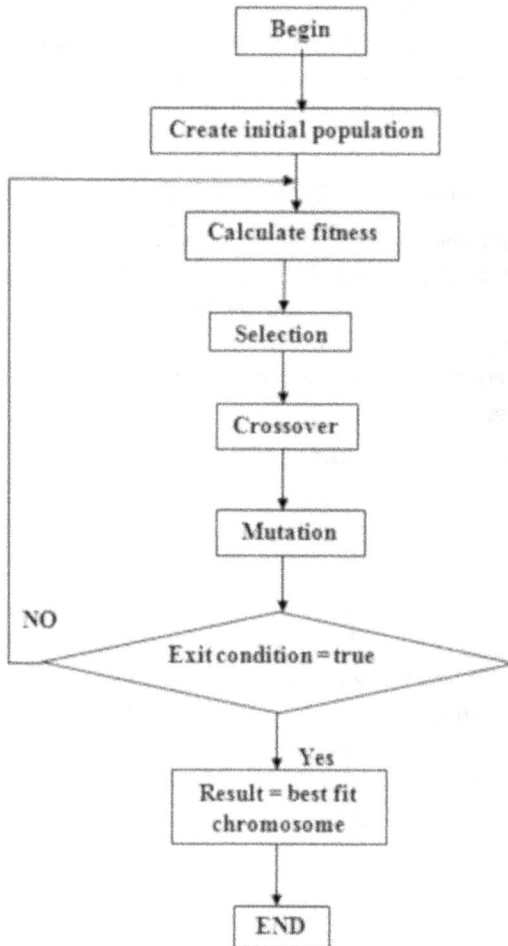

Fig.5.10: Flow chart of basic GA operation

The operation of GA is straight-forward. We start with a random population of n strings where each individual string in the population is known as a **Chromosome** and has its own **fitness** value. We copy strings with some bias towards the best i.e. high fit chromosomes are more likely to be copied. This process of copying strings is known as **selection** process. We then **crossover** the best strings i.e. mate best strings and partially swap substrings. Finally **mutation** process takes place where we mutate an occasional bit value of resulting string for good measure. Flow chart presented in figure 5.10 describes the basic GA.

Now let's model the operation of GA in terms of mechanics of natural selection and natural genetics. As stated above, chromosomes in a population with high fitness are more likely to be selected for the reproduction and consequently likely to produce more offspring in the next generation were as the less fitted chromosomes are more likely to die. This characteristic of GA models the concept of survival for the fittest. Crossover plays the role of mating process between parent chromosomes such that the reproduced child will have function of both of its parents. The mutation process represents the error in the reproduction process, occurrence of which may differ child from its parents. To analyse the behaviour of GA, the notion of schema has been introduced. Schema can be defined as a string containing all similar bits (defined bits) among highly fit chromosomes in a population, where non similar bits (non defined bits) are represented as '*' (Don't care) symbol. Let's see an example of a 4-bit schema with two defined bits and two non-defined bits:

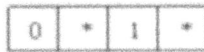

Fig.5.11: a 4-bit schema with two defined bits and two non-defined bits

The chromosomes in a current generation containing all defined bits of a schema are known as **instances** of that particular schema. Figure 5.11 shows a schema with two defined bits and two non defined bits. The possible instance of the schema is shown in figure 5.12.

Fig.5.12: Set of 4 bit chromosome matching schema shown in figure 5.11

Schema provides the basic means for analyzing the net effect of reproduction and genetic operators on Building Block contained within population [Goldberg 89]. The concept: important similarities among highly fit strings can help guide search, lead to the concept of schema (schemata in plural).

Given a current generation of chromosomes, *the Schema Theorem helps to predict the number of instances of schema in the next generation.* Let's give explanation to the above statement.

As we know that the probability of selection of a chromosome is proportional to its fitness, we can calculate the expected number of instances of a chromosome in next generation, which can be written as

$$m_x(i+1) = F_x(i) / \vec{F}(i) \tag{5.5}$$

Where, $m_x(i+1)$: Number of instances of chromosome x in $i+1$ generation

$F_x(i)$: Fitness of chromosome x in i generation

$\vec{F}(i)$: Average fitness of chromosome in i generation

Similarly by knowing chromosomes matching the schema in current generation, we can calculate the number of instances of that schema in next generation. It can be written as:

$$m_H(i+1) = [\vec{F}_H(i)/\vec{F}(i)]m_H(i) \qquad (5.6)$$

where, $m_H(i + 1)$: Number of instances of schema H in $i + 1$ generation

$m_H(i)$: Number of instances of schema H in i generation

$\vec{F}_H(i)$: Average fitness of chromosomes containing H in i generation

$\vec{F}(i)$: Average fitness of chromosomes in i generation

Equation 5.6 clearly states that, particular schema grows as the ratio of the average fitness of the schema to the average fitness of population, i.e. Selection process allocates increasing number of samples to above average fit schemata.

However, selection process alone does nothing to promote exploration of new regions of the search space. i.e. it only selects the chromosomes that are already presented in current generation. To avoid such case, crossover and mutation operators are needed. But crossover and mutation both can create schemata as well as can destroy them. Schema Theorem considers only destructive effect of crossover and mutation, i.e. the effect that decreases the number of instances of the schema to be occurred in next generation.

The probability that the schema H will survive after crossover can be expressed as

$$P_H(c) = 1 - P_c[l_d/(l-1)] \qquad (5.7)$$

Where:

P_c : Crossover probability

l: Chromosome length

l_d: Defining length which is calculated as the distance between outermost defined bits of schema H . If crossover takes place within defining length, the probability that the schema H will be disrupted will increase.

Now let us consider the destructive effect caused by the mutation. The probability that the schema H will survive after mutation can be expressed as

$$P_H(m) = (1 - P_m)^n \qquad (5.8)$$

Where,

P_m: Mutation probability

n: Order of schema H , which is equal to the number of defined bits in schema H.

Here, $(1 - P_m)$ represents the probability that an individual bit will not be mutated.

So taking to account the destructive effect of crossover and mutation, equation (5.6) can be reformulated as

$$m_H(i+1) = [F_H(i)/F(i)]m_H(i)[1 - P_c\{l_d/(l-1)\}][(1-P_m)^n] \qquad (5.9)$$

Equation (5.9) is known as the Schema Theorem, which gives lower bound on the expected number of schemata on next generation.

Let us analyse the individual component of schema theorem in more detail. Looking on the formula which calculates destructive effect of crossover, we see that if $l_d << l$, the probability that crossover will take place within l_d is low. So it is clear that the probability of survival of schemata after crossover is higher for the short schemata. Similarly looking on formula which calculates destructive effect of mutation, we see that if value of n is low, the probability that the mutation will take place within defined bits of schema H will be lower. So it is also clear that survival after mutation is high for the low ordered schemata. Finally we can see that if $\vec{F}_H(i) > \vec{F}(i)$, the probability of the schema H being selected for the next generation is high, which means the probability of selection for reproduction is high for above average fit schemata. Consequently we can make the conclusion that the short, low order, above average fit schemata receives increasing samples in subsequent generations. These short, low-order, above average fit schemata are known as **Building Blocks. Building Block Hypothesis** states that GA seeks the near optimal performance through the juxtaposition of these Building Blocks.

It is important to understand that the genetic algorithm depends upon the recombination of Building Blocks to seek the best point. However, if the Building Blocks are misleading due to the coding used or the function itself, the problem may require long waiting times to arrive at the near optimal solution.

5.6. Applications of GA

A genetic algorithm (GA) is a method for solving both constrained and unconstrained optimization problems based on a natural selection process that mimics biological evolution. The algorithm repeatedly modifies a population of individual solutions. At each step, the genetic algorithm randomly selects individuals from the current population and uses them as parents to produce the children for the next generation. Over successive generations, the population "evolves" toward an optimal solution.

You can apply the genetic algorithm to solve problems that are not well suited for standard optimization algorithms, including problems in which the objective function is discontinuous, non-differentiable, stochastic, or highly nonlinear. The genetic algorithm differs from a classical, derivative-based, optimization algorithm in two main ways, as summarized in the following table.

Classical Algorithm	Genetic Algorithm
Generates a single point at each iteration.	Generates a population of points at each iteration.
The sequence of points approaches an optimal solution.	The best point in the population approaches an optimal solution.
Selects the next point in the sequence by a deterministic computation.	Selects the next population by computation which uses random number generators.

5.6.1. Travelling salesman problem

The **Travelling Salesman Problem (TSP)** asks the following question: Given a list of cities and the distances between each pair of cities, what is the shortest possible route that visits each city exactly once and returns to the origin city? It is an **NP-hard** problem in combinatorial optimization, important in operations research and theoretical computer science. TSP is a special case of the travelling purchaser problem.

In the theory of computational complexity, the decision version of the TSP (where, given a length L, the task is to decide whether the graph has any tour shorter than L) belongs to the class of **NP-complete** problems. Thus, it is possible that the ***worst-case running time*** for any algorithm for the TSP increases superpolynomially (or perhaps exponentially) with the number of cities.

The problem was first formulated in 1930 and is one of the most intensively studied problems in optimization. It is used as a benchmark for many optimization methods. Even though the problem is computationally difficult, a large number of heuristics and exact methods are known, so that some instances with tens of thousands of cities can be solved completely and even problems with millions of cities can be approximated within a small fraction of 1%.

The TSP has several applications even in its purest formulation, such as **planning, logistics,** and the manufacture of **microchips.** Slightly modified, it appears as a sub-problem in many areas, such as **DNA sequencing.** In these applications, the concept *city* represents, for example, customers, soldering points, or DNA fragments, and the concept *distance* represents travelling times or cost, or a similarity measure between DNA fragments. In many applications, additional constraints such as limited resources or time windows may be imposed.

5.6.1.1. Description

TSP can be modelled as an undirected weighted graph, such that cities are the graph's vertices, paths are the graph's edges, and a path's distance is the edge's length. It is a minimization problem starting and finishing at a specified vertex after having visited each other vertex exactly once. Often, the model is a complete graph (*i.e.* each pair of vertices is connected by an edge). If no path exists between two cities, adding an arbitrarily long edge will complete the graph without affecting the optimal tour.

As a graph problem

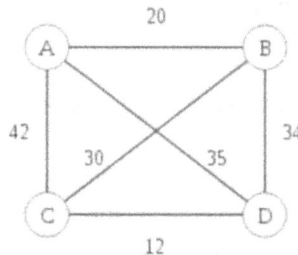

Fig.5.13: Symmetric TSP with four cities

Asymmetric and symmetric

In the *symmetric TSP*, the distance between two cities is the same in each opposite direction, forming an undirected graph. This symmetry halves the number of possible solutions. In the *asymmetric TSP*, paths may not exist in both directions or the distances might be different, forming a directed graph. Traffic collisions, one-way streets, and airfares for cities with different departure and arrival fees are examples of how this symmetry could break down.

Related problems

➢ An equivalent formulation in terms of graph theory is: Given a complete weighted graph (where the vertices would represent the cities, the edges would represent the roads, and the weights would be the cost or distance of that road), find a Hamiltonian cycle with the least weight.

➢ The requirement of returning to the starting city does not change the computational complexity of the problem.

➢ Another related problem is the bottleneck traveling salesman problem (bottleneck TSP): In a weighted graph find a Hamiltonian cycle with the minimum weight of the weightiest edge. The problem is considerably important for practical purpose, excluding the evident transportation and logistics areas. A conventional example is in printed circuit board manufacturing: organizing the route of the drill machine to drill holes in a PCB. In robotic machining or drilling applications, the "cities" are parts to machine or holes (of different sizes) to drill, and the "cost of travel" includes time for retooling the robot (single machine job sequencing problem).

➢ The generalized traveling salesman problem deals with "states" that have (one or more) "cities" and the salesman has to visit exactly one "city" from each "state". Also known as the "traveling politician problem". One application is encountered in ordering a solution to the cutting stock problem in order to minimize knife changes. Another is concerned with drilling in semiconductor manufacturing, see e.g., U.S. Patent 7,054,798. Surprisingly, Behzad and Modarres demonstrated that the generalized traveling salesman problem can be transformed into a standard traveling salesman problem with the same number of cities, but a modified distance matrix.

➢ The sequential ordering problem deals with the problem of visiting a set of cities where precedence relations between the cities exist.

➢ The traveling purchaser problem tackles a purchaser who is charged with buying a set of products. He can purchase these products in several cities, but at different prices and not all cities offer the same products. The objective is to find a route between a subset of the cities, which minimizes total cost (travel cost + purchasing cost) and which enables the purchase of all required products.

5.6.1.2. Integer linear programming formulation

TSP can be formulated as an integer linear program. Label the cities with the numbers $0, ..., n$ and define:

$$x_{ij} = \begin{cases} 1 & \text{the path goes from city } i \text{ to city } j \\ 0 & \text{otherwise} \end{cases}$$

For $i = 0, ..., n$, let u_i be an artificial variable, and finally take c_{ij} to be the distance from city i to city j. Then TSP can be written as the following integer linear programming problem:

$$\min \sum_{i=0}^{n} \sum_{j \neq i, j=0}^{n} c_{ij} x_{ij} \qquad\qquad 0 \leq x_{ij} \leq 1$$

$$u_i \in Z \qquad\qquad i = 0, ..., n$$

$$\sum_{i=0, i \neq j}^{n} x_{ij} = 1 \qquad\qquad j = 0, ... , n$$

$$\sum_{j=0, i \neq j}^{n} x_{ij} = 1 \qquad\qquad i = 0, ... , n$$

$$u_i - u_j + n x_{ij} \leq n - 1 \qquad\qquad 1 \leq i \neq j \neq n$$

The first set of equalities requires that each city be arrived at from exactly one other city, and the second set of equalities requires that from each city there is a departure to exactly one other city. The last constraints enforce that there is only a single tour covering all cities, and not two or more disjointed tours that only collectively cover all cities. To prove this, it is shown below (1) that every feasible solution contains only one closed sequence of cities, and (2) that for every single tour covering all cities, there are values for the dummy variables u_i that satisfy the constraints.

To prove that every feasible solution contains only one closed sequence of cities, it suffices to show that every subtour in a feasible solution passes through city 0 (noting that the equalities ensure there can only be one such tour). For if we sum all the inequalities corresponding to $x_{ij} = 1$ for any subtour of k steps not passing through city 0, we obtain:

$nk \leq (n - 1)k$,

this is a contradiction.

It now must be shown that for every single tour covering all cities, there are values for the dummy variables that satisfy the constraints. Without loss of generality, define the tour as originating (and ending) at city 0. Choose $u_i = t$, if city i is visited in step t (i, $t = 1, 2, ..., n$). Then,

$u_i - u_j \leq n - 1$

since u_i can be no greater than n and can be no less than 1; hence the constraints are satisfied whenever $x_{ij} = 0$. For $x_{ij} = 1$, we have:

$u_i - u_j + n x_{ij} = (t) - (t + 1) + n = n - 1$,

satisfying the constraint.

5.6.1.3. Computing a solution

The traditional lines of attack for the NP-hard problems are the following:

➤ Devising algorithms for finding exact solutions (they will work reasonably fast only for small problem sizes).

➤ Devising "suboptimal" or heuristic algorithms, i.e., algorithms that deliver either seemingly or probably good solutions, but which could not be proved to be optimal.

➤ Finding special cases for the problem ("subproblems") for which either better or exact heuristics are possible.

Computational complexity

The problem has been shown to be NP-hard (more precisely, it is complete for the complexity class FP^{NP};, and the decision problem version ("given the costs and a number x, decide whether there is a round-trip route cheaper than x") is NP-complete. The bottleneck travelling salesman problem is also NP-hard. The problem remains NP-hard even for the case when the cities are in the plane with Euclidean distances, as well as in a number of other restrictive cases. Removing the condition of visiting each city "only once" does not remove the NP-hardness, since it is easily seen that in the planar case there is an optimal tour that visits each city only once (otherwise, by the triangle inequality, a shortcut that skips a repeated visit would not increase the tour length).

Complexity of approximation

In the general case, finding a shortest travelling salesman tour is NPO-complete. If the distance measure is a metric and symmetric, the problem becomes APX-complete and Christofides's algorithm approximates it within 1.5.

If the distances are restricted to 1 and 2 (but still are a metric) the approximation ratio becomes 8/7. In the asymmetric, metric case, only logarithmic performance guarantees are known, the best current algorithm achieves performance ratio 0.814 $\log(n)$; it is an open question if a constant factor approximation exists.

The corresponding maximization problem of finding the *longest* travelling salesman tour is approximable within 63/38. If the distance function is symmetric, the longest tour can be approximated within 4/3 by a deterministic algorithm and within 1/25 (33 + ∈) by a randomized algorithm.

5.6.1.4. Exact algorithms

The most direct solution would be to try all permutations (ordered combinations) and see which one is cheapest (using brute force search). The running time for this approach lies within a polynomial factor of $O(n!)$, the factorial of the number of cities, so this solution becomes impractical even for only 20 cities. One of the earliest applications of dynamic programming is the Held–Karp algorithm that solves the problem in time $O(n^2 2^n)$.

Improving these time bounds seems to be difficult. For example, it has not been determined whether an exact algorithm for TSP that runs in time $O(1.9999^n)$ exists. Other approaches include:

➤ Various branch-and-bound algorithms, which can be used to process TSPs containing 40–60 cities.

➤ Progressive improvement algorithms which use techniques reminiscent of linear programming. Works well for up to 200 cities.

➤ Implementations of branch-and-bound and problem-specific cut generation (branch-and-cut); this is the method of choice for solving large instances. This approach holds the current record, solving an instance with 85,900 cities.

An exact solution for 15,112 German towns from TSPLIB was found in 2001 using the cutting-plane method proposed by George Dantzig, Ray Fulkerson, and Selmer M. Johnson in 1954, based on linear programming. The computations were performed on a network of 110 processors located at Rice University and Princeton University (see the Princeton external link). The total computation time was equivalent to 22.6 years on a single 500 MHz Alpha processor. In May 2004, the travelling salesman problem of visiting all 24,978 towns in Sweden was solved: a tour of length approximately 72,500 kilometers was found and it was proven that no shorter tour exists.

In March 2005, the travelling salesman problem of visiting all 33,810 points in a circuit board was solved using *Concorde TSP Solver*: a tour of length 66,048,945 units was found and it was proven that no shorter tour exists. The computation took approximately 15.7 CPU-years (Cook et al. 2006). In April 2006 an instance with 85,900 points was solved using *Concorde TSP Solver*, taking over 136 CPU-years.

5.6.1.5. Heuristic and approximation algorithms

Various heuristics and approximation algorithms, which quickly yield good solutions have been devised. Modern methods can find solutions for extremely large problems (millions of cities) within a reasonable time which are with a high probability just 2–3% away from the optimal solution. Several categories of heuristics are recognized.

5.6.1.5.1. Constructive heuristics

Nearest Neighbor algorithm for a TSP with 7 cities: The solution changes as the starting point is changed.The nearest neighbor (NN) algorithm (or so-called greedy algorithm) lets the salesman choose the nearest unvisited city as his next move. This algorithm quickly yields an effectively short route. For N cities randomly distributed on a plane, the algorithm on average yields a path 25% longer than the shortest possible path. However, there exist many specially arranged city distributions which make the NN algorithm give the worst route (Gutin, Yeo, and Zverovich, 2002). This is true for both asymmetric and symmetric TSPs (Gutin and Yeo, 2007). Rosenkrantz et al. [1977] showed that the NN algorithm has the approximation factor ô$(\log |V|)$ for instances satisfying the triangle inequality. A variation of NN algorithm, called Nearest Fragment (NF) operator, which connects a group (fragment) of nearest unvisited cities, can find shorter route with successive iterations. The NF operator can also be applied on an initial solution obtained by NN algorithm for further improvement in an elitist model, where only better solutions are accepted. Constructions based on a minimum spanning tree have an approximation ratio of 2. The Christofides algorithm achieves a ratio of 1.5.

The bitonic tour of a set of points is the minimum-perimeter monotone polygon that has the points as its vertices; it can be computed efficiently by dynamic programming. Another constructive heuristic, Match Twice and Stitch (MTS) (Kahng, Reda 2004), performs two sequential matchings, where the second matching is executed after deleting all the edges of the first matching, to yield a set of cycles. The cycles are then stitched to produce the final tour.

5.6.1.5.2. Iterative improvement

➢ **Pairwise exchange**

The pairwise exchange or *2-opt* technique involves iteratively removing two edges and replacing these with two different edges that reconnect the fragments created by edge removal into a new and shorter tour. This is a special case of the k-opt method.

➢ **k-opt heuristic, or Lin–Kernighan heuristics**

Take a given tour and delete k mutually disjoint edges. Reassemble the remaining fragments into a tour, leaving no disjoint subtours (that is, don't connect a fragment's endpoints together). This in effect simplifies the TSP under consideration into a much simpler problem. Each fragment endpoint can be connected to $2k - 2$ other possibilities: of $2k$ total fragment endpoints available, the two endpoints of the fragment under consideration are disallowed. Such a constrained $2k$-city TSP can then be solved with brute force methods to find the least-cost recombination of the original fragments. The k-opt technique is a special case of the V-opt or variable-opt technique. The most popular of the k-opt methods are 3-opt, and these were introduced by Shen Lin of Bell Labs in 1965. There is a special case of 3-opt where the edges are not disjoint (two of the edges are adjacent to one another). In practice, it is often possible to achieve substantial improvement over 2-opt without the combinatorial cost of the general 3-opt by restricting the 3-changes to this special subset where two of the removed edges are adjacent. This so-called two-and-a-half-opt typically falls roughly midway between 2-opt and 3-opt, both in terms of the quality of tours achieved and the time required to achieve those tours.

➢ *V-opt heuristic*

The variable-opt method is related to, and a generalization of the k-opt method. Whereas the k-opt methods remove a fixed number (k) of edges from the original tour, the variable-opt methods do not fix the size of the edge set to remove. Instead they grow the set as the search process continues. The best known method in this family is the Lin–Kernighan method (mentioned above as a misnomer for 2-opt). Shen Lin and Brian Kernighan first published their method in 1972, and it was the most reliable heuristic for solving travelling salesman problems for nearly two decades. More advanced variable-opt methods were developed at Bell Labs in the late 1980s by David Johnson and his research team. These methods (sometimes called Lin–Kernighan–Johnson) build on the Lin–Kernighan method, adding ideas from tabu search and evolutionary computing. The basic Lin–Kernighan technique gives results that are guaranteed to be at least 3-opt. The Lin–Kernighan–Johnson methods compute a Lin–Kernighan tour, and then perturb the tour by what has been described as a mutation that removes at least four edges and reconnecting the tour in a different way, then *V*-opting the new tour. The mutation is often enough to move the tour from the local minimum identified by Lin–Kernighan. *V*-opt methods are widely considered the most powerful heuristics for the problem, and are able to address special cases, such as the Hamilton Cycle Problem and other non-metric TSPs that other heuristics fail on. For many years Lin–Kernighan–Johnson had identified optimal solutions for all TSPs where an optimal solution was known and had identified the best known solutions for all other TSPs on which the method had been tried.

5.6.1.5.3. Randomized improvement

Optimized Markov chain algorithms which use local searching heuristic sub-algorithms can find a route extremely close to the optimal route for 700 to 800 cities.

TSP is a touchstone for many general heuristics devised for combinatorial optimization such as **genetic algorithms, simulated annealing, Tabu search, ant colony optimization, river formation dynamics** and **the cross entropy method**, we will discuss some of these in the upcoming chapter-6.

5.6.2. Job shop scheduling

Job shop scheduling (or job-shop problem) is an optimization problem in computer science and operations research in which ideal jobs are assigned to resources at particular times. The most basic version is as follows:

We are given n jobs $J_1, J_2, ..., J_n$ of varying sizes, which need to be scheduled on m identical machines, while trying to minimize the makespan. The makespan is the total length of the schedule (that is, when all the jobs have finished processing). Nowadays, the problem is presented as an online problem (dynamic scheduling), that is, each job is presented, and the online algorithm needs to make a decision about that job before the next job is presented.

This problem is one of the best known online problems, and was the first problem for which competitive analysis was presented, by Graham in 1966. Best problem instances for basic model with makespan objective are due to Taillard.

5.6.2.1. Problem variations

Many variations of the problem exist, including the following:

➢   Machines can be related, independent, equal
➢   Machines can require a certain gap between jobs or no idle-time
➢   Machines can have sequence-dependent setups
➢   Objective function can be to minimize the makespan, the L_p norm, tardiness, maximum lateness etc. It can also be multi-objective optimization problem
➢   Jobs may have constraints, for example a job i needs to finish before job j can be started (see workflow). Also, the objective function can be multi-criteria.

➢ Jobs and machines have mutual constraints, for example, certain jobs can be scheduled on some machines only

➢ Set of jobs can relate to different set of machines

➢ Deterministic (fixed) processing times or probabilistic processing times

v There may also be some other side constraints

If one already knows that the travelling salesman problem is NP-hard (as it is), then the job-shop problem with sequence-dependent setup is clearly also NP-hard, since the TSP is special case of the JSP with m=1 (the salesman is the machine and the cities are the jobs).

Problem representation

The disjunctive graph is one of the popular models used for describing the job shop scheduling problem instances. A mathematical statement of the problem can be made as follows:

Let $M = \{M_1, M_2, \ldots, M_m\}$ and $J = \{J_1, J_2, \ldots, J_n\}$ be two finite sets. On account of the industrial origins of the problem, the M_i are called **machines** and the J_j are called **jobs**.

Let X denote the set of all sequential assignments of jobs to machines, such that every job is done by every machine exactly once; elements $x \in X$ may be written as $n \times m$ matrices, in which column i lists the jobs that machine M_i will do, in order. For example, the matrix

$$x = \begin{pmatrix} 1 & 2 \\ 2 & 3 \\ 3 & 1 \end{pmatrix}$$

means that machine M_1 will do the three jobs J_1, J_2, J_3 in the order J_1, J_2, J_3 while machine M_2 will do the jobs in the order J_2, J_3, J_1.

Suppose also that there is some **cost function** $C: X \to [0, +\infty]$. The cost function may be interpreted as a "total processing time", and may have some expression in terms of times $C_{ij}: M \times J \to [0, +\infty]$, the cost/time for machine M_i to do job J_j.

The **job-shop problem** is to find an assignment of jobs $x \in X$ such that $C(x)$ is a minimum, that is, there is no $y \in X$ such that $C(x) > C(y)$.

The problem of infinite cost

One of the first problems that must be dealt with in the JSP is that many proposed solutions have infinite cost: i.e., there exists $x_\infty \in X$ such that $C(x_\infty) = +\infty$. In fact, it is quite simple to concoct examples of such x_∞ by ensuring that two machines will deadlock, so that each waits for the output of the other's next step.

5.6.2.2. Offline makespan minimization

➢ **Atomic jobs**

The simplest form of the offline makespan minimization problem deals with atomic jobs, that is, jobs that are not subdivided into multiple operations. It is equivalent to packing a number of items of various different sizes into a fixed number of bins, such that the maximum bin size needed is as small as possible. (If instead the number of bins is to be minimized, and the bin size is fixed, the problem becomes a different problem, known as the <u>bin packing problem</u>.)

Hochbaum and Shmoys presented a polynomial-time approximation scheme in 1987 that finds an approximate solution to the offline makespan minimization problem with atomic jobs to any desired degree of accuracy.

➢ **Jobs consisting of multiple operations**

The basic form of the problem of scheduling jobs with multiple (*M*) operations, over *M* machines, such that all of the first operations must be done on the first machine, all of the second operations on the second, etc., and a single job cannot be performed in parallel, is known as the **open shop scheduling** problem. Various algorithms exist, including genetic algorithms.

1. Johnson's algorithm

A heuristic algorithm by S. M. Johnson can be used to solve the case of a 2 machine N job problem when all jobs are to be processed in the same order. The steps of algorithm are as follows:

Job P_i has two operations, of duration P_{i1}, P_{i2}, to be done on Machine *M1*, *M2* in that sequence.

➢ *Step 1.* List A = { 1, 2, ..., N}, List *L1* = {}, List *L2* = {}.

➢ *Step 2.* From all available operation durations, pick the minimum.

If the minimum belongs to P_{k1}, Remove *K* from list *A*; Add *K* to end of List *L1*.

If minimum belongs to P_{k2}, Remove *K* from list *A*; Add *K* to beginning of List *L2*.

➢ *Step 3.* Repeat Step 2 until List *A* is empty.

➢ *Step 4.* Join List L1, List L2. This is the optimum sequence.

Johnson's method only works optimally for two machines. However, since it is optimal, and easy to compute, some researchers have tried to adopt it for *M* machines, (*M* > 2.)

The idea is as follows: Imagine that each job requires m operations in sequence, on *M1*, *M2* ... Mm. We combine the first *m*/2 machines into an (imaginary) Machining center, *MC1*, and the remaining Machines into a Machining Center *MC2*. Then the total processing time for a Job *P* on *MC1* = sum(operation times on first *m*/2 machines), and processing time for Job *P* on *MC2* = sum(operation times on last *m*/2 machines).

By doing so, we have reduced the m-Machine problem into a Two Machining center scheduling problem. We can solve this using Johnson's method.

Here is an example of a job shop scheduling problem formulated in AMPL as a mixed-integer programming problem with indicator constraints:

```
param N_JOBS;
param N_MACHINES;
```

```
set JOBS ordered = 1..N_JOBS;
set MACHINES ordered = 1..N_MACHINES;

param ProcessingTime{JOBS, MACHINES} > 0;

param CumulativeTime{i in JOBS, j in MACHINES} =
    sum {jj in MACHINES: ord(jj) <= ord(j)} ProcessingTime[i,jj];

param TimeOffset{i1 in JOBS, i2 in JOBS: i1 <> i2} =
    max {j in MACHINES}
    (CumulativeTime[i1,j] - CumulativeTime[i2,j] +
    ProcessingTime[i2,j]);

var end >= 0;
var start{JOBS} >= 0;
var precedes{i1 in JOBS, i2 in JOBS: ord(i1) < ord(i2)} binary;

minimize makespan: end;

subj to makespan_def{i in JOBS}:
    end >= start[i] + sum{j in MACHINES} ProcessingTime[i,j];

subj to no12_conflict{i1 in JOBS, i2 in JOBS: ord(i1) < ord(i2)}:
    precedes[i1,i2] ==> start[i2] >= start[i1] + TimeOffset[i1,i2];

subj to no21_conflict{i1 in JOBS, i2 in JOBS: ord(i1) < ord(i2)}:
 !precedes[i1,i2] ==> start[i1] >= start[i2] + TimeOffset[i2,i1];

data;

param N_JOBS := 4;
param N_MACHINES := 3;

param ProcessingTime:
1 2 3 :=
1 4 2 1
2 3 6 2
3 7 2 3
4 1 5 8;
```

5.6.3. Network Design Routing

The mobile ad hoc network is a decentralized and self organized wireless network which does not work on any fixed infrastructure so it is having a time variant topology which varies time to time due to the mobility of the nodes. In the same way the natural world is enormous, dynamic, incredibly diverse, and highly complex. Inspite of the immanent challenges of surviving in such a adaptive world, biological organisms evolve, self-codify, renovate, navigate, and prosper. They do so without any centralized control and with just the local knowledge. Our Mobile Ad hoc networks are increasingly facing the similar challenges as they grow larger in size. Many research efforts have been made based on the Genetic Algorithms for the development of the various data routing techniques for MANETs. As a result, genetically inspired research in Mobile Ad hoc Networks is a quickly growing field. This section begins by exploring why Genetics and MANETs research are such natural counterparts. We then present a broad overview of genetically inspired research in MANETs. We concluded how genetics concepts have been most successfully applied in MANETs.

In the last few years there are various GA based protocols design techniques have been suggested and implemented by the research community some of the proposed techniques are discussed below:

1. **GA in solving the dynamic multicast problem in mobile adhoc networks MANETs:**
    In a MANET, the network topology keeps changing due to its inherent characteristics such as the node mobility and energy conservation. Therefore, an effective multicast algorithm should track the topological changes and adapt the best multicast tree to the changes accordingly. So the use of genetic algorithms with immigrants schemes to solve the dynamic QoS multicast problem in MANETs. Extensive experiments are conducted based on both of the dynamic network models. The experimental results show that these immigrants based genetic algorithms can quickly adapt to the environmental changes (i.e., the network topology changes) and produce high quality solutions following each change.

2. **GA for energy-efficient based multicast routing on MANETs:**
    In ad hoc networks, mobile node battery energy is limited and is one of the important constraints for designing multicast routing protocols. An energy-efficient genetic algorithm mechanism to resolve these problems was proposed. To design a source-tree-based routing algorithm and build the shortest-path multicast tree to minimize delay time by using a small population size in the genetic algorithm. Only a few nodes are involved in the route computation. The simulation results show that the proposed method based on GA is an efficient and robust algorithm for multicast route selection.

3. **GA in routing optimization in Ad hoc Networks:**
    Ad hoc networks require a highly adoptive routing scheme to deal with the frequent topology changes. So the proposed algorithm for improving routing in clustering algorithm based on both Clusterhead gateway switching protocol (CGSR) and the mechanisms of a genetic algorithm (GA).As the GA mechanisms allow for self configuration quickly and efficiently to adjust an ever changing local topology, thus initiating fewer link breakages. Also the proposed Genetic algorithm shows that GA's are able to find if not the shortest, at least a very good path between source and destination nodes in MANETs.

4. **GA in QoS Route Selection for Mobile Ad -hoc Networks:**
    It is a challenging issue designing a QoS routing protocol for mobile ad hoc networks. Because in selecting the most optimal route from source to destination, one has to select from a set of routes with corresponding connectivity qualities.

The QoS routing scheme that selects a source to destination route using genetic algorithm such that the route need to satisfy the node bandwidth, node delay, end –to-end delay and node connectivity index. The simulation results shows that QoS routing can successfully utilized GA in finding the optimal route.

5. **GA for Path Bandwidth calculation in TDMA-based MANETs:**

    As the development of routing protocols for Mobile Ad Hoc Networks (MANETs) has become an important research field because of the promising applications provided by the MANETs. In a TDMA - based MANETs, routing protocols should be designed such that it meets the QoS constraints like bandwidth in addition to finding the shortest path. As most of the existing protocols concentrate only on finding the shortest path. Therefore with an aim to satisfy the QoS requirements by maximizing the path bandwidth found between the source and destination. Thus the efficient GA approach uses genetic algorithm to solve the problem of finding the path with maximum bandwidth.

6. **GA based approach in Genetic Zone Routing Protocol (GZRP):**

    GZRP applies the Genetic Algorithm (GA) to Zone Routing Protocol (ZRP) for finding a limited set of multiple alternative routes to the destinations, in order to provide load balancing and fault tolerance during node or link failure by using the routing database available at the border nodes.

    Thus we sum up few of the applications out of the various applications of the GA based Approach ,which is best suitable from the point of view of MANETs, in the design of routing protocols.

    A number of research efforts have attempted to design self-organizing mobile networks based on Genetic Algorithms. A great deal of successful research in the field of Mobile Ad Hoc

    Networks have been inspired by Genetic Algorithms. Yet, we believe genetically inspired mobile ad hoc networking still has much room to grow. In particular, there are great opportunities in exploring a new approach. Whether successful or not, current research tends to follow the same general philosophy:

    Observe some high-level behavior in nature which has a direct parallel to a desirable behavior for mobile ad hoc networks (MANETs).

    Explore the basic biology of this behavior – what individual components make up the system, the processes these components perform, what mathematical models have been used to describe this behavior, and so on. Look for components, processes, or models that seem like they could map well to the computer networking domain. Turn these components, processes, or models into algorithms, new mathematical models, or software implementations. Generally attempt to stay as close as possible to the biological

    Therefore, the goal of bio-inspired research should be to find broader lessons and principles in the way large biological systems are built, then determine how to apply these lessons and principles to the design of networked systems such as MANETs.

5.6.4.   Time Tabling Problem

Let *P* be a population of *N* chromosomes (*individuals* of *P*). Let *P*(0) be the initial population, randomly generated, and *P*(*t*) the population at time *t*. The GA generates a new population *P*(*t* + 1) from the old population *P*(*t*) applying some *genetic operators*. The new population is created by means of the *reproduction* operator, that gives higher reproduction probability to higher fitted individuals, and by the subsequent application of the *crossover* and of the *mutation* operators, which modify randomly chosen individuals of population *P*(*t*) into new ones. The overall effect of GAs work is to move the population P towards areas of the solution space with higher values of the fitness function.

The computational speed-up that we obtain using GAs with respect to random search is due to the fact that our search is directed by the fitness function. This direction is not based on whole chromosomes, but on their parts which are strongly related to high values of the fitness function; these parts are called *building blocks*. It has been demonstrated that GAs are very efficient at processing building blocks. GAs are therefore useful for every problem where an optimal solution is composed of a collection of building blocks. This computational paradigm allows an effective search in very large search spaces. It has been recently applied to various kinds of optimization problems, including NP-complete problems, e.g. Traveling Salesman and Satisfiability, with satisfactory results.

The three basic genetic operators are:

➢ **reproduction**, an operator which allocates in the population *P*(*t* + 1) an increasing number of copies of the individuals with a *f.f.* above the average in population *P*(*t*);

➢ **crossover**, a genetic operator activated with a probability p_c, independent of the specific individuals on which it is applied; it takes as input two randomly chosen individuals (parents) and combines them to generate two sons;

➢ **mutation**, an operator that causes, with probability p_m, the change of an allelic value of a randomly chosen gene; for instance, if the alphabet were {0, 1}, an allelic value of 0 would be modified into 1 and vice versa.

The main goal of our research is to understand the limitations of the GA and its potentialities in addressing highly constrained problems, that is optimization problems where a minimal change to a feasible solution is very likely to generate an infeasible one. As a test problem we have chosen the timetable problem (TTP), that is known to be NP-hard, but which has been intensively investigated given its great practical relevance.

5.6.4.1. Time Timetable Problem

We will use the construction of a timetable, or schedule of classes, for an Italian high school as the medium for our investigation. The ideas introduced in this paper can be applied, of course, to the solution of other, and possibly very different, instances of the timetable problem. The possibility of "on field" testing has been the main reason for the choice of this particular problem example. (In a typical Italian high-school, a class receives five hours of lessons, six days a week. Teachers may teach one or more subjects, usually in two or more classes. In addition to their eighteen-hour teaching demand, they have other activities, as described in the paper. Also, every teacher has the right to take one day-off per week, in addition to Sundays.)

The construction of the lesson timetable for an Italian high school may be decomposed in the formulation of several interrelated timetables. In fact, sections are always coupled in pairs, with a couple of sections sharing many teachers and resources (e.g. laboratories). Two coupled sections can therefore be processed as an "atomic unit", not further decomposable given its high internal dependencies, but relatively isolated from other sections.

Given these premises, the problem is described by:

1. a list of m teachers (20-24 in our case);
2. a list of p classes involved (10 for the two coupled sections);
3. a list of n weekly teaching hours for each class (30);
4. the *curriculum* of each class, that is the list of the frequencies of the teachers working in the class;
5. some external conditions (for example the hours during which some teachers are involved in other sections or activities).

A formal representation of the TTP is the following. Given the 5-tuple $< T, A, H, R, f >$ where

T is a finite set $\{T_1, T_2, .. , T_j, .. , T_m\}$ of m resources (teachers);

A is a set of jobs (teaching in the p classes and other activities) to be accomplished by the teachers;

H is a finite set $\{H_1, H_2, .. , H_j, .. , H_n\}$ of n time-intervals (hours);

R is a $m\,n$ matrix of $r_{ij} \in A$ (a timetable);

f is a function to be minimized, $f: R \Rightarrow ^\circledR$; we want to compute; $\min f (\sigma, \Delta, \Omega, \Pi)$, where, σ is the number of *infeasibilities*, as defined in the following;

Δ is the set of didactic costs (e.g., not having the hours of the same subject spread over the whole week);

Ω is a set of organizational costs (e.g., not having at least one teacher available for possible temporary teaching posts);

Π is a set of personal costs (e.g., not having a specific day-off).

Every solution (timetable) generated by our algorithm is *feasible* if it satisfies the following constraints:

➤ every teacher and every class must be present in the timetable in a predefined number of hours;

➤ there may not be more than one teacher in the same class in the same hour;

➤ no teacher can be in two classes in the same hour;

➢ there can be no "uncovered hours" (that is, hours when no teacher has been assigned to a class).

The problem has been approached by means of linear programming with binary variables, using some heuristics. In fact, if it were approached with standard algorithms, i.e. defining binary variables x_{ijk} (where, according to the parameters previously specified, i identifies a teacher, j identifies a time-interval and k identifies a class) the problem would be represented by 6000 variables ($i = 1, \ldots , 20; j = 1, \ldots , 30; k = 1, \ldots , 10$), which makes it intractable. We have decided to approach it by means of an evolutionary stochastic algorithm, namely a Genetic Algorithm (GA), introduced in the next section.

5.6.4.2. The genetic approach to the timetable problem

Some difficulties are encountered when applying GAs to constrained combinatorial optimization problems. The most relevant of them is that crossover and mutation operators, as previously defined, may generate infeasible solutions.

The following corrections to this drawback have been proposed.

1. change the representation of a solution in such a way that crossover can be applied consistently;
2. define new crossover and mutation operators which generate only feasible solutions;
3. apply the crossover and mutation operators and then make some kind of *genetic repair* that changes the infeasible solutions to feasible ones through the use of a filtering algorithm.

In the traveling salesman case the most successful approaches have been the introduction of a new crossover operator and the application of genetic repair. The redefinition of mutation is in this case particularly straightforward: it is sufficient to exchange the position of two cities in the string. In the TTP on the other hand, even after the redefinition of both crossover and mutation, it has been necessary to implement genetic repair.

We now describe how we approached the problem of generating a school timetable for a pair of sections of an Italian high school.

The alphabet we chose is the set **A** of the jobs that teachers have to perform: its elements are the classes to be covered and other activities. We indicate:

➢ with the characters 1, 2, 3, .. ,0 the ten classes where the lessons have to be taught;
➢ with the character *D* the hours at disposal for temporary teaching posts;
➢ with the character *A* the hours for the professional development;
➢ with the character *S* the hours during which lessons are taught in classes of sections different from the two considered; this hours are fixed in the initialization phase and are called *fixed hours*;
➢ with the character ⃞ the hours in which the teacher does not have to work;
➢ with the characters —— the teacher's day-off.

Our alphabet is therefore A = {1,2,3,4,5,6,7,8,9,0,D,A,S,□,-}. This alphabet allows us to represent the problem as a matrix R (an m·n matrix of r_{ij}□A) where each row corresponds to a teacher and each column to a hour. Every element r_{ij} of the matrix R is a gene; its allelic value may vary on the subset of A specific to the teacher corresponding to the row containing the gene.

The problem is therefore represented by matrices similar to that proposed in Table 5.2. To be a feasible timetable a matrix must satisfy the constraints discussed in Section 1.

Teacher-Subject	Mon	Tue	Wed	Thu	Fri	Sat
Literature - 1	□11□1	112□□	□□□11	2212□	11111	————
Literature - 2	□6□□6	7777□	□□□77	66□□7	——-	7777□
Literature - 3	□□□2□	6666	2□□22	——-	6266□	6622□
Literature - 4	□8□□□	44□□□	——-	□□4□8	84888	88444
Literature - 5	——-	□5555	□□355	□□353	3□33□	33□□□
Literature - 6	000□0	——-	0□999	0099□	9□□□□	□9□□□
English	152□5	32411	53□□□	□□□□5	43422	——-
German	77997	98800	607□6	——-	□6□□□	□□08□
History and Philosophy - 1	5□33□	□3343	——-	55□44	□□□4□	4555□
History and Philosophy - 2	9□□8□	——-	□88□0	990□□	0□009	908□8
Math and Physics - 1	——-	5□□□□	45434	4453□	5□55□	□4333
Math and Physics - 2	□9□09	09998	□□□08	88800	□9□□0	——-
Math - 1	SSSS2	2S1AA	112□□	□□□1□	——-	22□1□
Math - 2	6S66S	SS□AA	□7S6□	——-	7777□	□□□6□
Natural sciences	33444	80022	——-	7378□	□8995	5□9□□
Art	84518	——-	96643	37279	2□□□□	01□05
Experimental Physics	2277S	S□□67	——-	1166□	□□2SS	SS1□□
Gymnastic - 1	SSS□□	□□□34	345SS	□□□SS	S5□□□	——-
Gymnastic - 2	SSS□□	□□□89	890SS	□□□SS	SO□□□	——-
Religion	4S853	□□□□□	721S□	SS□□□	——-	SS690

Table 5.2: Example of a matrix representing a timetable

The constraints are managed as follows.

➢ by the *genetic operators*, so that the set of hours to be taught by each teacher, allocated in the initialization phase, cannot be changed by the application of the genetic operators (which have been specifically redefined for this purpose);

➢ by the *filtering algorithm*, so that the infeasibilities caused by the application of genetic operators are, totally or partially, eliminated by filtering;

➢ by the *objective function*, so that selective pressure is used to limit the number of individuals with infeasibilities (infeasibilities are explicitly considered in the objective function, by means of high penalties).

➤ It is possible to distinguish between two kinds of constraints: rows and columns. *Row constraints* are incorporated in the genetic operators and are therefore always satisfied; *column constraints* (infeasibilities due to superimpositions or uncovered classes) are managed by means of a combination of fitness function and genetic repair. Single-teacher solutions (i.e. solutions which satisfy a single teacher) are constrained each other by column constraints. Genetic repair must convert infeasible timetables into feasible ones, modifying them as little as possible.

We decided to manage the infeasibilities by means of both filtering and fitness function penalties because in this way the algorithm has a greater degree of freedom in moving through the search space. This choice is due to the difficulty of the problem: in our application, in fact, every teacher represents a TSP-like problem (consisting of the analysis of the permutations of a predefined symbol set), which has a search space of dimension

$$k = \left(\sum_h n_h\right)! / \prod_h (n_h!) = \prod_h^{n!} (n_h!)$$

where n_h is the number of repetitions of the h-th character in the row representing the teacher, and n is the total number of weekly hours. A teacher working in several classes has a value of k greater than that of a teacher working in fewer classes, the total number of teaching hours being the same.

5.7. Implementation of GA using MATLAB

In this section we describe the procedure of implementing the canonical genetic algorithm using MATLAB. For simplicity, we assume that the task is to achieve the maximum of a one-variable multi-modal function, $f(x) > 0$, for x belonging to the domain $[a, b]$. The implementation steps are as follows.

5.7.1. Initialization

For CGA, a binary representation is needed to describe each individual in the population of interest. Each individual is made up of a sequence of binary bits (0 and 1). Let stringlength and popsize denote the length of the binary sequence and the number of individuals involved in the population. Each individual uses a string codification of the form shown in Fig. 3. Using MATLAB, the whole data structure of the population is implemented by a matrix of size popsize×(stringlength+2):

$$Pop = \begin{pmatrix} binary\ string\ 1 & x1 & f(x1) \\ binary\ string\ 2 & x2 & f(x2) \\ binary\ string\ popsize & xpopsize & f(xpopsize) \end{pmatrix}$$

Fig.5.14: Binary string representation for the optimization of a one-variable function.

The first stringlength column contains the bits which characterize the binary codification of the real variable x. The strings are randomly generated, but a test must be made to ensure that the corresponding values belong to the function domain. The crossover and mutation operators will be applied on this stringlength-bit sub-string. The (stringlength+1)-th and (stringlength+2)-th columns contain the real x value, used as auxiliary information in order to check the algorithm's evolution, and the corresponding f(x), which is assumed to be the fitness value of the string in this case. Then the initialization process can be completed using the following code:

```
function [pop]=initialise(popsize, stringlength, fun);
pop=round(rand(popsize, stringlength+2));
pop(:, stringlength+1)=sum(2.^(size(pop(:,1:stringlength),2)
"1:"1:0).
*pop(:,1:stringlength))*(b"a)/(2.^stringlength"1)+a;
pop(;, stringlength+2)=fun(pop(;, stringlength+1));
end
```

In the above routine, we first generate the binary bits randomly, and then replace the (stringlength+1)-th and (stringlength+2)-th columns with real x values and objective function values, where fun is the objective function, usually denoted by a .m file.

5.7.2 Crossover

Crossover takes two individuals parent1, parent2, and produces two new individuals child1, child2. Let pc be the probability of crossover, then the crossover operator can be implemented as follows:

```
function [child1, child2]=crossover(parent1, parent2, pc); if
(rand<pc)
cpoint=round(rand*(stringlength"2))+1;
child1=[parent1(:,1:cpoint) parent2(:,cpoint1+1:stringlength)];
child2=[parent2(:,1:cpoint) parent1(:,cpoint1+1:stringlength)];
child1(:, stringlength+1)=sum(2.^(size(child1(:,1:stringlength),2)
"1:"1:0).
*child1(:,:stringlength))*(b"a)/(2.^stringlength"1)+a;
child2(:, stringlength+1)=sum(2.^(size(child2(:,1:stringlength),2)
"1:"1:0).
*child2(:,1:stringlength))*(b"a)/(2.^stringlength"1)+a;
child1(:, stringlength+2)=fun(child1(:, stringlength+1)); child2(:,
stringlength+2)=fun(child2(:, stringlength+1));
else
child1=parent1; child2=parent2;
end
end
```

At the top of the crossover routine, we determine whether we are going to perform crossover on the current pair of parent chromosomes. Specifically, we generate a random number and compare it with the probability parameter pc. If the random number is less than pc, a crossover operation is performed; otherwise, no crossover is performed and the parent individuals are returned. If a crossover operation is called for, a crossing point cpoint is selected between 1 and stringlength. The crossing point cpoint is selected in the function round, which returns a pseudorandom integer between specified lower and upper limits (between 1 and stringlength "1). Finally, the partial exchange of cross-over is carried out and the real values and fitness of the new individuals child1, child2, are computed.

5.7.3. Mutation

Mutation alters one individual, parent, to produce a single new individual, child. Let pm be the probability of mutation, then as in the crossover routine, we first determine whether we are going to perform mutation on the current pair of parent chromosomes. If a mutation operation is called for, we select a mutating point mpoint, and then change a true to a false (1 to 0) or vice versa. The real value and fitness of the new individual child are then computed:

```
function [child]=mutation(parent, pm): if
rand<pm)
mpoint=round(rand*(stringlength"1))+1; child=parent;
child[mpoint]=abs(parent[mpoint]"1);
child(:, stringlength+1)=sum(2.⁹ (size(child(:,1:stringlength),2)
"1:"1:0).
*child(:,1:stringlength))*(b"a)/ (2.⁹stringlength"1)+a;
child(:, stringlength+2)=fun(child(:, stringlength+1)); else
child=parent;
end
end
```

5.7.4. Selection

The selection operator determines which of the individuals will survive and continue in the next generation. The selection operator implemented here is roulette wheel selection and this is perhaps the simplest way to implement selection. We first calculate the probabilities of each individual being selected, based on equation (1). Then the partial sum of the probabilities is accumulated in the vector prob. We also generate a vector rns containing normalized random numbers, by comparing the elements of the two vectors rns and prob, we decide the individuals which will take part in the new population:

```
function [newpop]=roulette(oldpop);
totalfit=sum(oldpop(:,stringlength+2));
prob=oldpop(:,stringlength+2) / totalfit;
prob=cumsum(prob);
rns=sort(rand(popsize,1)); ®tin=1; newin=1;
while newin<=popsize
```

```
if  (rns(newin)<prob(®tin))  newpop(newin,:)=oldpop(®tin,:);
newin=newin+1;
else
fitin=fitin+1;
end
```

5.7.5. Accessing on-line information

We have shown how the three main pieces of CGA may be easily coded and easily understood. After implementing the key genetic operators, implementation of the main program is straightforward. At the moment, the World Wide Web and the Internet provide some quality MATLAB source codes for different kinds of genetic algorithms. Chris Houck, Jeff Joines, and Mike Kay at North Carolina State University have developed two versions of the genetic algorithm for function optimization using both MATLAB 4 and MATLAB 5. The WWW site is: http://www.ie.ncsu.edu/mirage. Andrew F. Potvin has also implemented a simple version of genetic algorithm which is available on the WWW site: http://unix.hensa.ac.uk/ftp/mirrors/matlab/contrib/v4/optim/genetic/.

It should be pointed out that although the above Toolboxes are very useful in solving many engineering problems, they are sometimes too comprehensive for the students. In many situations, the students need to modify the genetic operators to meet their own problem-dependent requirements. However, they found it very difficult to change some parts of the above GA Toolboxes, because the whole package is heavily interconnected. With the source codes provided in this section, the students found it quite easy to modify the genetic operators and invent some new genetic operators. This is helpful in promoting the students' creativity, which is necessary and important in the new teaching process.

Review Questions

1.   What is Evolutionary Algorithm?
2.   Explain the generation cycle of genetic algorithm.
3.   Write short notes on crossover operator and mutation operator.
4.   Explain briefly the applications of genetic algorithms and how genetic algorithms differ from traditional algorithms.
5.   Short note on reproduction operators.

CHAPTER 6

Few Auxiliary Algorithms

"Let us change our traditional attitude to the construction of programs. Instead of imagining that our main task is to instruct a computer what to do, let us concentrate rather on explaining to human beings what we want a computer to do."

-Donald Knuth
American Computer Scientist

"True optimization is the revolutionary contribution of modern research to decision processes."

-George Bernhard Dantzig
Computer Scientist

6.1.   Simulated Annealing

In metallurgy annealing is a process in which metals are gradually cooled down to make them reach a state of low energy where they are very strong. Annealing process includes increasing as well as decreasing the temperature of a material to modify its physical properties due to the variations in its basic structure. As the metal settles down to low temperature or in other words cools down, its new structure becomes stable and, consequently provoking the metal to retain its newly obtained characteristics. Simulated annealing is an analogous method for optimization. It is typically described in terms of thermodynamics. In simulated annealing we constantly vary the temperature to simulate this heating process. The random movement corresponds to high temperature; at low temperature, there is little randomness. Initially the temperature is set at high and then it is allowed to gradually 'cool' as the algorithm runs. This subtle 'cooling' process makes the simulated annealing algorithm remarkably effective at finding a close to optimum solution when dealing with large problems which contain numerous local optimums. While this temperature variable is high the algorithm will be allowed, with more frequency, to accept solutions that are worse than our current solution. This gives the algorithm the ability to jump out of any local optimums it finds itself in early on in execution. As the temperature is reduced so is the chance of accepting worse solutions, therefore allowing the algorithm to gradually focus in on a area of the search space in which hopefully, a close to optimum solution can be found.

Simulated annealing is a process where the temperature is reduced slowly, starting from a random search at high temperature eventually becoming pure greedy descent as it approaches zero temperature. The randomness should tend to jump out of local minima and find regions that have a low heuristic value; greedy descent will lead to local minima. At high temperatures, worsening steps are more likely than at lower temperatures.

Simulated annealing maintains a current assignment of values to variables. At each step, it picks a variable at random, then picks a value at random. If assigning that value to the variable is an improvement or does not increase the number of conflicts, the algorithm accepts the assignment and there is a new current assignment. Otherwise, it accepts the assignment with some probability, depending on the temperature and how much worse it is than the current assignment. If the change is not accepted, the current assignment is unchanged.

To control how many worsening steps are accepted, there is a positive real-valued temperature T. Suppose A is the current assignment of a value to each variable. Suppose that $h(A)$ is the evaluation of assignment A to be minimized. For solving constraints, h is typically the number of conflicts. Simulated annealing selects a neighbor at random, which gives a new assignment A'. If $h(A') \leq h(A)$, it accepts the assignment and A' becomes the new assignment. Otherwise, the assignment is only accepted randomly with probability

$$e^{(h(A)-h(A'))/T} \qquad (6.1)$$

Thus, if $h(A')$ is close to $h(A)$, the assignment is more likely to be accepted. If the temperature is high, the exponent will be close to zero, and so the probability will be close to 1. As the temperature approaches zero, the exponent approaches ∞, and the probability approaches zero.

Temperature	Probability of acceptance		
	1-worse	2-worse	3-worse
10	0.9	0.82	0.74
1	0.37	0.14	0.05
0.25	0.018	0.0003	0.000006
0.1	0.00005	2×10^{-9}	9×10^{-14}

Table 6.1: Probability of simulated annealing accepting worsening steps

Table 6.1 shows the probability of accepting worsening steps at different temperatures. In this figure, k-worse means that $h(A')-h(A) = k$. For example, if the temperature is 10 (i.e., $T = 10$), a change that is one worse (i.e., if $h(a) - h(a') = -1$) will be accepted with probability $e^{-0.1}$ approx 0.9; a change that is two worse will be accepted with probability $e^{-0.2}$ approx 0.82. If the temperature T is 1, accepting a change that is one worse will happen with probability e^{-1} approx 0.37. If the temperature is 0.1, a change that is one worse will be accepted with probability e^{-10} approx 0.00005. At this temperature, it is essentially only performing steps that improve the value or leave it unchanged.

If the temperature is high, as in the $T = 10$ case, the algorithm tends to accept steps that only worsen a small amount; it does not tend to accept very large worsening steps. There is a slight preference for improving steps. As the temperature is reduced (e.g., when $T = 1$), worsening steps, although still possible, become much less likely. When the temperature is low (e.g., 0.1), it is very rare that it chooses a worsening step.

Simulated annealing requires an **annealing schedule**, which specifies how the temperature is reduced as the search progresses. Geometric cooling is one of the most widely used schedules. An example of a geometric cooling schedule is to start with a temperature of 10 and multiply by 0.97 after each step; this will have a temperature of 0.48 after 100 steps. Finding a good annealing schedule is an art.

Travelling salesman problem, which we had discussed in chapter-5 can also be dealt with simulated annealing algorithm. In TSP, the salesman is looking to visit a set of cities in the order that minimizes the total number of miles he travels. As the number of cities gets large, it becomes too computationally intensive to check every possible itinerary. At that point, you need an algorithm.

6.1.1. How simulated annealing is better than other algorithms

There are many optimization algorithms, including hill climbing, genetic algorithms, gradient descent, and more. Simulated annealing's strength is that it avoids getting caught at local maxima - solutions that are better than any others nearby, but aren't the very best.

You can visualize this by imagining a 2D graph like the one shown below in figure 6.1. Each *x*-coordinate represents a particular solution (e.g., a particular itinerary for the salesman). Each *y*-coordinate represents how good that solution is (e.g., the inverse of that itinerary's mileage).

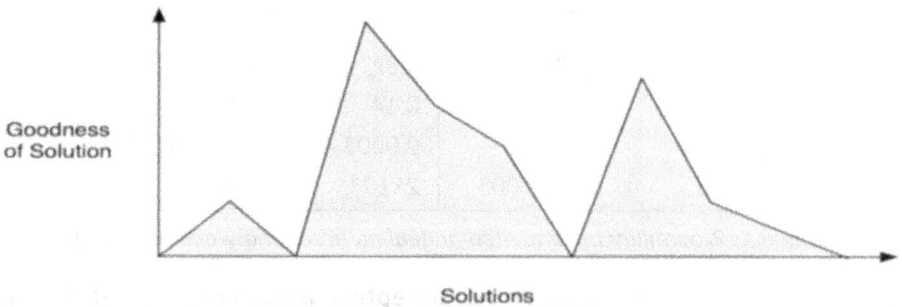

Fig.6.1: a 2D graph showing itinerary for the salesman

Broadly, an optimization algorithm searches for the best solution by generating a random initial solution and "exploring" the area nearby. If a neighboring solution is better than the current one, then it moves to it. If not, then the algorithm stays put.

This is perfectly logical, but it can lead to situations where you're stuck at a sub-optimal place. In the graph depicted in figure 6.2, the best solution is at the yellow star on the left. But if a simple algorithm finds its way to the green star on the right, it won't move away from it: all of the neighboring solutions are worse. The green star is a local maximum.

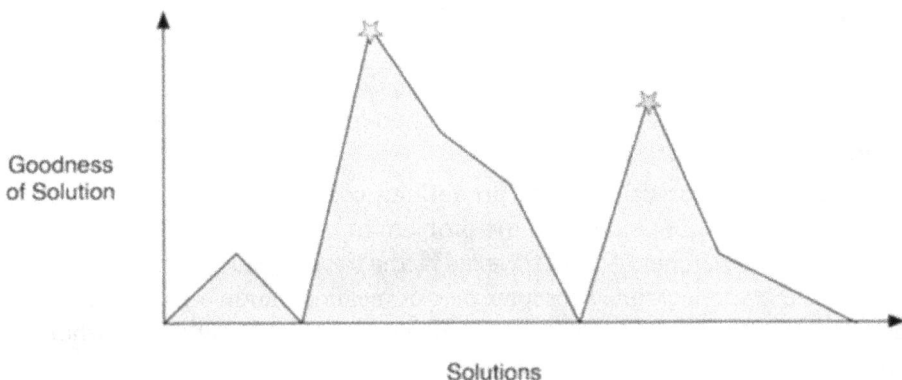

Fig.6.2: depiction of best-solution and local maxima

Simulated annealing injects just the right amount of randomness into things to escape local maxima early in the process without getting off course late in the game, when a solution is nearby. This makes it pretty good at tracking down a decent answer, no matter its starting point.

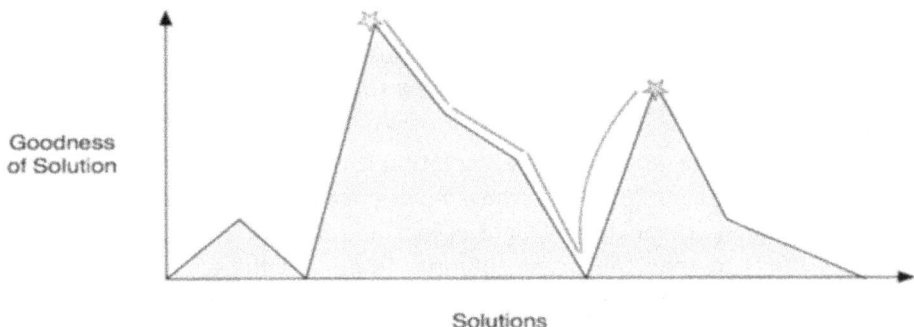

Fig.6.3: utilization of simulated annealing to avoid local-maxima problem

On top of this, simulated annealing is not that difficult to implement, despite its somewhat scary name.

6.1.2.   The basic simulated annealing algorithm

1. First, generate a random solution
2. Calculate its cost using some cost function you've defined
3. Generate a random neighboring solution
4. Calculate the new solution's cost
5. Compare them:

➤   If $c_{new} < c_{old}$: move to the new solution

➤   If $c_{new} > c_{old}$: *maybe* move to the new solution

6.   Repeat steps 3 to 5 above until a satisfactory solution is obtained or we attain some maximum number of iterations.

First, generate a random solution We can do this however we want. The main point to be noted here is that it is random in nature i.e, it doesn't required being the best guess at the optimal solution.

Calculate its cost using some predefined cost function This, too, depends completely up to us. Depending on the problem to be solved, it could be as easy as counting the total number of miles travelled by the traveling salesman. Or on the other hand it could be an incredibly complex task of melding multiple factors. Computing the cost of each solution is found to be the most complex part of the algorithm, so it's hard to keep it simple.

Produce a random neighboring solution "Neighboring" means there's only one thing that vary between the old solution and the new solution. Effectively, you switch two elements of your solution and re-calculate the cost. The main requirement is to get it done randomly.

Calculate the new solution's cost Use the same cost function as above. We can observe why it needs to perform well - it gets called with each successive iteration of the algorithm.

If $c_{new} < c_{old}$: move to the new solution If the new solution has a smaller cost than the old solution, the new one is better. This makes the algorithm happy - it's getting closer to an optimum. It will "move" to that new solution, saving it as the base for its next iteration.

If $c_{new} > c_{old}$: *maybe* move to the new solution This is where things get interesting. Most of the time, the algorithm will eschew moving to a worse solution. If it did that all of the time, though, it would get caught at local maxima. To avoid that problem, it sometimes elects to keep the worse solution. To decide, the algorithm calculates something called the 'acceptance probability' and then compares it to a random number.

The explanation above leaves out an extremely important parameter called the "temperature". The temperature is a function of which iteration you're on; its name comes from the fact that this algorithm was inspired by a method of heating and cooling metals.

Usually, the temperature is started at 1.0 and is decreased at the end of each iteration by multiplying it by a constant called α. You get to decide what value to use for α; typical values are between 0.8 and 0.99. Furthermore, simulated annealing does better when the neighbor-cost-compare-move process is carried about many times (typically somewhere between 100 and 1,000) at each temperature. So the production-grade algorithm is somewhat more complicated than the one discussed above. It is implemented in the example Python code given below.

Example Code

This python code is for the most fundamental version of the simulated annealing algorithm. The auxiliary optimization is to always supervise the optimal solution found so far so that it can be repeated if the algorithm terminates at a sub-optimal place.

```python
from random import random
def anneal(sol):
    old_cost = cost(sol)
    T = 1.0
    T_min = 0.00001
    alpha = 0.9
    while T > T_min:
    i = 1
    while i <= 100:
    new_sol = neighbor(sol)
    new_cost = cost(new_sol)
    ap = acceptance_probability(old_cost, new_cost, T)
    if ap > random():
    sol = new_sol
    old_cost = new_cost
    i += 1
    T = T*alpha
    return sol, cost
```

This framework leaves a few gaps to be filled in by you: `neighbor()`, in which you generate a random neighboring solution, cost(), to apply your cost function, and `acceptance_probability()`, which is basically defined for you.

6.1.3. The acceptance probability function

The acceptance probability function receives the old cost, new cost, and current temperature and reveals a number between 0 and 1, i.e., a kind of recommendation on whether or not to switch to the new solution. For example:

➢ 1.0: definitely switch (the new solution is better)

➢ 0.0: definitely stay put (the new solution is infinitely worse)

➢ 0.5: the odds are 50-50

Once the acceptance probability is calculated, it's compared to a randomly-generated number between 0 and 1. If the acceptance probability is larger than the random number, you're switching!

Calculating the acceptance probability

The equation typically used for the acceptance probability is:

$$a = e^{(c_{new} - c_{old})/T} \tag{6.2}$$

where a is the acceptance probability, $(c_{new} - c_{old})$ is the difference between the new cost and the old one, T is the temperature, and e is 2.71828, that mathematical constant that pops up in all sorts of unexpected places.

This equation is the part of simulated annealing that was inspired by metalworking. Throw in a constant and it describes the embodied energy of metal particles as they are cooled slowly after being subjected to high heat. This process allows the particles to move from a random configuration to one with a very low embodied energy. Computer scientists borrow the annealing equation to help them move from a random solution to one with a very low cost.

This equation means that the acceptance probability:

➢ is always > 1 when the new solution is better than the old one. Since you can't have a probability greater than 100%, we use $á$ = 1 in this case.

➢ gets smaller as the new solution gets more worse than the old one.

➢ gets smaller as the temperature decreases (if the new solution is worse than the old one)

What this means is that the algorithm is more likely to accept sort-of-bad jumps than really-bad jumps, and is more likely to accept them early on, when the temperature is high.

6.2.   Ant Colony Optimization

Ant colony optimization is a technique for optimization that was introduced in the early 1990's. The inspiring source of ant colony optimization is the foraging behavior of real ant colonies. This behavior is exploited in artificial ant colonies for the search of approximate solutions to discrete optimization problems, to continuous optimization problems, and to important problems in telecommunications, such as routing and load balancing. First, we deal with the biological inspiration of ant colony optimization algorithms. We show how this biological inspiration can be transferred into an algorithm for discrete optimization. Then, we outline ant colony optimization in more general terms in the context of discrete optimization, and present some of the nowadays best-performing ant colony optimization variants. After summarizing some important theoretical results, we demonstrate how ant colony optimization can be applied to continuous optimization problems. Finally, we provide examples of an interesting recent research direction: The hybridization with more classical techniques from artificial intelligence and operations research.

Optimization problems are of prominent today, both in the case of industrial world and for the scientific world. Examples of practical optimization problems include train scheduling, time tabling, shape optimization, telecommunication network design, or problems from computational biology. The researchers have simplified many of these complications with the objective to obtain scientific test cases such as the popular travelling salesman problem (TSP). The TSP models the situation of a travelling salesman who is required to travel through a number of cities. The goal of the travelling salesman is to traverse these cities (visiting each city exactly once) so that the total travelling distance is minimal. Another example is the problem of protein folding, which is one of the most challenging problems in computational biology, molecular biology, biochemistry and physics. It consists of finding the functional structure or conformation of a protein in two- or three-dimensional space, for example, under simplified lattice models such as the hydrophobic-polar model. The TSP and the protein folding problem under lattice models belong to an important class of optimization problems known as combinatorial optimization (CO).

According to Papadimitriou and Steiglitz, a CO problem $P = (S, f)$ is an optimization problem in which are given a finite set of objects S (also called the search space) and an objective function $f : S \rightarrow R+$ that assigns a positive cost value to each of the objects $s \in S$. The goal is to find an object of minimal cost value. The objects are typically integer numbers, subsets of a set of items, permutations of a set of items, or graph structures. CO problems can be modelled as discrete optimization problems in which the search space is defined over a set of decision variables X_i, $i = 1,...,n$, with discrete domains. Therefore, we will hence forth use the terms CO problem and discrete optimization problem interchangeably.

Due to the practical importance of CO problems, many algorithms to tackle them have been developed. These algorithms can be classified as either complete or approximate algorithms. Complete algorithms are guaranteed to find for every finite size instance of a CO problem an optimal solution in bounded time. Yet, for CO problems that are NP-hard, no polynomial time algorithm exists, assuming that $P \neq NP$ .Therefore, complete methods might require exponential computation time in the worst-case. This often leads to practically too high computation times. Thus, the development of approximate methods—in which we sacrifice the guarantee of finding optimal solutions for the sake of getting good solutions in a significantly reduced amount of time—has received more and more attention in the last 30 years.

Ant colony optimization (ACO) is one of the most recent techniques for approximate optimization. The inspiring source of ACO algorithms are real ant colonies. More specifically, ACO is inspired by the ants' foraging behavior. At the core of this behavior is the indirect communication between the ants by means of chemical pheromone trails, which enables them to find short paths between their nest and food sources. This characteristic of real ant colonies is exploited in ACO algorithms in order to solve, for example, discrete optimization problems. Depending on the point of view, ACO algorithms may belong to different classes of approximate algorithms. Seen from the artificial intelligence (AI) perspective, ACO algorithms are one of the most successful strands of swarm intelligence. The goal of swarm intelligence is the design of intelligent multi-agent systems by taking inspiration from the collective behavior of social insects such as ants, termites, bees, wasps, and other animal societies such as flocks of birds or fish schools. Examples of "swarm intelligent" algorithms other than ACO are those for clustering and data mining inspired by ants' cemetery building behavior those for dynamic task allocation inspired by the behavior of wasp colonies, and particle swarm optimization.

Seen from the operations research (OR) perspective, ACO algorithms belong to the class of metaheuristics.The term metaheuristic, first introduced in, derives from the composition of two Greek words. Heuristic derives from the verb heuriskein (!νρισκ!ιν) which means "to find", while the suffix meta means "beyond, in an upper level". Before this term was widely adopted, metaheuristics were often called modern heuristics. In addition to ACO, other algorithms such as evolutionary computation iterated local search, simulated annealing, and tabu search, are often regarded as metaheuristics.

6.2.1. The origins of ant colony optimization

Marco Dorigo and colleagues introduced the first ACO algorithms in the early 1990's.Thedevelopment of these algorithms was inspired by the observation of ant colonies. Ants are social insects. They live in colonies and their behavior is governed by the goal of colony survival rather than being focused on the survival of individuals. The behavior that provided the inspiration for ACO is the ants' foraging behavior, and in particular, how ants can find shortest paths between food sources and their nest. When searching for food, ants initially explore the area surrounding their nest in a random manner. While moving, ants leave a chemical pheromone trail on the ground. Ants can smell pheromone. When choosing their way, they tend to choose, in probability, paths marked by strong pheromone concentrations. As soon as an ant finds a food source, it evaluates the quantity and the quality of the food and carries some of it back to the nest. During the return trip, the quantity of pheromone that an ant leaves on the ground may depend on the quantity and quality of the food. The pheromone trails will guide other ants to the food source. It has been shown in that the indirect communication between the ants via pheromone trails—known as stigmergy—enables them to find shortest paths between their nest and food sources. This is explained in an idealized setting in Fig. 6.4.

As a first step towards an algorithm for discrete optimization we present in the following a discretized and simplified model of the phenomenon explained in Fig. 6.4. After presenting the model we will outline the differences between the model and the behavior of real ants. Our model consists of a graph $G = (V, E)$, where V consists of two nodes, namely v_s (representing the nest of the ants), and v_d (representing the food source). Furthermore, E consists of two links, namely e_1 and e_2, between v_s and v_d. To $e1$ we assign a length of l_1, and to e_2 a length of l_2 such that $l_2 > l_1$. In other words, $e1$ represents the short path between v_s and v_d, and e_2 represents the long path. Real ants deposit pheromone on the paths on which they move. Thus, the chemical pheromone trails are modeled as follows. We introduce an artificial pheromone value τ_i for each of the two links e_i, $i = 1, 2$. Such a value indicates the strength of the pheromone trail on the corresponding path. Finally, we introduce n_a artificial ants. Each ant behaves as follows: Starting from v_s (i.e., the nest), an ant chooses with probability

$$P_i = \tau_i / (\tau_1 + \tau_2), i = 1, 2, \tag{6.3}$$

between path e_1 and path e_2 for reaching the food source v_d. Obviously, if $\tau_1 > \tau_2$, the probability of choosing e_1 is higher, and vice versa. For returning from v_d to v_s, an ant uses the same path as it chose to reach v_d, and it changes the artificial pheromone value associated to the used edge. More in detail, having chosen edge e_i an ant changes the

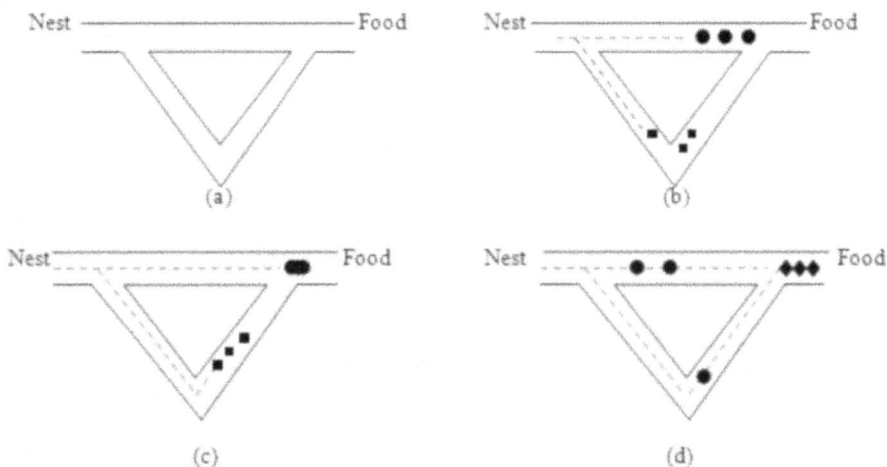

Fig.6.4: An experimental setup to demonstrate the shortest path finding capability of ant colonies. (a) All ants are in the nest, there is no pheromone in the environment. (b) The foraging starts, in probability 50% of the ants take the short path (symbolized by circles), and 50% takes the long path to the food source (symbolized by rhombs). (c) the ants that have taken the short path have arrived earlier at the food source, therefore when returning, the probability to take again the short path is higher. (d) the pheromone trail on the short path receives, in probability, a stronger reinforcement, and the probability to take the path grows. Finally, due to the evaporation of the pheromone, on the long path the whole colony will, in probability, use the short path.

artificial pheromone value τi as follows:

$$\tau \leftarrow \tau + Q / l_i , \tag{6.4}$$

where the positive constant Q is a parameter of the model. In other words, the amount of artificial pheromone that is added depends on the length of the selected path: the shorter the path, the higher the amount of added pheromone.

The foraging of an ant colony is in this model iteratively simulated as follows: At each step (or iteration) all the ants are initially placed in node v_s. Then, each ant moves from v_s to v_d as outlined above. As mentioned in the caption of Figure 6.4, in nature the deposited pheromone is subject to an evaporation over time. We simulate this pheromone evaporation in the artificial model as follows:

$$\tau \leftarrow (1-\rho) \cdot \tau, \; i = 1, \, 2. \tag{6.5}$$

The parameter $\rho \in (0,1]$ is a parameter that regulates the pheromone evaporation. Finally, all ants conduct their return trip and reinforce their chosen path as outlined above. We implemented this system and conducted simulations with the following settings: $l_1 = 1$, $l_2 = 2$, $Q = 1$. The two pheromone values were initialized to 0.5 each.

Note that in our artificial system we cannot start with artificial pheromone values of 0. This would lead to a division by 0 in Eq.(6.3). over time the artificial colony of ants converges to the short path, i.e., after sometime all ants use the short path. In the case of 10 ants the random fluctuations are bigger than in the case of 100 ants. This indicates that the shortest path finding capability of ant colonies results from a cooperation between the ants.

The main differences between the behavior of the real ants and the behavior of the artificial ants in our model are as follows:

1.   While real ants move in their environment in an asynchronous way, the artificial ants are synchronized, i.e., at each iteration of the simulated system, each of the artificial ants moves from the nest to the food source and follows the same path back.

2.   While real ants leave pheromone on the ground whenever they move, artificial ants only deposit artificial pheromone on their way back to the nest.

3.   The foraging behavior of real ants is based on an implicit evaluation of a solution (i.e., a path from the nest to the food source). By implicit solution evaluation we mean the fact that shorter paths will be completed earlier than longer ones, and therefore they will receive pheromone reinforcement more quickly. In contrast, the artificial ants evaluate a solution with respect to some quality measure which is used to determine the strength of the pheromone reinforcement that the ants perform during their return trip to the nest.

6.2.2.   Ant System for the TSP: The first ACO algorithm

The model that we used in the previous section to simulate the foraging behavior of real ants in the setting of Figure 6.4 cannot directly be applied to CO problems. This is because we associated pheromone values directly to solutions to the problem (i.e., one parameter for the short path, and one parameter for the long path). This way of modeling implies that the solutions to the considered problem are already known. However, in combinatorial optimization we intend to find an unknown optimal solution. Thus, when CO problems are considered, pheromone values are associated to solution components instead. Solution components are the units from which solutions to the tackled problem are assembled. Generally, the set of solution components is expected to be finite and of moderate size. As an example we present the first ACO algorithm, called Ant System (AS), applied to the TSP, which we mentioned in the introduction and which we define in more detail in the following:

Definition 1. In the TSP is given a completely connected, undirected graph $G = (V, E)$ with edge-weights. The nodes V of this graph represent the cities, and the edge weights represent the distances between the cities. The goal is to find a closed path in G that contains each node exactly once (henceforth called a tour) and whose length is minimal. Thus, the search space S consists of all tours in G. The objective function value $f(s)$ of a tour $s \in S$ is defined as the sum of the edge-weights of the edges that are in s. The TSP can be modeled in many different ways as a discrete optimization problem.

The most common model consists of a binary decision variable X_e for each edge in G. If in a solution $X_e = 1$, then edge e is part of the tour that is defined by the solution. Concerning the AS approach, the edges of the given TSP graph can be considered solution components, i.e., for each $e_{i,j}$ is introduced a pheromone value $\tau_{i,j}$. The task of each ant consists in the construction of a feasible TSP solution, i.e., a feasible tour. In other words, the notion of task of an ant changes from "choosing a path from the nest to the food source" to "constructing a feasible solution to the tackled optimization problem". Note that with this change of task, the notions of nest and food source loose their meaning. Each ant constructs a solution as follows. Initially, one of the nodes of the TSP graph is randomly selected as the start node. Later, the ant frames a tour in the TSP graph by moving in each construction step from its current node (i.e., the city in which she is located) to another node which she has not visited yet. At each step the traversed edge is added to the solution under construction. When no unvisited nodes are left the ant closes the tour by moving from her current node to the node in which she started the solution construction. This way of constructing a solution implies that an ant has a memory T to store the already visited nodes.

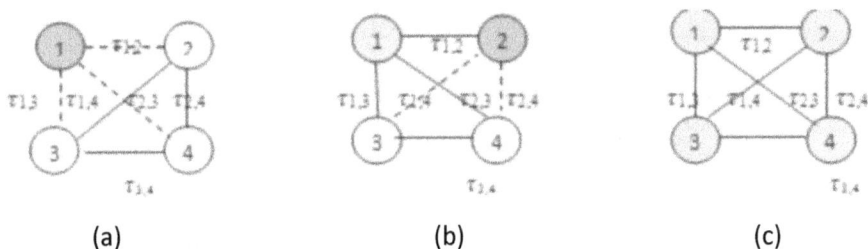

(a) (b) (c)

Fig. 6.5: Example of the solution construction for a TSP problem consisting of 4 cities (modelled by a graph with 4 nodes; see Definition 1). The solution construction starts by randomly choosing a start node for the ant; in this case node 1. Figures (a) and (b) show the choices of the first, respectively the second, construction step. Note that in both cases the current node (i.e., location) of the ant is marked by dark gray color, and the already visited nodes are marked by light gray color (respectively yellow color, in the online version of this article). The choices of the ant (i.e., the edges she may traverse) are marked by dashed lines. The probabilities for the different choices (according to Eq.(6.6))are given underneath the graphics. Note that after the second construction step, in which we exemplary assume the ant to have selected node 4, the ant can only move to node 3, and then back to node 1 in order to close the tour.

Each solution construction step is performed as follows. Assuming the ant to be in node v_i, the subsequent construction step is done with probability

$$P(e_i, j) = \tau_{i,j} / \left[\sum_{\{k \in \{1,\dots,|V|\} v k \notin T\}} \tau_{i,k} \right] \; \forall \, j \in \{,\dots,|V|\},\, v_j \in \{1,\dots,|V|\},\, v_j \notin T$$

(6.6)

For an example of such a solution construction see Figure 6.5. Once all ants of the colony have completed the construction of their solution, pheromone evaporation is performed as follows:

$$\tau_{i,j} \leftarrow (1-\rho) \cdot \tau_{i,j}, \forall \tau_{i,j} \in T, \tag{6.7}$$

where T is the set of all pheromone values. Then the ants perform their return trip. Hereby, an ant having constructed a solution s—performs for each $e_{i,j} \in s$ the following pheromone deposit:

$$\tau_{i,j} \leftarrow \tau_{i,j} + Q/f(s), \tag{6.8}$$

where Q is again a positive constant and $f(s)$ is the objective function value of the solution s. As explained in the previous section, the system is iterated—applying n_a ants per iteration—until a stopping condition (e.g., a time limit) is satisfied. Even though the AS algorithm has proved that the ants foraging behavior can be transferred into an algorithm for discrete optimization, it was generally found to be inferior to state-of-the-art algorithms. Therefore, over the years several extensions and improvements of the original AS algorithm were introduced. They are all covered by the definition of the ACO metaheuristic, which we will outline in the following section.

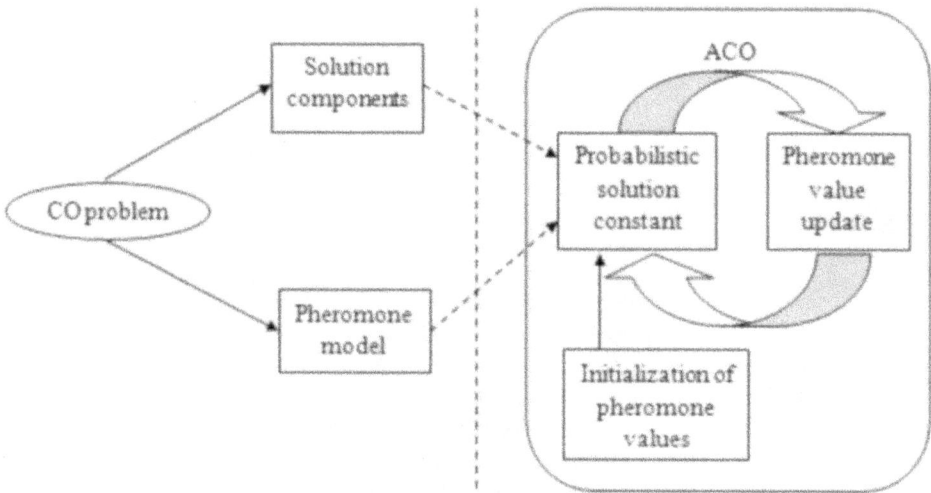

Fig.6.6: the working of ACO metaheuristic

6.2.3.   The ant colony optimization metaheuristic

The ACO metaheuristic, as we know it today, was first formalized by Dorigo and colleagues in 1999.The recent book by Dorigo and Stützle gives a more comprehensive description. The definition of the ACO metaheuristic covers most—if not all—existing ACO variants for discrete optimization problems. In the following, we give a general description of the framework of the ACO metaheuristic. The basic way of working of an ACO algorithm is graphically shown in figure 6.6. Given a CO problem to be solved, one first has to derive a finite set C of solution components which are used to assemble solutions to the CO problem. Second, one has to define a set of pheromone values T.

This set of values is commonly called the pheromone model, which is—seen from a technical point of view—a parameterized probabilistic model. The pheromone model is one of the central components of the ACO metaheuristic. The pheromone values τ_i $\in T$ are usually associated to solution components. The pheromone model is used to probabilistically generate solutions to the problem under consideration by assembling them from the set of solution components. In general, the ACO approach attempts to solve an optimization problem by iterating the following two steps:

➢ candidate solutions are constructed using a pheromone model, that is, a parameterized probability distribution over the solution space;

➢ the candidate solutions are used to modify the pheromone values in a way that is deemed to bias future sampling toward high quality solutions.

The pheromone update aims to concentrate the search in regions of the search space containing high quality solutions. In particular, the reinforcement of solution components depending on the solution quality is an important ingredient of ACO algorithms. It implicitly assumes that good solutions consist of good solution components. To learn which components contribute to good solutions can help assembling them into better solutions.

Algorithm1. *Ant colony optimization (ACO)*

```
While termination conditions not met do
    ScheduleActivities
    AntBasedSolutionConstruction() {see Algorithm 2}
    PheromoneUpdate()
    DaemonActions() {optional}
    end ScheduleActivities
end while
```

In the following, we give a more technical description of the general ACO metaheuristic whose framework is shown in Algorithm 1. ACO is an iterative algorithm whose runtime is controlled by the principal while-loop of Algorithm 1.In each iteration the three algorithmic components AntBasedSolutionConstruction(), PheromoneUpdate(), and DaemonActions()—gathered in the ScheduleActivities construct—must be scheduled. The ScheduleActivities construct does not specify how these three activities are scheduled and synchronized. This is up to the algorithm designer. In the following we outline these three algorithmic components in detail.

Algorithm 2. *Procedure AntBasedSolutionConstruction() of Algorithm1*

```
S =<>
Determine N(s)
while N(s)≠ϕ do
    c ← ChooseFrom(N(s))
    s ← extend s by appending solution component c
    Determine N(s)
end while
```

AntBasedSolutionConstruction() (see also Algorithm 2): Artificial ants can be regarded as probabilistic constructive heuristics that assemble solutions as sequences of solution components. The finite set of solution components $C = \{c1,...,cn\}$ is hereby derived from the discrete optimization problem under consideration. For example, in the case of AS applied to the TSP (see previous section) each edge of the TSP graph was considered a solution component. Each solution construction starts with an empty sequence $s = <>$. Then, the current sequence s is at each construction step extended by adding a feasible solution component from the set $N(s)$ † $\subseteq C\backslash s$. The specification of $N(s)$ depends on the solution construction mechanism. In the example of AS applied to the TSP (see previous section) the solution construction mechanism restricted the set of traversable edges to the ones that connected the ants' current node to unvisited nodes. The choice of a solution component from $N(s)$ (see function ChooseFrom($N(s)$) in Algorithm 2) is at each construction step performed probabilistically with respect to the pheromone model. In most ACO algorithms the respective probabilities—also called the transition probabilities—are defined as follows:

$$P(C_i \mid S) = \{[\tau_i]^\alpha \cdot [\eta C(i)]^\beta\} / \sum_{Cj \in N(s)} [\tau_j]^\alpha \cdot [\eta(C_j)]^\beta, \forall c_i \in N(s) \tag{6.9}$$

Where η is an optional weighting function, that is, a function that, sometimes depending on the current sequence, assigns at each construction step a heuristic value $\eta(c_j)$ to each feasible solution component $C_j \in N(s)$. The values that are given by the weighting function are commonly called the heuristic information. Furthermore, the exponents α and β are positive parameters whose values determine the relation between pheromone information and heuristic information. In the previous sections' TSP example, we chose not to use any weighting function η, and we have set α to 1. It is interesting to note that by implementing the function Choose From ($N(s)$) in Algorithm 2 such that the solution component that maximizes Eq.(6.9) is chosen deterministically (i.e., $c \leftarrow$ argmax $\{\eta(c_i) \mid c_i \eta \in N(s)\}$), we obtain a deterministic greedy algorithm.

Pheromone Update(): Different ACO variants mainly differ in the update of the pheromone values they apply. In the following, we outline a general pheromone update rule in order to provide the basic idea. This pheromone update rule consists of two parts. First, a pheromone evaporation, which uniformly decreases all the pheromone values, is performed. From a practical point of view, pheromone evaporation is needed to avoid a too rapid convergence of the algorithm toward a sub-optimal region. It implements a useful form of forgetting, favoring the exploration of new areas in the search space. Second, one or more solutions from the current and/or from earlier iterations are used to increase the values of pheromone trail parameters on solution components that are part of these solutions:

$$\tau_i \leftarrow (1-\rho) \cdot \tau_i + \rho \cdot \sum_{\{s \in Supd \mid Ci \in S\}} w_s \cdot F(s) \tag{6.10}$$

For $i = 1,...,n$. Hereby, S_{upd} denotes the set of solutions that are used for the update. Furthermore, $\rho \in (0, 1]$ is a parameter called evaporation rate, and $F : S + \rightarrow R+$ is a so-called quality function such that $f(s) < f(s') \Longrightarrow F(s) \mathbin{!} F(s'),\ \forall\, s \neq s' \in S$. In other words, we could say that, if the value of objective function of a solution s is better than the objective function value of a solution s', at least the quality of solution s will be as high as the quality of solution s'. Eq. (6.10) also allows an additional weighting of the quality function, i.e., $w_s \in R+$ denotes the weight of a solution s. Epitome of this update rule are obtained by different specifications of S_{upd} and by different weight settings. In several cases, S_{upd} consists of some of the solutions produced in the respective iteration (henceforth denoted by S_{iter}) and the best solution found since the start of the algorithm (hence forth denoted by s_{bs}). Solution s_{bs} is often called the best-so-far solution. A well-known example is the AS-update rule, that is, the update rule of AS. The AS-update rule, which is well-known due to the fact that AS was the first ACO algorithm to be proposed in the literature, is obtained from update rule (6.10) by setting

$$S_{upd} \leftarrow S_{iter \text{ and } w_s = 1\forall} \in S_{upd}, \tag{6.11}$$

that is, by using all the solutions that were generated in the respective iteration for the pheromone update, and by setting the weight of each of these solutions to 1. An example of a pheromone update rule that is more used in practice is the IB-update rule (where IB stands for iteration-best). The IB-update rule is given by:

$$S_{upd} \leftarrow \{ s_{ib} = \arg\max\{ F(s) \,|\, s \in S_{iter} \} \} \text{ with } w_{sib} = 1, \tag{6.12}$$

that is, by choosing only the best solution generated in the respective iteration for updating the pheromone values. This solution, denoted by s_{ib}, is weighted by 1. The IB update rule introduces a much stronger bias towards the good solutions found than the AS-update rule. However, this increases the danger of premature convergence. An even stronger bias is introduced by the BS-update rule, where BS refers to the use of the best-so-far solution s_{bs}. In this case, S_{upd} is set to $\{ s_{bs} \}$ and s_{bs} is weighted by 1, that is, $w_{sbs} = 1$. In practice, ACO algorithms that use variations of the IB-update or the BS-update rule and that additionally include mechanisms to avoid premature convergence achieve better results than algorithms that use the AS-update rule. Examples are given in the following section.

DaemonActions(): Daemon actions can be used to implement centralized actions which cannot be performed by single ants. Examples are the application of local search methods to the constructed solutions, or the collection of global information that can be used to decide whether it is useful or not to deposit additional pheromone to bias the search process from a non-local perspective. As a practical example, the daemon may decide to deposit extra pheromone on the solution components that belong to the best solution found so far.

6.2.4. Applications of ACO

The ACO technique had been widely used in a number of real life applications. Ant Colony Optimization (ACO) is the best example of how studies aimed at understanding and modeling the behavior of ants and other social insects can provide inspiration for the development of computational algorithms for the solution of difficult mathematical problems. Introduced by Marco Dorigo in his PhD thesis (1992) and initially applied to the travelling salesman problem, the ACO field has experienced a tremendous growth, standing today as an important nature-inspired stochastic metaheuristic for hard optimization problems. Recent contributions of ACO to diverse fields, such as traffic congestion and control, structural optimization, manufacturing, and genomics had been seen. Feature selection is one of the important application domain of ACO and in this section we'll discuss feature selection and the contribution of ACO in feature selection in detail.

6.2.4.1. Feature Selection

Over the past decades, there is an explosion of data composed by huge information, because of rapid growing up of computer and database technologies. Ordinarily, this information is hidden in the cast collection of raw data. Because of that, we are now drowning in information, but starving for knowledge. As a solution, data mining successfully extracts knowledge from the series of data-mountains by means of data preprocessing. In case of data preprocessing, feature selection (FS) is ordinarily used as a useful technique in order to reduce the dimension of the dataset. It significantly reduces the spurious information, that is to say, irrelevant, redundant, and noisy features, from the original feature set and eventually retaining a subset of most salient features. As a result, a number of good outcomes can be expected from the applications, such as, speeding up data mining algorithms, improving mining performances (including predictive accuracy) and comprehensibility of result.

In the available literature, different types of data mining are addressed, such as, regression, classification, and clustering. The task of interest in this study is classification. In fact, classification problem is the task of assigning a data-point to a predefined class or group according to its predictive characteristics. In practice, data mining for classification techniques are significant in a wide range of domains, such as, financial engineering, medical diagnosis, and marketing.

In details, FS is, however, a search process or technique in data mining that selects a subset of salient features for building robust learning models, such as, neural networks and decision trees. Some irrelevant and/or redundant features generally exist in the learning data that not only make learning harder, but also degrade generalization performance of learned models. More precisely, good FS techniques can detect and ignore noisy and misleading features. As a result, the dataset quality might even increase after selection. There are two feature qualities that need to be considered in FS methods: relevancy and redundancy. A feature is said to be relevant if it is predictive of the decision feature(s); otherwise, it is irrelevant. A feature is considered to be redundant if it is highly correlated with other features. An informative feature is the one that is highly correlated with the decision concept(s), but is highly uncorrelated with other features.

For a given classification task, the problem of FS can be described as follows: given the original set, N, of n features, find a subset F consisting of f relevant features, where $F \subset N$ and $f < n$. The aim of selecting F is to maximize the classification accuracy in building learning models. The selection of relevant features is important in the sense that the generalization performance of learning models is greatly dependent on the selected features. Moreover, FS assists for visualizing and understanding the data, reducing storage requirements, reducing training times and so on.

It is found that, two features to be useless individually and yet highly predictive if taken together. In FS terminology, they may be both redundant and irrelevant on their own, but their combination provides important information. For instance, in the Exclusive-OR problem, the classes are not linearly separable. The two features on their own provide no information concerning this separability, because they are uncorrelated with each other. However, considering together, the two features are highly informative and can provide good predictive accuracy. Therefore, the search of FS is particularly for high-quality feature subsets and not only for ranking of features.

6.2.4.2. Applications of Feature Selection

Feature selection has a wide-range of applications in various fields since the 1970s. The reason is that, many systems deal with datasets of large dimensionality. However, the areas, in which the task of FS can mainly be applied, are categorized into the following ways (see Figure 6.7.).

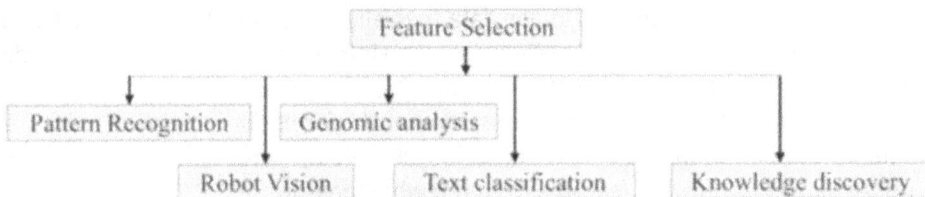

Fig.6.7: Applicable areas of Feature Selection

In the pattern recognition paradigm, the FS tasks are mostly concerned with the classification problems. Basically, pattern recognition is the study of how machines can monitor the environment, learn to differentiate patterns of interest, and make decision correctly about the categories of patterns. A pattern, ordinarily, contains some features based on classifying a target or object. As an example, a classification problem, that is to say, sorting incoming fish on a conveyor belt in a fish industry according to species. Assume that, there are only two kinds of only two kinds of fish available, such as, salmon and sea bass, exhibited in Figure 6.8. A machine gives the decision in classifying the fishes automatically based on training of some features, for example, length, width, weight, number and shape of fins, tail shape, and so on. But, problem is that, if there are some irrelevant, redundant, and noisy features are available, classification performance then might be degraded. In such cases, FS has a significant performance to recognize the useless features from the patterns, delete the features, and finally bring the improved classification performance significantly in the context of pattern recognition.

Fig.6.8: Picture taken by camera from a fish processing industry

FS technique has successfully been implemented in mobile robot vision to generate efficient navigation trajectories with an extremely simple neural control system. In this case, evolved mobile robots select the salient visual features and actively maintain them on the same retinal position, while the useless image features are discarded. According to the analysis of evolved solutions, it can be found that, robots develop simple and very efficient edge detection to detect obstacles and to move away among them. Furthermore, FS has a significant role in image recognition systems. In these systems, patterns are designed by image data specially describing the image pixel data. There could be hundreds of different features for an image. These features may include: *color* (in various channels), *texture* (dimensionality, line likeness, contrast, roughness, coarseness), *edge, shape, spatial relations, temporal information, statistical measures* (moments- mean, variance, standard deviation, skewness, kurtosis). The FS expert can identify a subset of relevant features from the whole feature set.

In analysis of human genome, gene expression microarray data have increased many folds in recent years. These data provide the opportunity to analyze the expression levels of thousand or tens of thousands of genes in a single experiment. A particular classification task distinguishes between healthy and cancer patients based on their gene expression profile. On the other hand, a typical gene expression data suffer from three problems:

a.   limited number of available examples,

b.   very high dimensional nature of data,

c.   noisy characteristics of the data.

Therefore, suitable FS methods are used upon these datasets to find out a minimal set of gene that has sufficient classifying power to classify subgroups along with some initial filtering.

Text classification is, nowadays, a vital task because of the presence of the proliferated texts in the digital form. We need to access these texts in the flexible ways. A major problem regarding the text classification is the feature space's high dimensionality. It is found that, text feature space has several tens of thousands of features, among which most of them are irrelevant and spurious for the text classification tasks. This high number of features resulting the reduction of classification accuracy and of learning speed of the classifiers. Because of those features, a number of classifiers are being unable to utilize in their learning tasks. For this, FS is such a technique that is very much efficient for the text classification task in order to reduce the feature dimensionality and to improve the performance of the classifiers.

Knowledge discovery (KD) is an efficient process of identifying valid, novel, potentially useful, and ultimately understandable patterns from the large collections of data. Indeed, the popularity of KD is caused due to our daily basis demands by federal agencies, banks, insurance companies, retail stores, and so on. One of the important KD steps is the data mining step. In the context of data mining, feature selection cleans up the dataset by reducing the set of least significant features. This step ultimately helps to extract some rules from the dataset, such as, *if—then* rule. This rule signifies the proper understanding about the data and increases the human capability to predict what is happening inside the data.

It is now clear that, FS task has an important role in various places, where one can easily produce better performances from the systems by distinguishing the salient features. Among the various applications, in this chapter, we are interested to discuss elaborately in a particular topic of "pattern recognition", in which how FS task can play an important role especially for the classification problem. The reason is that, in the recent years, dealing with classification problem using FS is a crucial source for the data mining paradigm.

ACO is prevalently a useful technique, considered as a modern algorithm that has been used in several studies for selecting salient features. During the operation of this algorithm, a number of artificial ants traverse the feature space to construct feature subsets iteratively. During subset construction (SC), the existing approaches define the size of the constructed subsets by a fixed number for each iteration, whereas the SFS strategy has been followed. In order to measure the heuristic values of features during FS, some of the algorithms use filter tools. Evaluating the constructed subsets is, on the other hand, a vital part in the study of ACO-based FS, since most algorithms design the pheromone update rules on the basis of outcomes of subset evaluations. In this regard, a scheme of training classifiers (i.e., wrapper tools) has been used in almost all of the above ACO-based FS algorithms, except for the two cases, where rough set theory and the latent variable model (i.e., filter tools) are considered, which are in and, respectively.

A recently proposed FS approach is based on rough sets and a particle swarm optimization (PSO) algorithm. A PSO algorithm is used for finding a subset of salient features over a large and complex feature space. The main heuristic strategy of PSO in FS is that particles fly up to a certain velocity through the feature space. PSO finds an optimal solution through the interaction of individuals in the population. Thus, PSO finds the best solution in the FS as the particles fly within the subset space. This technique is found more efficient than a GA in the sense that it does not require crossover and mutation operators; simple mathematical operators are required only.

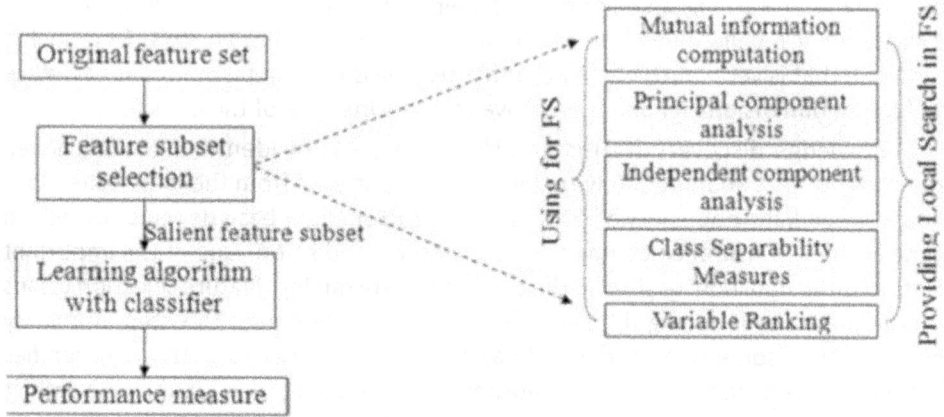

Fig.6.9 (a): Schematic diagram of filter approach. Each approach incorporates the specific search strategies.

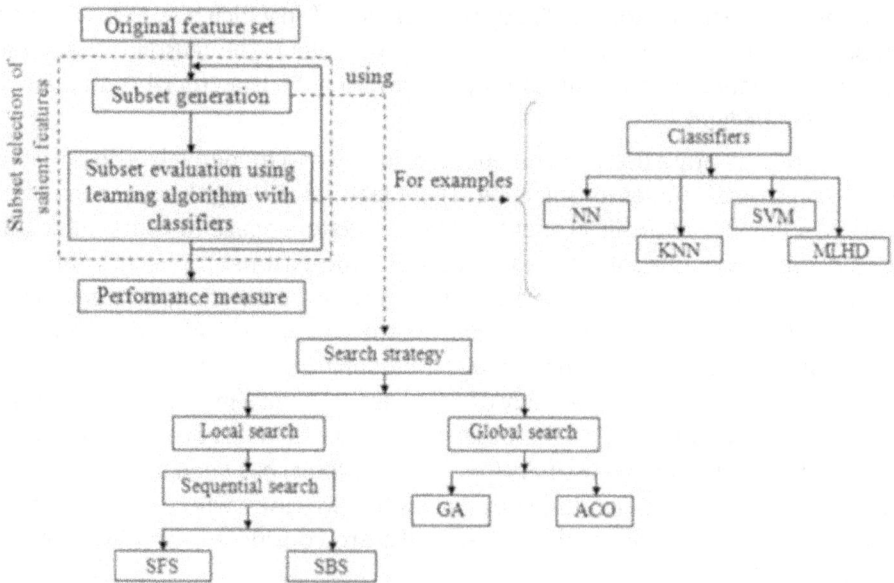

Fig.6.9 (b): Schematic diagram of wrapper approach. Each approach incorporates the specific search strategies and classifiers. Here, NN, KNN, SVM, and MLHD refer to the neural network, K-nearest neighbour, support vector machine, and maximum likelihood classifier, respectively.

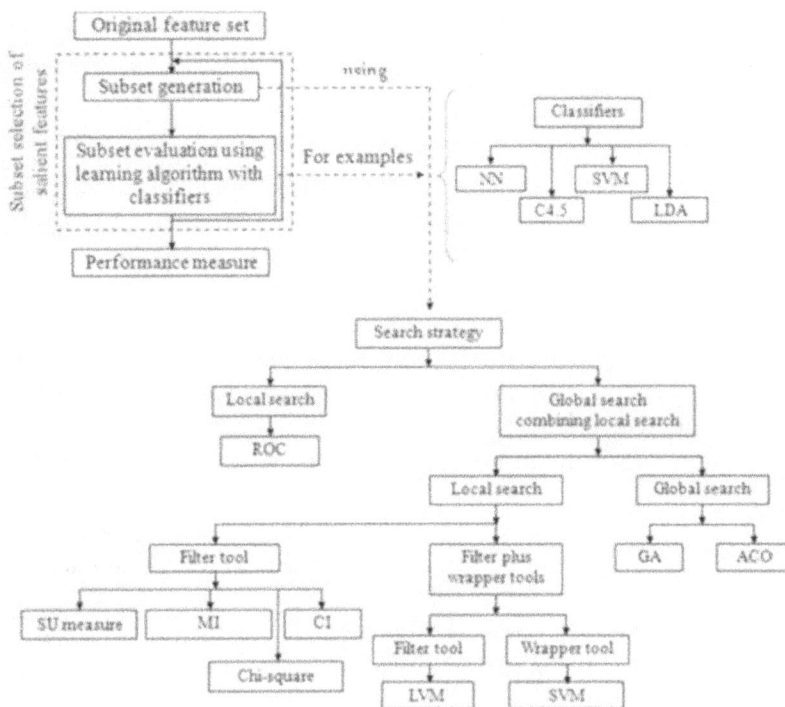

Fig.6.9 (c): Schematic diagram of hybrid approach. Each approach incorporates the specific search strategies and classifiers. Here, LDA, ROC, SU, MI, CI, and LVM, refer to the linear discriminant analysis classifier, receiver operating characteristic method, symmetrical uncertainty, mutual information, correlation information, and latent variable model, respectively.

6.2.4.3. Common Problems

Most of the afore-mentioned search strategies, however, attempt to find solutions in FS that range between sub-optimal and near optimal regions, since they use local search throughout the entire process, instead of global search. On the other hand, these search algorithms utilize a partial search over the feature space, and suffer from computational complexity. Consequently, near-optimal to optimal solutions are quite difficult to achieve using these algorithms. As a result, many research studies now focus on global search algorithms (or, metaheuristics). The significance of global search algorithms is that they can find a solution in the full search space on the basis of activities of multi-agent systems that use a global search ability utilizing local search appropriately, thus significantly increasing the ability of finding very high-quality solutions within a reasonable period of time. To achieve global search, researchers have attempted simulated annealing, genetic algorithm, ant colony optimization, and particle swarm optimization algorithms in solving FS tasks.

On the other hand, most of the global search approaches discussed above do not use a bounded scheme to decide the size of the constructed subsets. Accordingly, in these algorithms, the selected subsets might be larger in size and include a number of least significant features. Furthermore, most of the ACO-based FS algorithms do not consider the random and probabilistic behavior of ants during SCs. Thus, the solutions found in these algorithms might be incomplete in nature. On the other hand, the above sequential search-based FS approaches suffer from the nesting effect as they try to find subsets of salient features using a sequential search strategy. It is said that such an effect affects the generalization performance of the learning model.

6.2.5.   A New Hybrid ACO-based Feature Selection Algorithm-ACOFS

It is found that, hybridization of several components gives rise to better overall performance in FS problem. The reason is that hybrid techniques are capable of finding a good solution, even when a single technique is often trapped with an incomplete solution. Furthermore, incorporation of any global search strategy in a hybrid system (called as hybrid meta-heuristic approach) can likely provide high-quality solution in FS problem. In this section, a new hybrid meta-heuristic approach for feature selection (ACOFS) has been presented that utilizes ant colony optimization. The main focus of this algorithm is to generate subsets of salient features of reduced size. ACOFS utilizes a hybrid search technique that combines the wrapper and filter approaches. In this regard, ACOFS modifies the standard pheromone update and heuristic information measurement rules based on the above two approaches. The reason for the novelty and distinctness of ACOFS versus previous algorithms lie in the following two aspects.

First, ACOFS emphasizes not only the selection of a number of salient features, but also the attainment of a reduced number of them. ACOFS selects salient features of a reduced number using a subset size determination scheme. Such a scheme works upon a bounded region and provides sizes of constructed subsets that are smaller in number. Thus, following this scheme, an ant attempts to traverse the node (or, feature) space to construct a path (or, subset). This approach is quite different from those of the existing schemes, where the ants are guided by using the SFS strategy in selecting features during the feature subset construction. However, a problem is that, SFS requires an appropriate stopping criterion to stop the SC. Otherwise, a number of irrelevant features may be included in the constructed subsets, and the solutions may not be effective. To solve this problem, some algorithms define the size of a constructed subset by a fixed number for each iteration for all ants, which is incremented at a fixed rate for following iterations. This technique could be inefficient if the fixed number becomes too large or too small. Therefore, deciding the subset size within a reduced area may be a good step for constructing the subset while the ants traverse through the feature space.

```
┌─────────────────────┐
│   Initialization    │
└─────────────────────┘
          │
          ▼
┌─────────────────────┐
│ Measure information  │
│ gain of individual   │
│ features             │
└─────────────────────┘
          │
          ▼
┌─────────────────────┐
│   Generate k ants    │
└─────────────────────┘
          │
          ▼
┌─────────────────────┐
│ For each of k,       │
│ constants a subset   │◄──────────────┐
│ using transition rule│               │
└─────────────────────┘               │
          │                            │
          ▼                            │
      ◇ All constructions ◇───NO──────┘
         finished
          │
          ▼
┌─────────────────────┐
│ Evaluate all         │
│ constructed subsets  │
└─────────────────────┘
          │
          ▼
┌─────────────────────┐
│ Select the local     │
│ best and global      │
│ best subsets         │
└─────────────────────┘
          │
          ▼
    ◇ Termination ◇──NO──►┌──────────────┐
   criterion satisfied?   │ Update τ and η│
          │               └──────────────┘
        YES                      ▲
          │               ┌──────────────┐
          ▼               │Generate new k │
┌─────────────────────┐   │     ants      │
│ Return best subsets  │   └──────────────┘
└─────────────────────┘
```

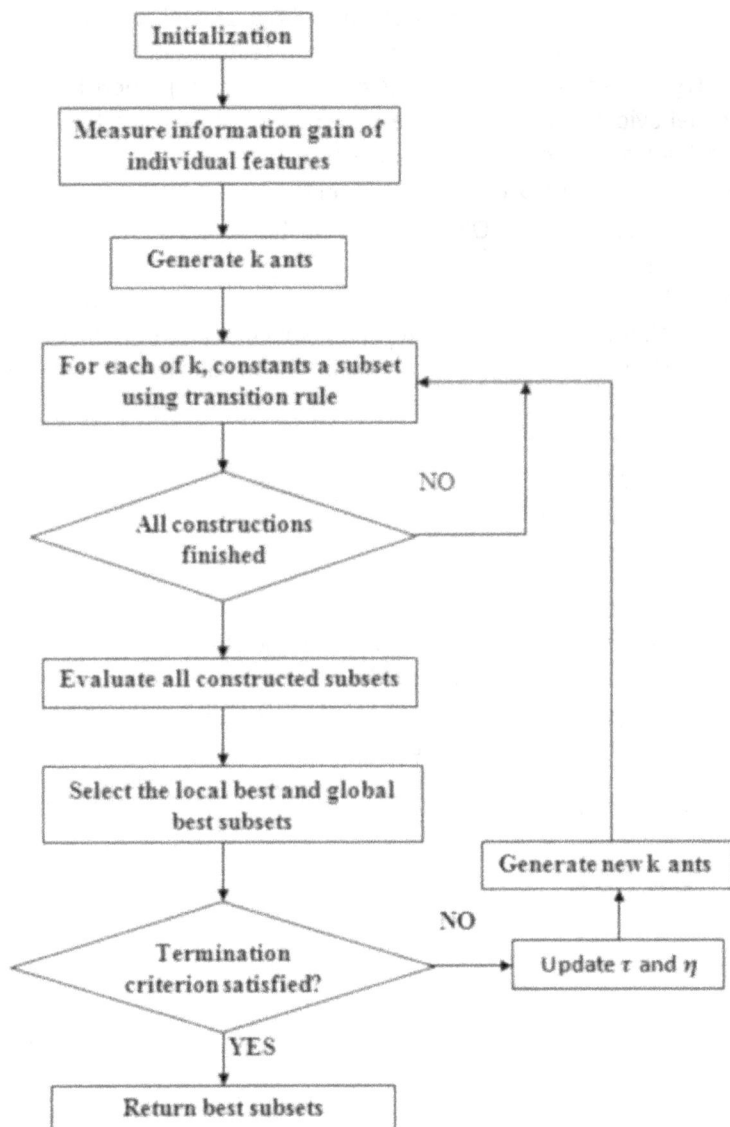

Fig.6.10: Major steps of ACOFS

Second, ACOFS utilizes a hybrid search technique for selecting salient features that combines the advantages of the wrapper and filter approaches. An alternative name for such a search technique is "ACO search". This technique is designed with two sets of new rules for pheromone update and heuristic information measurement. The idea of these rules is based mainly on the random and probabilistic behaviors of ants while selecting features during SC. The aim is to provide the correct information to the features and to maintain an effective balance between exploitation and exploration of ants during SC. Thus, ACOFS achieves a strong search capability that helps to select a smaller number of the most salient features among a feature set. In contrast, the existing approaches try to design rules without distinguishing between the random and probabilistic behaviors of ants during the construction of a subset. Consequently, ants may be deprived of the opportunity of utilizing enough previous experience or investigating more salient features during SC in their solutions.

The main structure of ACOFS is shown in figure 6.10, in which the detailed description can be found in. However, at the first stage, while each of the k ants attempt to construct subset, it decides the subset size r first according to the subset size determination scheme. This scheme guides the ants to construct subsets in a reduced form. Then, it follows the conventional probabilistic transition rule. for selecting features as follows,

$$P_i^k(t) = \begin{cases} \dfrac{[\tau i(t)]^\alpha [\eta i(t)]^\beta}{\sum_{u \in j^{\wedge} k} [\tau u(t)]^\alpha [\eta u(t)]^\beta} \\ 0 \end{cases}$$

(6.13)

where j^k is the set of feasible features that can be added to the partial solution, τ_i and η_i are the pheromone and heuristic values associated with feature i (i 1, 2,.....,n), and α and β are two parameters that determine the relative importance of the pheromone value and heuristic information. Note that, since the initial value of and for all individual features are equal, equation 6.13 shows random behaviour in SC initially. The approach used by the ants in constructing individual subsets during SC can be seen in figure 6.11.

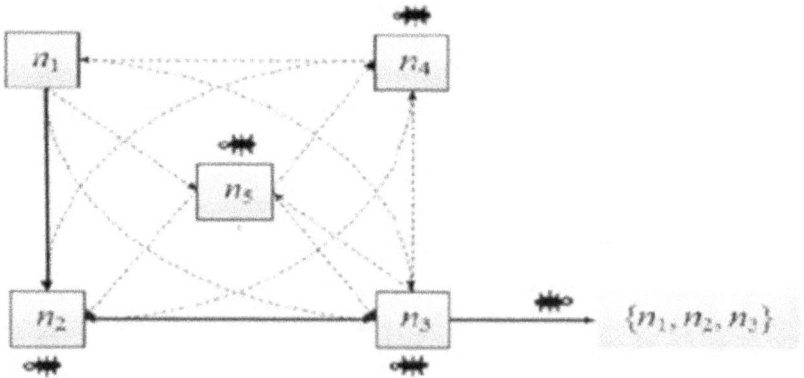

Fig.6.11: Representation of subset constructions by individual ants in ACO algorithm for FS. Here, n_1, n_2,..., n_5 represent the individual features. As an example, one ant placed in n_1 constructed one subset $\{n_1, n_2, n_3\}$.

ACOFS imposes a confinement upon the determination of the subset size, which is not an immanent constraint. Because, other than such restrictions, similarly, the conventional approaches, the above determination scheme works on an expanded boundary beyond a definite range that leads to ineffective solutions for FS. In order to solve other problem, say, incomplete solutions to ACO-based FS algorithms; our ACOFS utilizes a hybrid search strategy (i.e., a combination of the wrapper and filter approaches) by designing different rules to enhance the global search ability of the ants. Fusion of these two approaches leads to an ACOFS that gains high-quality solutions for FS from a given dataset. A more detailed elaboration about each aspect of ACOFS is now given in the following sections.

6.2.5.1. Computation of Subset Size

In an ACO algorithm, the activities of ants have significance for dealing with different combinatorial optimization problems. Therefore, in entangling the FS problem, guiding ants in the right directions is very beneficial in this sense. Contrary to other existing ACO- based FS algorithms, ACOFS uses a simple mechanism to determine the subset size r. It employs a simpler probabilistic formula that consists of a constraint and a random function. The objective of employing such a probabilistic formula is to impart information to the random function in a way that the minimum size of subset has a higher probability of being selected. This is important because ACOFS can be guided toward a particular direction by the choice of which reduced-size subset of salient features is likely to be generated. The subset size determination scheme used can be described in two ways as follows.

First, ACOFS uses a probabilistic formula modified to decide the size of a subset r $(d \leq n)$ as follows:

$$P_r = \frac{n-r}{\sum_{i=1}^{l}(n-i)} \tag{6.14}$$

Here, P_r is maximized linearly as r is minimized, and the value of r is restricted by a constraint, namely, $2 \leq r \leq \delta$. Therefore, r 2, 3,......, δ, where $\delta = \mu x_n$ and $l = n - r$. Here, μ is a user-specified parameter that controls δ. Its value depends on the n for a given dataset. If is closed to n, then the search space of determining the salient features enlarges that certainly causes a high computational cost, and raises the risk that ineffective feature subsets might be generated. Since the aim of ACOFS is to select a subset of salient features within a smaller range, the length of the selected subset is preferred to be between 3 and 12 depending on the given dataset. Thus, is set as [0.1, 0.6]. Then, normalize all the values of P_r in such a way that the summation of all possible values of P_r is equal to 1.

Second, ACOFS utilizes all the values of P_r for the random selection scheme mentioned in figure 6.12 to determine the size of the subset, r eventually. This selection scheme is almost similar to the classical roulette wheel procedure.

```
Random_selection
{
        generate random value h [0,1];
        sum=0;P₀=0;P₁=0;
        for(r=2 to δ){
                sum=sum+Pᵣ;
                if(h<=sum)
                        break;
        }
        return r;
}
```

Fig.6.12: Pseudo-code of the random selection procedure.

6.2.5.2. Subset Evaluation

Subset evaluation has a significant role, along with other basic operations of ACO for selecting salient features in FS tasks. In common practices, filter or wrapper approaches are involved for evaluation tasks. However, it is found in that the performance of a wrapper approach is always better than that of a filter approach. Therefore, the evaluation of the constructed subsets is inspired by a feed-forward NN training scheme for each iteration. Such a NN classifier is not an inherent constraint; instead of NN, any other type of classifier, such as SVM, can be used as well for this evaluation tasks. In this study, the evaluation of the subset is represented by the percentage value of NN classification accuracy (CA) for the testing set. A detailed discussion of the evaluation mechanism integrated into ACOFS as follows.

First, during training the features of a constructed subset, the NN is trained partially for τ_p epochs. Training is performed sequentially using the examples of a training set and a back-propagation (BP) learning algorithm. The number of training epochs, τ_p, is specified by the user. In partial training, which was first used in conjunction with an evolutionary algorithm, the NN is trained for a fixed number of epochs, regardless of whether the algorithm has converged on a result.

Second, check the progress of training to determine whether further training is necessary. If training error is reduced by a predefined amount, ε, after the τ_p training epochs (as mentioned in equation 6.16), we assume that the training process has been progressing well, and that further training is thus necessary, and then proceed to the first step. Otherwise, we go to the next step for adding a hidden neuron. The error, E, is calculated as follows:

$$E = \frac{1}{2}\sum_{p=1}^{p}\sum_{c=1}^{c}(O_c(p) - t_c(p))^2 \qquad (6.15)$$

where $o_c(p)$ and $t_c(p)$ are the actual and target responses of the c-th output neuron for the training example p. The symbols P and C represent the total number of examples and of output neurons in the training set, respectively. The reduction of training error can be described as follows:

$$E(t) - E(t + \tau_p) > \varepsilon, t = \tau, 2\tau, 3\tau, \ldots \ldots \tag{6.16}$$

On the other hand, in the case of adding the hidden neuron, the addition operation is guided by computing the contributions of the current hidden neurons. If the contributions are high, then it is assumed that another one more hidden neuron is required. Otherwise, freeze the extension of the hidden layer size for further partial training of the NN. Analysis of the contribution of previously added hidden neurons in the NN depends on the validation set CA. The CA can be calculated as follows:

$$\text{CA} = 100 \, (P_{vc} / P_v) \tag{6.17}$$

where P_{vc} refers to the number of examples in the validation set correctly classified by the NN and P_v is the total number of patterns in the validation set.

At this stage, the ACOFS measures error and CA in the validation set using equations 6.15 and 6.17 after every τ_p epochs of training. It then terminates training when either the validation CA decreases or the validation error increases or both are satisfied for T successive times, which are measured at the end of each of T successive τ_p epochs of training. Finally, the testing accuracy of the current NN architecture is checked with selected hidden neurons, using the example of the testing set according to equation 6.17.

The idea behind this evaluation process is straightforward: minimize the training error, and maximize the validation accuracy. To achieve these goals, ACOFS uses a constructive approach to determine NN architectures automatically. Although other approaches, such as, pruning and regularization could be used in ACOFS, the selection of an initial NN architecture in these approaches is difficult. This selection, however, is simple in the case of a constructive approach. For example, the initial network architecture in a constructive approach can consist of a hidden layer with one neuron. On the other hand, an input layer is set with r neurons, and an output layer with c neurons. More precisely, among r and c neurons, one neuron for each feature of the corresponding subset and one neuron for each class, respectively. If this minimal architecture cannot solve the given task, hidden neurons can be added one by one. Due to the simplicity of initialization, the constructive approach is used widely in multi-objective learning tasks.

6.2.5.3. Best Subset Selection

Generally, finding salient subsets with a reduced size is always preferable due to the low cost in hardware implementation and less time consumed in operation. Unlike other existing algorithms, in ACOFS, the best salient feature subset is recognized eventually as a combination of the local best and global best selections as follows:

Local best selection: Determine the local best subset, $S'(t)$ for a particular t ($t \in 1$,

2, 3,......) iteration according to Max($S^k(t)$), where $S^k(t)$ is the number of subsets constructed by k ants, and k 1, 2,...,n.

Global best selection: Determine the global best subset (S^g), that is, the best subset of salient features from the all local best solutions in such a way that S^g is compared with the currently decided local best subset, $S^l(t)$ at every t iteration by their classification performances. If $S^l(t)$ is found better, then $S^l(t)$ is replaced by S^g. One thing is that, during this selection process, if the performances are found similar at any time, then select the one among the two, i.e., S^g and $S^l(t)$ as a best subset that has reduced size. Note that, at the first iteration $S^l(t)$ is considered as S^g.

6.2.5.4. Hybrid Search Process

The new hybrid search technique, incorporated in ACOFS, consists of wrapper and filter approaches. A significant advantage of this search technique is that ants achieve a significant ability of utilizing previous successful moves and of expressing desirability of moves towards a high-quality solution in FS. This search process is composed of two sets of newly designed rules, such as, the pheromone update rule and the heuristic information rule, which are further described as follows.

6.2.5.4.1. Pheromone Update Rule

Pheromone updating in the ACO algorithm is a vital aspect of FS tasks. Ants exploit features in SC that have been most suitable in prior iterations through the pheromone update rule, consisting of local update and global update. More precisely, global update applies only to those features that are a part of the best feature subset in the current iteration. It allows the features to receive a large amount of pheromone update in equal shares. The aim of global update is to encourage ants to construct subsets with a significant CA. In contrast to the global update, local update not only causes the irrelevant features to be less desirable, but also helps ants to select those features, which have never been explored before. This update either decreases the strength of the pheromone trail or maintains the same level, based on whether a particular feature has been selected.

In ACOFS, a set of new pheromone update rules has been designed on the basis of two basic behaviors (that is to say, random and probabilistic) of ants during SCs. These rules have been modified from the standard rule, which aims to provide a proper balance between exploration and exploitation of ants for the next iteration. Exploration is reported to prohibit ants from converging on a common path. Actual ants also have a similar behavioral characteristic, which is an attractive property. If different paths can be explored by different ants, then there is a higher probability that one of the ants may find a better solution, as opposed to all ants converging on the same tour.

Random case: The rule presenting in equation 618 is modified only in the second term, which is divided by m_i. Such a modification provides for sufficient exploration of the ants for the following constructions. The reason is that during the random behavior of the transition rule, the features are being selected randomly, rather than depending to their experiences. Thus, to provide an exploration facility for the ants, the modification has been adopted as follows:

$$\tau_i(t+1) = (1-\rho)\tau_i(t) + \frac{1}{mi}\sum_{k=1}^{n}\Delta\,\tau_i^k(t) + e\Delta\tau_i^g(t)$$

$$\Delta\tau_i^k(t) = \begin{cases} \gamma(s^k(t)) & if\ i\in S^k(t) \\ 0 & otherwise \end{cases}$$

(6.18)

$$\Delta\tau_i^g(t) = \begin{cases} \gamma(S^l(t)) & if\ \in s^l(t) \\ 0 & otherwise \end{cases}$$

Here, *i* refers to the number of feature (*i* 1, 2,......*n*), and m_i is the value for the specifically selected feature i in the current iteration.

$\Delta\tau ki(t)$ is the amount of pheromone received by the local update for feature *i*, which is included in $S^k(t)$ at iteration *t*. Similarly, the global update, $\Delta\tau gi(t)$, is the amount of pheromone for feature i that is included in $S^l(t)$. Finally, ρ and e refer to the pheromone decay value, and elitist parameter, respectively.

Probabilistic case: equation 6.19 shows the modified pheromone rule for the probabilistic case. The rule is similar to the original form, but actual modification has been made only for the inner portions of the second and third terms.

$$\tau_i(t+1) = (1-\rho)\tau_i(t) + \sum_{k=1}^{n}\Delta\,\tau_i^k(t) + e\Delta\,\tau_i^g(t)$$

$$\Delta\tau_i^k(t) = \begin{cases} \gamma(S^k(t))\times\gamma i & if\ i\in S^k(t) \\ 0 & otherwise \end{cases}$$

(6.19)

$$\Delta\tau_i^g(t) = \begin{cases} \gamma(S^l(t))\times\lambda i & if\ i\in S^l(t) \\ 0 & otherwise \end{cases}$$

Here, feature *i* is rewarded by the global update, and $\Delta\,\tau^g$ is in the third term, where $i\in S^l(t)i$. It is important to emphasize that, *i* is maintained strictly here. That is, *i* at iteration *i* t_i is compared with *i* at iteration $(t_t\text{-}\tau_p)$, where $t_t = t + \tau_p$, and τ_p 1, 2, 3,...... In this regard, if $\gamma(S^l(t_t))$ max$((\gamma S^l(t_{t_p}\varepsilon)),)$, where ε refers to the number of CAs for those local best subsets that maintain $|S^l(t_t)| = |S^l(t_{t_p})|$, then a number of features, n_c are ignored to get $\Delta\tau^g$, since those features are available in $S^l(t_t)$, which causes to degrade its performance. Here, $n_c \in S^l(t_t)$ but $n_c \notin S^{lb}$, where S^{lb} provides max$((\gamma S^l(t_{t_p})),)$, and $|S^l(t_t)|$ implies the size of the subset $S^l(t_t)$. Note that, the aim of this restriction is to provide $\Delta\tau^g$ only to those features that are actually significant, because, global update has a vital role in selecting the salient features in ACOFS. Distinguish such salient features and allow them to receive $\Delta\tau^g$ by imposing the above restriction.

6.2.5.4.2. Heuristic Information Measurement

A heuristic value, η, for each feature generally represents the attractiveness of the features, and depends on the dependency degree. It is therefore necessary to use ; otherwise, the algorithm may become too greedy, and ultimately a better solution may not be found. Here, a set of new rules is introduced for measuring heuristic information using the advantages of wrapper and filter tools. More precisely, the outcome of subset evaluations using the NN is used here as a wrapper tool, whereas the value of information gain for each feature is used as a filter tool. These rules are, therefore, formulated according to the random and probabilistic behaviors of the ants, which are described as follows.

Random case: In the initial iteration, while ants are involved in constructing the feature subsets randomly, the heuristic value of all features i can be estimated as follows:

$$\eta_i = \frac{1}{mi} \sum\nolimits_{k=1}^{n} \gamma(S^k(t)) \left(1 + \varphi \frac{|S^k(t)|}{n} \right) \qquad if \; i \in S^k(t) \tag{6.20}$$

Probabilistic case: In the following iterations, when ants complete the feature SCs on the basis of the probabilistic behavior, the following formula is used to estimate for all features i:

$$\eta_i = mi \; \phi i \sum\nolimits_{k=1}^{n} \gamma a(S^k(t)) \lambda i \left(1 + \varphi e \frac{-|S^k(t)|}{n} \right) \; if \; i \in S^k(t) \tag{6.21}$$

In these two rules, φ_i refers to the number of a particular selected feature i that is a part of the subsets that are constructed within the currently completed iterations, except for the initial iteration. The aim of multiplying m_i and φ_i is to provide a proper exploitation capability for the ants during SCs. φ_i refers to the information gain for feature i. A detailed discussion on measurement of information gain can be seen in. However, the aim of including is based on the following two factors:

a.   reducing the greediness of some particular feature i in n during SCs, and

b.   increasing the diversity between the features in n.

Thus, different features may get an opportunity to be selected in the SC for different iterations, thus definitely enhancing the exploration behavior of ants. Furthermore, one additional exponential term has been multiplied by these rules in aiming for a reduced size subset. Here, is the user specified parameter that controls the exponential term.

6.2.5.4.3. Computational Complexity

In order to understand the actual computational cost of a method, an exact analysis of computational complexity is required. In this sense, the big-O notation is a prominent approach in terms of analyzing computational complexity. Thus, ACOFS here uses the above process for this regard. There are seven basic steps in ACOFS, namely, information gain measurement, subset construction, subset evaluation, termination criterion, subset determination, pheromone update, and heuristic information measurement. The following paragraphs present the computational complexity of ACOFS in order to show that inclusion of different techniques does not increase computational complexity in selecting a feature subset.

1. **Information Gain Measurement:** In this step, information gain (IG) for each feature is measured according to. If the number of total features for a given dataset is n, then the cost of measuring IG is $O(n \times P)$, where P denotes the number of examples in the given dataset. It is further mentioning that this cost is required only once, specifically, before starting the FS process.

2. Subset Construction: Subset construction shows two different types of phenomena according to equation 6.13 For the random case, if the total number of features for a given dataset is n, then the cost of an ant constructing a single subset is $O(r \times n)$. Here, r refers to the size of subsets. Since the total number of ants is k, the computational cost is $O(r \times k \times n)$ operations. However, in practice, $r < n$; hence, the cost becomes $O(k \times n)$ Hd $O(n^2)$. In terms of the probabilistic case, ACOFS uses the equation 6.13 for selecting the features in SC, which shows a constant computational cost of $O(1)$ for each ant. If the number of ants is k, then the computational cost becomes $O(k)$.

3. In ACOFS, five types of operations are necessarily required for evaluating a single subset using a constructive NN training scheme: (a) partial training, (b) stopping criterion, (c) further training, (d) contribution computation, and (e) addition of a hidden neuron. The subsequent paragraphs describe these types in details.

   a. **Partial training:** In case of training, standard BP is used. During training each epoch BP takes $O(W)$ operations for one example. Here, W is the number of weights in the current NN. Thus, training all examples in the training set for τ_p epochs requires $O(\tau_p \times P_t \times W)$ operations, where P_t denotes the number of examples in the training set.

   b. **Stopping criterion:** During training, the stopping criterion uses either validation accuracy or validation errors for subset evaluation. Since training error is computed as a part of the training process, evaluating the termination criterion takes $O(P_v \times W)$ operations, where P_v denotes the number of examples in the validation set. Since $P_v < P_t$, $O(P \times_v \times W) < O(_p \times kP_t \times W)$.

   c. **Further training:** ACOFS uses equation 6.16 to check whether further training is necessary. The evaluation of equation 6.16 takes a constant number of computational operations $O(1)$, since the error values used in equation 6.15 have already been evaluated during training.

   d. **Contribution computation:** ACOFS computes the contribution of the added hidden neuron using equation 6.17. This computation takes $O(P_v)$ operations, which is less than $O(\tau_p \times P_t \times W)$.

   e. **Addition of a hidden neuron:** The computational cost for adding a hidden neuron is $O(r \times c)$ for initializing the connection weights, where r is the number of features in the current subset, and c is the number of neurons in the output layer. Also note that $O(r + c) < O(_p \times P_t \times W)$.

The aforementioned computation is done for a partial training session consisting of τ_p epochs. In general, ACOFS requires a number, say M, of such partial training sessions for evaluating a single subset. Thus, the cost becomes $O(\tau_p \times M \times P_p \times W)$. Furthermore, by considering all subsets, the computational cost required is $O(k \times \tau_p \times M \times P_t \times W)$ operations.

i.   Termination criterion: A termination criterion is employed in ACOFS for terminating the FS process eventually. Since only one criterion is required to be executed (i.e., the algorithm achieves a predefined accuracy, or executes a iteration threshold, I), the execution of such a criterion requires a constant computational cost of $O(1)$.

ii.   Subset determination: ACOFS requires two steps to determine the best subset, namely, finding the local best subset and the global best subset. In order to find the local best subset in each iteration t, ACOFS requires $O(k)$ operations. The total computational cost for finding the local best subsets thus becomes $O(k \times t)$. In order to find the global best subset, ACOFS requires $O(1)$ operations. Thus, the total computational cost for subset determination becomes $O(k \times t)$, which is less than $O(k \times \tau_p \times M \times P_t \times W)$.

iii. Pheromone update rule: ACOFS executes equations 6.18 and 6.19 to update the pheromone trails for each feature in terms of the random and probabilistic cases. Since the number of features is n for a given learning dataset, the computation takes $O(n)$ constant operations, which is less than $O(k \times \tau_p \times M \times P_t \times W)$.

iv.   Heuristic information measurement: Similar to the pheromone update operation, ACOFS uses equations 6.20 and 6.21 to update the heuristic value of n features. Thereafter, the computational cost becomes $O(n)$. Note that, $O(n)$ $O(k \times \tau_p \times M \times P_t \times W)$.

In accordance with the above analysis, summarize the different parts of the entire computational cost as $O(n \times P) + O(n^2) + O(k) + O(k \times \tau_p \times M \times P_t \times W)$. It is important to note here that the first and second terms, namely, $n \times P$ and $\times n^2$, are the cost of operations performed only once, and are much less than $k \times \tau_p \times M \times P_t \times P$. On the other hand, $O(k) << O(k \times \tau_p \times M \times P_t \times W)$. Hence, the total computational cost of ACOFS is $O((\tau_p \times M \times P_t \times W)$, which is similar to the cost of training a fixed network architecture using BP, and that the total cost is similar to that of other existing ACO-based FS approaches. Thus, it can be said that incorporation of several techniques in ACOFS does not increase the computational cost.

6.3.   Tabu Search Algorithm

Tabu Search is a meta-heuristic that guides a local heuristic search procedure to explore the solution space beyond local optimality. One of the main components of Tabu Search is its use of adaptive memory, which creates a more flexible search behavior. Memory-based strategies are therefore the hallmark of tabu search approaches, founded on a quest for "integrating principles," by which alternative forms of memory are appropriately combined with effective strategies for exploiting them. In this chapter we address the problem of training multilayer feed-forward neural networks. These networks have been widely used for both prediction and classification in many different areas. Although the most popular method for training these networks is back propagation, other optimization methods such as tabu search have been applied to solve this problem. This section describes two training algorithms based on the tabu search. The experimentation shows that the procedures provide high quality solutions to the training problem, and in addition consume a reasonable computational effort.

Before introducing the basic concepts of TS, we believe it is useful to go back in time to try to better understand the genesis of the method and how it relates to previous work.

Heuristics or approximate solution technique, have been prominently used since the very beginning of operations research to tackle difficult combinatorial problems. With the invention of the theory of complexity in the early 70's, it became clear that, since most of these problems were indeed *NP-hard*, there were very little chances of ever finding efficient exact solution procedures for them. This realization emphasized the role of heuristics for solving the combinatorial problems that were encountered in real-life applications and that needed to be tackled, whether or not they were *NP-hard*. While many different approaches were proposed and experimented with, the most popular one was based on Local Search (LS) improvement techniques. LS can be roughly summarized as an iterative search procedure that, starting from an initial feasible solution, progressively improves it by applying a series of local modifications (or *moves*). At each iteration, the search moves to an improving feasible solution that differs only slightly from the current one (in fact, the difference between the previous and the new solutions amounts to one of the local modifications mentioned above). The search terminates when it encounters a local optimum with respect to the transformations that it considers, an important limitation of the method: unless one is extremely lucky, this local optimum is often a fairly mediocre solution. In LS, the quality of the solution obtained and computing times are usually highly dependent upon the "richness" of the set of transformations (moves) considered at each iteration of the heuristic.

In 1983, the world of combinatorial optimization was shattered by the appearance of a paper in which the authors (Kirkpatrick, Gelatt and Vecchi) were describing a new heuristic approach called *Simulated Annealing* (SA) that could be shown to converge to an optimal solution of a combinatorial problem, albeit in infinite computing time. Based on analogy with statistical mechanics, SA can be interpreted as a form of controlled random walk in the space of feasible solutions. The emergence of SA indicated that one could look for other ways to tackle combinatorial optimization problems and spurred the interest of the research community. In the following years, many other new approaches, mostly based on analogies with natural phenomena, were proposed (TS, *Ant Systems, Threshold Methods)* and, together with some older ones, such as *Genetic Algorithms* (Holland, 1975), they gained an increasing popularity. Now collectively known under the name of *Meta-Heuristics* (a term originally coined by Glover in 1986), these methods have become over the last fifteen years the leading edge of heuristic approaches for solving combinatorial optimization problems.

6.3.1.   Tabu Search

Building upon some of his previous work, Fred Glover proposed in 1986 a new approach, which he called Tabu Search, to allow LS methods to overcome local optima. (In fact, many elements of this first TS proposal, and some elements of later TS elaborations, were introduced in Glover, 1977, involving short term memory to prevent the turnaround of recent moves, and longer term frequency memory to fortify attractive components.) The fundamental concept of TS is to follow LS each time it encounters a local optimum by permitting un-advancing moves; *cycling* back to pre-visited solutions is restricted by the use of *memories*, known as *tabu lists*, that keeps a record of the recent history of the search, an important idea that can be linked to Artificial Intelligence concepts. It is interesting to note that, the same year, a similar approach was proposed by Hansen, which he named *steepest ascent/mildest descent*. It is also important to noticeable that Glover disapproved TS, by considering it as an improper heuristic, but rather as a Meta-Heuristic, i.e., a general methodology for managing and controlling "inner" heuristics specifically designed to the problems at hand.

6.3.2.   Search space and neighborhood structure

As we just mentioned, TS is the further extension of classical LS methods. The generic TS can be understood as simply the fusion of LS with short-term memories. It follows that the first two basic elements of any TS heuristic are the definition of its *search space* and its *neighborhood structure*.

The LS search space or TS heuristic is generally the space of all possible solutions that can be considered (visited) at the time of the search. For instance, in the CVRP example previously described, the search space could be considered as the set of feasible solutions to the problem, where each specific point in the search space corresponds to a set of vehicles routes satisfying all the identified constraints. Although in that case the definition of the search space seems to be quite natural, it is not always so. Consider now the CPLP example: the feasible space includes both integer location and continuous flow variables that are linked by strict conditions; moreover, as already indicated previously, for any reasonable set of values for the location variables, one could easily retrieve optimal values for the flow variables by solving the associated transportation problem. In this context, one could obviously use as a search space the full feasible space; this would involve manipulating both location and flow variables, which is not that easy task. A more attractive search space is the set of feasible vectors of location variables, i.e., feasible vectors in $\{0, 1\}^{|J|}$, any solution in that space being "completed" to yield a feasible solution to the original problem by computing the associated optimal flow variables. It is worth noticed that these two possible definitions are not the only ones. Indeed, one could also decide to search instead the set of extreme points of the set of feasible flow vectors, retrieving the associated location variables by simply noting that a plant must be open whenever some flow is allocated to it. It is also important to consider that it is not always a good approach to confine the search space to reasonable solutions; in most of the cases, allowing the search to move to unrealistic or unreasonable solutions is desirable, and sometimes even necessary.

Closely linked to the definition of the search space is that of the neighborhood structure. At each iteration of LS or TS, the local transformations that can be applied to the current solution, denoted by S, define a set of neighboring solutions in the search space, denoted $N(S)$ (the neighborhood of S). Formally, $N(S)$ is a subset of the search space defined by:

$N(S) = \{solutions\ obtained\ by\ applying\ a\ single\ local\ transformation\ to\ S\}$.

In general, for any specific problem at hand, there are many more possible (and even, attractive) neighborhood structures than search space definitions. This follows from the fact that there may be several plausible neighborhood structures for a given definition of the search space. This is easily illustrated on our CVRP example that has been the object of several TS implementations. In order to simplify the discussion, we suppose in the following that the search space is the feasible space.

Simple neighborhood structures for the CVRP involve moving at each iteration a single customer from its current route; the selected customer is inserted in the same route or in another route with sufficient residual capacity. An important feature of these neighborhood structures is the way in which insertions are performed: one could use random insertion or insertion at the best position in the target route; alternately, one could use more complex insertion schemes that involve a partial re-optimization of the target route, such as GENI insertions (see Gendreau, Hertz and Laporte, 1994). Before proceeding any further it is important to stress that while we say that these neighborhood structures involve moving a *single* customer, the neighborhoods they define contain all the feasible route configurations that can be obtained from the current solution by moving *any* customer and inserting it in the stated fashion. Examining the neighborhood can thus be fairly demanding.

More complex neighborhood structures for the CVRP, such as the λ-interchange of Osman (1993), are obtained by allowing simultaneously the movement of customers to different routes and the swapping of customers between routes. In Rego and Roucairol (1996), moves are defined by *ejection chains* that are sequences of coordinated movements of customers from one route to another; for instance, an ejection chain of length 3 would involve moving a customer v_1 from route R_1 to route R_2, a customer v_2 from R_2 to route R_3 and a customer v_3 from R_3 to route R_4. Other neighborhood structures involve the swapping of sequences of several customers between routes, as in the Cross-exchange of Taillard *et al.* (1997). These types of neighborhoods have seldom be used for the CVRP, but are common in TS heuristics for its time-windows extension, where customers must be visited within a pre-specified time interval. We refer the interested reader to Gendreau, Laporte and Potvin (2002) and Bräysy and Gendreau (2001) for a more detailed discussion of TS implementations for the CVRP and the Vehicle Routing Problem with Time-Windows.

When different definitions of the search space are considered for any given problem, neighborhood structures will inevitably differ to a considerable degree. This can be illustrated on our CPLP example. If the search space is defined with respect to the location variables, neighborhood structures will usually involve the so-called *"Add/ Drop"* and *"Swap"* moves that respectively change the status of one site (i.e., either opening a closed facility or closing an open one) and proceed an open provision from one site to another (this move amounts to performing simultaneously an Add move and a Drop move). Although, the search space is the set of extreme points of the set of reasonable flow vectors, these moves become meaningless, instead One should consider moves defined by the application of pivots to the linear programming formulation of the transportation problem, since with each pivot operation the current solution moves to an adjacent extreme point.

The preceding discussion depicted a major point: selecting a search space and a neighborhood structure is by far the most crucial step in the design of a TS heuristic. It is at this step that one could most optimally utilize the understanding and knowledge of the problem at hand.

6.3.3. Tabus

Tabus are one of the distinctive constituents of TS when compared to LS. As we had already discussed, tabus are specifically used to prevent cycling when proceeding away from local optima through non-improving proceedings. The key realization here is that when this situation takes place, something is requires to be done to prevent the search from tracing back its steps to where it came from. This could be achieved by declaring *tabu* (disallowing) moves that turnaround the effect of recent moves. For instance, in the CVRP example, if customer v_1 has just been moved from route R_1 to route R_2, one could declare tabu proceeding back v_1 from R_2 to R_1 for some number of epochs (this number is called the *tabu tenure* of the move). Tabus are also useful to help the search move away from previously visited portions of the search space and thus perform more extensive exploration.

Tabus are stored in a *short-term memory* of the search (the *tabu list*) and usually only a fixed and fairly limited quantity of information is recorded. In any given context, there are several possibilities regarding the specific information that is recorded. One could record complete solutions, but this requires a lot of storage and makes it expensive to check whether a potential move is tabu or not; it is therefore seldom used. The most commonly used tabus involve recording the last few transformations performed on the current solution and prohibiting reverse transformations (as in the example above); others are based on key characteristics of the solutions themselves or of the moves.

To better understand how tabus work, let us go back to our reference problems. In the CVRP, one could define tabus in several ways. To continue our example where customer v_1 has just been moved from route R_1 to route R_2, one could declare tabu specifically moving back v_1 from R_2 to R_1 and record this in the short-term memory as the triplet (v_1, R_2, R_1). Note that this type of tabu will not constrain the search much, but that cycling may occur if v_1 is then moved to another route R_3 and then from R_3 to

R_1. A stronger tabu would involve prohibiting moving back v_1 to R_1 (without consideration for its current route) and be recorded as (v_1, R_1). An even stronger tabu would be to disallow moving v_1 to any other route and would simply be noted as (v_1).

In the CPLP, when searching the space of location variables, tabus on Add/Drop moves should prohibit changing the status of the affected location variable and can be recorded by noting its index; tabus for Swap moves are more complex: they could be declared with respect to the site where the facility was closed, to the site where the facility was opened, to both locations (i.e., changing the status of both location variables is tabu), or to the specific swapping operation. When searching the space of flow variables, one can take advantage of the fact that a pivot operation is associated with a unique pair of entering and leaving variables to define tabus; while here again several combinations are possible, experience has shown that when dealing with pivot neighborhood structures, tabus imposed on leaving variables (to prevent them from coming back in the basis) are usually much more effective.

Multiple tabu lists can be used simultaneously and are sometimes advisable. For instance, in the CPLP, if one uses a neighborhood structure that contains both Add/Drop and Swap moves, it might be a good idea to keep a separate tabu list for each type of moves.

Standard tabu lists are usually implemented as circular lists of fixed length. It has been shown, however, that fixed-length tabus cannot always prevent cycling, and some authors have proposed varying the tabu list length during the search (Glover, 1989, 1990; Skorin-Kapov, 1990; Taillard, 1990 and 1991). Another solution is to randomly generate the tabu tenure of each move within some specified interval; using this approach requires a somewhat different scheme for recording tabus that are then usually stored as *tags* in an array (the entries in this array will usually record the iteration number until which a move is tabu; see Gendreau, Hertz and Laporte, 1994, for more details).

6.3.4. Aspiration criteria

While central to TS, tabus are sometimes too powerful: they may prohibit attractive moves, even when there is no danger of cycling, or they may lead to an overall stagnation of the searching process. It is thus necessary to use algorithmic devices that will allow one to *revoke* (cancel) tabus. These are called *aspiration criteria*. The simplest and most commonly used aspiration criterion (found in almost all TS implementations) consists in allowing a move, even if it is tabu, if it results in a solution with an objective value better than that of the current best-known solution (since the new solution has obviously not been previously visited). Much more complicated aspiration criteria have been proposed and successfully implemented (see, for instance, de Werra and Hertz, 1989, or Hertz and de Werra, 1991), but they are rarely used. The key rule in this respect is that if cycling cannot occur, tabus can be disregarded.

6.3.5. A template for simple tabu search

We are now in the position to give a general template for TS, integrating the elements we have seen so far. We suppose that we are trying to minimize a function $f(S)$ over some domain and we apply the so-called "best improvement" version of TS, i.e., the version in which one chooses at each iteration the best available move (this is the most commonly used version of TS). Fig.6.13 depicts the steps involved in a standard TS algorithm.

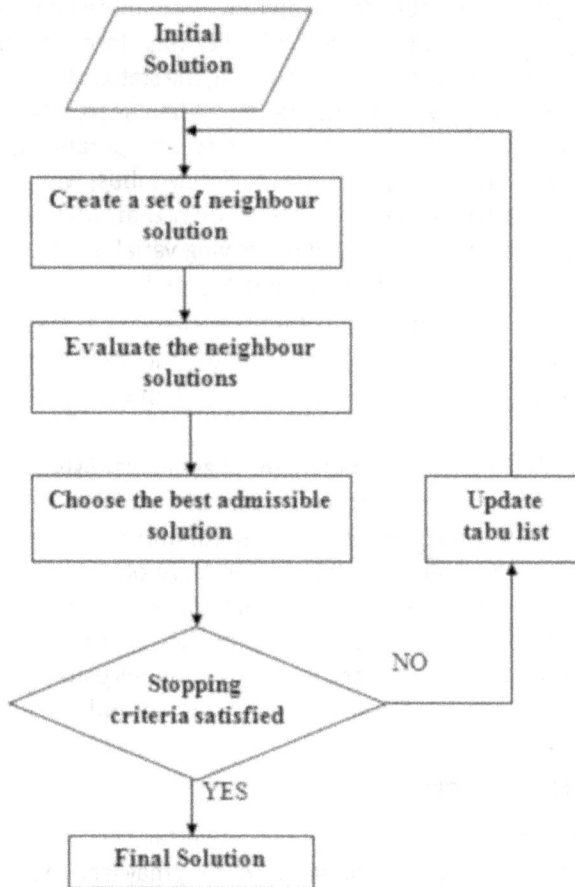

Fig.6.13: Flowchart of a standard TS algorithm

Notation

- ➢ S,   the current solution,
- ➢ S^*,   the best-known solution,
- ➢ f^*,   value of S^*,
- ➢ $N(S)$, the neighborhood of S,
- ➢ $\tilde{N}(S)$, the "admissible" subset of $N(S)$ (i.e., non-tabu or allowed by aspiration).

Initialization

Choose (construct) an initial solution S_0.

Set $S := S_0$, $f^* := f(S_0)$, $S^* := S_0$, $T := \Theta$.

Search

While *termination criterion not satisfied* do

➤   Select S in *argmin* $[f(S')]$;
     $S' \varepsilon \, \tilde{N}(S)$

➤   if $f(S) < f^*$, then set $f^* := f(S)$, $S^* := S$;

➤   record tabu for the current move in T (delete oldest entry if necessary);
     endwhile.

6.3.6.   Termination criteria

One may have noticed that we have not specified in our template above a termination criterion. In theory, the search could go on forever, unless the optimal value of the problem at hand is known beforehand. In practice, obviously, the search has to be stopped at some point. The most commonly used stopping criteria in TS are:

➤   after a fixed number of iterations (or a fixed amount of CPU time);

➤   after some number of iterations without an improvement in the objective function value (the criterion used in most implementations);

➤   when the objective reaches a pre-specified threshold value.

In complex tabu schemes, the search is usually stopped after completing a sequence of *phases*, the duration of each phase being determined by one of the above criteria.

6.3.7.   Probabilistic TS and candidate lists

In "regular" TS, one must evaluate the objective for every element of the neighborhood $N(S)$ of the current solution. This can prove extremely expensive from the computational standpoint. An alternative is to instead consider only a random sample $N'(S)$ of $N(S)$, thus reducing significantly the computational burden. Another attractive feature of this alternative is that the added randomness can act as an anti-cycling mechanism; this allows one to use shorter tabu lists than would be necessary if a full exploration of the neighborhood was performed. One the negative side, it must be noted that, in that case, one may miss excellent solutions. Probabilities may also be applied to activating tabu criteria.

Another way to control the number of moves examined is by means of *candidate list* strategies, which provide more strategic ways of generating a useful subset $N'(S)$ of $N(S)$. (The probabilistic approach can be considered to be one instance of a candidate list strategy, and may also be used to modify such a strategy.) Failure to adequately address the issues involved in creating effective candidate lists is one of the more conspicuous shortcomings that differentiates a naive TS implementation from one that is more solidly grounded. Relevant designs for candidate list strategies are discussed in

Glover and Laguna (1997). We also discuss a useful type of candidate generation approach in Section 3.4.

6.3.8. Intermediate Concepts

Simple TS as described above can sometimes successfully solve difficult problems, but in most cases, additional elements have to be included in the search strategy to make it fully effective. We now briefly review the most important of these.

6.3.8.1. Intensification

The idea behind the concept of search intensification is that, as an intelligent human being would probably do, one should explore more thoroughly the portions of the search space that seem "promising" in order to make sure that the best solutions in these areas are indeed found. From time to time, one would thus stop the normal searching process to perform an intensification phase. In general, intensification is based on some *intermediate-term memory*, such as a *recency memory*, in which one records the number of consecutive iterations that various "solution components" have been present in the current solution without interruption. For instance, in the CPLP application, one could record how long each site has had an open facility. A typical approach to intensification is to restart the search from the best currently known solution and to "freeze" (fix) in it the components that seem more attractive. To continue the CPLP example, one could thus freeze a number of facilities in the sites that have had them for the largest number of iterations and perform a restricted search on the other sites. Another technique that is often used consists in changing the neighborhood structure to one allowing more powerful or more diverse moves. In the CVRP example, one could therefore allow more complex insertion moves or switch to an ejection chain neighborhood structure. In the CPLP example, if Add/Drop moves were used, Swap moves could be added to the neighborhood structure. In probabilistic TS, one could increase the sample size or switch to searching without sampling.

Intensification is used in many TS implementations, but it is not always necessary. This is because there are many situations where the search performed by the normal searching process is thorough enough. There is thus no need to spend time exploring more carefully the portions of the search space that have already been visited, and this time can be used more effectively as we shall see right now.

6.3.8.2. Diversification

One of the main problems of all methods based on Local Search approaches, and this includes TS in spite of the beneficial impact of tabus, is that they tend to be too "local" (as their name implies), i.e., they tend to spend most, if not all, of their time in a restricted portion of the search space. The negative consequence of this fact is that, although good solutions may be obtained, one may fail to explore the most interesting parts of the search space and thus end up with solutions that are still pretty far from the optimal ones. *Diversification* is an algorithmic mechanism that tries to alleviate this problem by forcing the search into previously unexplored areas of the search space. It is usually based on some form of *long-term memory* of the search, such as a *frequency memory*, in which one records the total number of iterations (since the beginning of the search) that various "solution components" have been present in the current solution or have been involved in the selected moves. For instance, in the CPLP application, one could record during the number of iterations during which each site has had an open facility. In the CVRP application, one could note how many times each customer has been moved from its current route. In cases where it is possible to identify useful "regions" of the search space, the frequency memory can be refined to track the number of iterations spent in these different regions.

There are two major diversification techniques. The first, called *restart diversification*, involves forcing a few rarely used components in the current solution (or the best known solution) and restarting the search from this point. In CPLP procedures, one could thus open one or a few facilities at locations that have seldom had them up to that point and resume searching from that plant configuration (one could also close facilities at locations that have been used the most frequently). In a CVRP heuristic, customers that have not yet been moved frequently could be forced into new routes. The second diversification method, *continuous diversification*, integrates diversification considerations directly into the regular searching process. This is achieved by *biasing* the evaluation of possible moves by adding to the objective a small term related to component frequencies (see Soriano and Gendreau, 1996, for an extensive discussion on these two techniques). A third way of achieving diversification is *strategic oscillation* as we will see in the next subsection.

Before closing this subsection, we would like to stress that ensuring proper search diversification is possibly **the most critical issue** in the design of TS heuristics. It should be addressed with extreme care fairly early in the design phase and revisited if the results obtained are not up to expectations.

6.3.8.3. Allowing infeasible solutions

Accounting for all problem constraints in the definition of the search space often restricts the searching process too much and can lead to mediocre solutions. This occurs, for example, in CVRP instances where the route capacity or duration constraints are too tight to allow moving customers effectively between routes. In such cases, *constraint relaxation* is an attractive strategy, since it creates a larger search space that can be explored with "simpler" neighborhood structures. Constraint relaxation is easily implemented by dropping selected constraints from the search space definition and adding to the objective weighted penalties for constraint violations. However, this could raise the issue of finding correct weights for constraint violations. An attractive way of circumventing this problem is to use *self-adjusting penalties*, i.e., weights are adjusted dynamically on the basis of the recent history of the search: weights are increased if only infeasible solutions were encountered in the last few iterations, and decreased if all recent solutions were feasible (see, for instance, Gendreau, Hertz and Laporte, 1994, for further details). Penalty weights can also be altered in a systematic fashion to drive the search to cross the feasibility borderline of the search space and hence induce diversification. This methodology, called as *strategic oscillation*, was brought in light in 1977 by Glover and employed since then in several successful TS procedures. (A prominent early variant oscillates among alternative types of proceedings, hence neighborhood structures, while another oscillates around a selected value for a critical function.)

6.3.8.4. Surrogate and auxiliary objectives

There are many problems for which the true objective function is quite costly to evaluate, a typical example being the CPLP when one searches the space of location variables. (Remember that, in this case, computing the objective value for any potential solution entails solving the associated transportation problem.) When this occurs, the evaluation of moves may become prohibitive, even if sampling is used. An effective approach to handle this issue is to evaluate neighbors using a *surrogate objective*, i.e., a function that is correlated to the true objective, but is less computationally demanding, in order to identify a (small) set of promising candidates (potential solutions achieving the best values for the surrogate). The true objective is then computed for this small set of candidate moves and the best one selected to become the new current solution.

Another frequently encountered difficulty is that the objective function may not provide enough information to effectively drive the search to more interesting areas of the search space. A typical depiction of this situation is the variant of the CVRP in which the size of the fleet is not constant, but is rather the basic aim (i.e., one is looking for the minimal fleet size allowing a feasible solution). In this problem, except for the solutions where a route has only a few number of customers assigned to it, most neighborhood structures will lead to the situation where all elements in the neighborhood score equally with respect to the primary objective (i.e., all allowable moves produce solutions with the same number of vehicles). In such a case, it is absolutely necessary to define an *auxiliary objective function* to orient the search. Such a function must measure in some way the desirable attributes of solutions. In our example, one could, for instance, use a function that would favor solutions with routes having just a few customers, thus increasing the likelihood that a route can be totally emptied in a subsequent iteration. It should be noted that coming up with an effective auxiliary objective is not always easy and may require a lengthy trial and error process. In some other cases, fortunately, the auxiliary objective is obvious for anyone familiar with the problem at hand.

Review Questions

1. Write a short note on simulated annealing and illustrate how, it is found better than other algorithms for solving optimization problem.
2. Write down the steps involved in simulated annealing algorithm along with the example code.
3. Briefly explain Ant Colony Optimization and its contribution in feature selection, give an introductory note on feature selection.
4. Explain tabu search algorithm, along with the steps involved.
5.   Explain briefly, the concepts, intensification and diversification involved in tabu search.

Course-wide Test-Bank

Chapter 1

1. Explain Biological Neuron and Artificial Neuron on the basis of structure and function of a single neuron.
2. Discuss the various techniques/ aspects of soft computing in short.
3. Discuss the taxonomy of neural network architecture.
4. Write short note on Activation Function.
5. Describe briefly Artificial Neural Network (ANN), and the first Artificial Neuron model.
6. Explain Biological Neural Networks along with the steps involved in neuronal-processing.
7. Differentiate between hard computing and soft computing.

Chapter 2

1. Explain supervised and unsupervised learning with the help of examples.
2. Explain the Gradient descent learning rule.
3. State and explain the Hebb's leaning rule.
4. Describe Delta rule for the training of Neural Networks.
5. Draw and discuss the configuration of recurrent network.
6. Explain Feedforward networks and feedback networks.
7. Explain the problem of linear separability. How XOR gate problem can be implemented using Artificial Neural Networks.
8. Explain linear separability. Why a single layer of perceptron can-not be used to solve linearly inseparable problem?
9. Illustrate using an example that Multilayer perceptron can successfully implement XOR logic, while simple perceptron can-not.
10. Distinguish between linearly separable and linearly inseparable problems, giving example for each.
11. Explain ADALINE and MADALINE networks, with their algorithms.
12. Explain back propagation networks along with the backpropagation algorithm.

Chapter 3

1. Explain Counter Propagation Networks.
2. Describe briefly, the architecture of ART, with the help of schematic diagram.
3. Write short notes on:

    (a)   Associative Memory

    (b)   Boltzmann Machine

    (c)   Hopfield Network

4.   Explain how, Boltzmann machine can be employed to solve the problems associated with Hopfield network.

5.   Explain the architecture of Counter propagation network, how it works in normal and training mode?

6.   Explain the significance of hidden layer in pattern recognition.

7.   Explain Kohonen Self organizing feature map.

Chapter 4

1.   Write a short note on Fuzzy Logic and its consequences in artificial intelligence.

2.   Explain Fuzzy sets, and highlight the points, how these are different from the classical sets.

3.   Describe briefly the set-theoretic operations and various membership functions.

4.   Write a short note on Extension principle, along with the monotonic and non-monotonic functions.

5.   What do you mean my Fuzzy – relations? Explain operations on fuzzy relations and properties.

6.   Briefly explain Fuzzy if-then rules, and summarize the procedure of interpretation using them, also explain Fuzzy reasoning.

7.   Describe Fuzzy inference systems, along with Mamdani type and Sugeno type FIS,

8.   What are hybrid systems, explain different types of hybridization, and how it is useful in artificial intelligence.

9.   Explain Fuzzy Logic controlled genetic algorithm.

Chapter 5

1.   What is Evolutionary Algorithm?

2.   Explain the generation cycle of genetic algorithm.

3.   Write short notes on crossover operator and mutation operator.

4.   Explain briefly the applications of genetic algorithms and how genetic algorithms differ from traditional algorithms.

5.   Short note on reproduction operators.

Chapter 6

1.   Write a short note on simulated annealing and illustrate how, it is found better than other algorithms for solving optimization problem.

2.   Write down the steps involved in simulated annealing algorithm along with the example code.

3. Briefly explain Ant Colony Optimization and its contribution in feature selection, give an introductory note on feature selection.

4. Explain tabu search algorithm, along with the steps involved.

5. Explain briefly, the concepts, intensification and diversification involved in tabu search.